From
Coach
to
Awakener

by

Robert Dilts

Meta Publications
P.O. Box 1910
Capitola, California 95010
(831) 464-0254
FAX (831) 464-0517
E-Mail: metapub@prodigy.net
Homepage: http://www.meta-publications.com

Library of Congress Card Number 2003104426
I.S.B.N. 0-916990-45-1

Contents

Dedication

This book is dedicated with affection and respect to my many caretakers, guides, coaches, teachers, mentors, sponsors and awakeners; and in particular to

Gregory Bateson

who helped me to awaken at many levels.

Acknowledgments

I would like to acknowledge:

Stephen Gilligan for his profoundly important contribution of the notion of therapeutic sponsorship and for his personal sponsorship of me and my work.

Judith DeLozier, Todd Epstein, Robert McDonald, Tim Hallbom, Suzi Smith and Richard Clarke for their friendship, support and for their contributions in terms of several of the tools and processes described in this book.

John Grinder and Richard Bandler who awakened my calling with respect to coaching and NLP, and who have been sponsors and guardians for me at key times during my journey.

Jenny D'Angelo, who devoted her sharp eyes and strong literary sensibility to help with the proof reading, editing and production of this book from cover to cover. She has been the guardian angel and project manager for this undertaking in many ways.

Alain Moenart and Anne Pierard for suggesting the topic and title of *From Coach to Awakener* and for sponsoring the first workshop that became the basis for this book. I want to also acknowledge Anne for her ideas and suggestions related to the notion of survival strategies.

To Anita, Drew and Julia Dilts for their support during the times of sometimes intense focus that it takes to write a book.

Preface

From Coach to Awakener can be considered, in many ways, a workbook for coaches. In fact, the book started as a manual for a workshop sponsored by Anne Pierard and Alain Moenart of Institute Ressources in Brussels, Belgium, in May of 1999. As they have done so many times, Anne and Alain wanted to help me create a program that pushed the edge of the envelope of training for people interested in helping others and themselves to grow and improve.

The purpose of the seminar was to provide coaches, consultants, trainers, counselors and therapists with a set of tools to help their clients address goals, issues and change at different levels in their lives.

The structure of the seminar, and thus this book, is founded upon the NeuroLogical Levels model, which was inspired by the work of Gregory Bateson. (The relationship between NeuroLogical Levels and Bateson's work is covered in depth in *Appendix A*.) The basic idea of this model is that there is a hierarchy of levels of learning and change in our lives—each level transcending but including processes and relationships on the level beneath it. The range of levels in this hierarchy includes our environment, behavior, capabilities, beliefs, values, identity and purpose with respect to the larger system or "field" of which we are a part.

The premise of the NeuroLogical Levels model is that each level in this hierarchy has a different structure and function in our lives. Consequently, different types of support are needed in order to effectively produce or manage change at the various levels. We *guide* people to learn about new environments, for instance; *coach* them to improve specific behavioral competencies; *teach* them new cognitive capabilities; *mentor* empowering beliefs and values; *sponsor* growth at the identity level; and *awaken* people's awareness of the larger system or "field."

To succeed in reaching desired outcomes at each of these levels, we also need effective tools. Thus, one of the main objectives of *From Coach to Awakener* is to provide specific toolboxes for each level of change to be addressed.

An important implication of the approach taken in this book is that different tools have different uses and purposes; and it is important to select the right tools for the job. Tools that are effective for producing change at one level, for instance, may be of limited value at a different level. As an analogy, a surgeon's scalpel would be of little use to attempt to alter the genetic code of a cell. Attempting to update beliefs using behavior level techniques could be likened to trying to use a hammer to drive in a screw or cut a board in half when using a screwdriver or saw would be much easier and more effective.

It is also important to point out that the "tools" described in this book are intended to be more than just one-time techniques which are used to fix something that is broken. A tool is something that can be used time and again to build something new, as well as to improve and repair what already exists.

The overall goal is for coaches and clients to use these tools together to help clients build the future they desire and activate the resources necessary to reach that future. The role of the coach is to help clients learn to apply the tools for themselves. As clients become more proficient with each tool in the toolbox, they are able to utilize those tools for themselves with progressively less dependence on the coach for their success. In this regard, this book can be as valuable to clients as it is to coaches.

While the chapters have been organized sequentially, beginning with the tools and support needed for change at an environmental level and culminating with the spiritual level, it is not necessary to read or use the materials in a sequential fashion. Feel free to skip around and focus on the area of change that is most relevant to you.

Robert Dilts
March, 2003
Santa Cruz, California

Introduction

In general, *coaching* is the process of helping people and teams to perform at the peak of their abilities. It involves drawing out people's strengths, helping them to bypass personal barriers and limits in order to achieve their personal best, and facilitating them to function more effectively as members of a team. Thus, effective coaching requires an emphasis on both task and relationship.

Coaching emphasizes generative change, concentrating on defining and achieving specific goals. Coaching methodologies are outcome-oriented rather than problem-oriented. They tend to be highly solution focused, promoting the development of new strategies for thinking and acting, as opposed to trying to resolve problems and past conflicts. Problem solving, or remedial change, is more associated with counseling and therapy.

Origins of Coaching

The term "coach" comes from the Middle English word *coche*, which meant "a wagon or carriage." In fact, the word still carries this meaning today—such as when a person travels "coach" on a railway or airline. A "coach" is literally a vehicle which carries a person or group of people from some starting location to a desired location.

The notion of coaching in the educational sense derived from the concept that the tutor "conveys" or "transports" the student through his or her examinations. An educational coach is defined as "a private tutor," "one who instructs or trains a performer or a team of performers," or "one who instructs players in the fundamentals of a competitive sport and directs team strategy." The process of being a coach is defined as "to train intensively (as by instruction and demonstration)."

Thus, historically, coaching is typically focused toward achieving improvement with respect to a specific behavioral performance. An effective coach of this type (such as a "voice coach," an "acting coach," a "pitching coach") observes a person's behavior and gives him or her tips and guidance about how to improve in specific contexts and situations. This involves promoting the development of that person's behavioral competence through careful observation and feedback.

The Coaching Revolution

In recent years, starting in the 1980s, the notion of coaching has taken on a more generalized and expanded meaning. Coaching in organizations involves a variety of ways of helping people perform more effectively, including project, situational and transitional coaching. *Project coaching* involves the strategic management of a team in order to reach the most effective result. *Situational coaching* focuses on the specific enhancement or improvement of performance within a context. *Transitional coaching* involves helping people move from one job or role to another.

Many companies and organizations are opting for coaching of these types, in place of or in addition to training. Because coaching is more focused, contextualized and individually targeted, it is frequently more cost effective than traditional training methods in producing real change.

The essential question to be addressed by all types of organizational coaching is, "How can the organization be made more effective through the personal development of individual managers and leaders, acting independently and in teams?" To provide the practical answer to this question, executive coaching for organizations covers a range of activities, including:

- Personal development in a non-therapeutic context, which is aligned with the goals of the organization.

- Business consulting on a one-to-one basis.

- Organizational transformation through individual and organizational alignment toward future goals.

Common issues dealt with in executive coaching involve those necessary in order to reach desired outcomes in key areas of business and entrepreneurship including:

   * Generating possibilities
   * Making choices
   * Setting expectations (self/other)
   * Communicating clearly
   * Managing time
   * Learning from past mistakes
   * Solving problems
   * Improving working relationships
   * Managing up/down
   * Balancing personal and professional life

Another rapidly developing area of coaching is that of life coaching. *Life coaching* involves helping people to reach personal goals, which may be largely independent from professional or organizational objectives. Similar to transitional coaching, life coaching involves helping people deal effectively with a variety of performance issues which may face them as they move from one life phase to another.

Large "C" and Small "c" Coaching

Clearly, personal coaching, executive coaching and life coaching provide support on a number of different levels: behaviors, capabilities, beliefs, values and even identity. These new and more general forms of coaching—executive coaching and life coaching—can be referred to as capital "C" Coaching.

Small "c" coaching is more focused at a behavioral level, referring to the process of helping another person to achieve or improve a particular behavioral performance. Small "c" coaching methods derive primarily from a sports training model, promoting conscious awareness of resources and abilities, and the development of conscious competence.

Large "C" Coaching involves helping people effectively achieve outcomes on a range of levels. It emphasizes generative change, concentrating on strengthening identity and values, and bringing dreams and goals into reality. This encompasses the skills of small "c" coaching, but also includes much more.

This book is about the range of tools and skills necessary to be an effective large "C" Coach.

NLP and Coaching

The techniques and methods presented in this book are drawn largely from the field of Neuro-Linguistic Programming (NLP). The skills and tools of NLP are uniquely suited for promoting effective coaching. NLP's focus on well-formed outcomes, its foundation in modeling exceptional performers, and its ability to produce step-by-step processes to promote excellence, make it one of the most important and powerful resources for both large "C" and small "c" coaches.

Common NLP skills, tools and techniques that support effective coaching include: establishing goals and well-formed outcomes, managing internal states, taking different perceptual positions, identifying moments of excellence, mapping across resources, and providing high quality feedback.

The Coaching-Modeling Loop

While the focus of coaching is typically upon *what* a person is doing and needs to do in order to perform effectively, the focus of NLP and the NLP modeling process is on *how* to perform optimally. *Modeling* involves identifying and analyzing examples of successful performances (a type of combination of benchmarking and success analysis); sometimes by making comparisons to unsuccessful performances. (See *Modeling With NLP*, Dilts, 1999.)

Coaching and modeling are thus two essential and complementary processes for achieving optimal performance in any area, forming a loop between what needs to be done and how to do it. Modeling augments coaching by defining how key tasks and activities may best be done, and coaching augments modeling by helping people to internalize and put into practice what has been modeled. (See *Modeling and Coaching*, Dilts and DeLozier, 2002.)

The 'coaching-modeling' loop is an example of *double loop learning*. There is an old adage which states that "if you give

xvii

a person a fish, you have fed him for a day; but if you teach a person how to fish, you have fed him for the rest of his life." "Double loop learning" would involve helping a person to catch a fish, and in doing so, teaching the person how to fish at the same time. Thus, it involves achieving two simultaneous outcomes—learning *what to do* and, at the same time, *how to do it*.

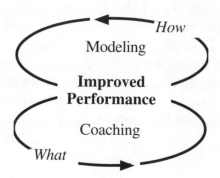

Double Loop Learning Involves Two Simultaneous Levels of Learning

In a sense, double loop learning involves getting "two for the price of one." In a double loop creative process, for example, a person would be coached to come up with an important and innovative idea or solution, and at the same time learn a strategy or "recipe" for generating other creative ideas that could be applied in other situations later on.

The objective of the tools and processes in this book is to provide this double loop capability, combining coaching and modeling to enrich and enhance effective performance.

Levels of Learning and Change in Individuals and Organizations

One of the most useful NLP models for capital "C" coaches is that of NeuroLogical Levels (see *Appendix A*). Both coaching and modeling frequently need to address multiple levels of learning and change in order to be successful. According to the *NeuroLogical Levels* model (Dilts, 1989, 1990, 1993, 2000), the life of people in any system, and indeed, the life of the system itself, can be described and understood on a number of different levels: environment, behavior, capabilities, values and beliefs, identity and spiritual.

At the most basic level, coaching and modeling must address the *environment* in which a system and its members act and interact—i.e., *when* and *where* the operations and relationships within a system or organization take place. Environmental factors determine the context and constraints under which people operate. An organization's environment, for instance, is made up of such things as the geographical locations of its operations, the buildings and facilities which define the "work place," office and factory design, etc. In addition to the influence these environmental factors may have on people within the organization, one can also examine the influence and impact that people within an organization have upon their environment, and what products or creations they bring to the environment.

At another level, we can examine the specific *behaviors* and actions of a group or individual—i.e., *what* the person or organization does within the environment. What are the particular patterns of work, interaction or communication? On an organizational level, behaviors may be defined in terms of general procedures. On the individual level, behaviors take the form of specific work routines, working habits or job related activities.

Another level of process involves the strategies, skills and *capabilities* by which the organization or individual selects and directs actions within their environment—i.e., *how* they generate and guide their behaviors within a particular context. For an individual, capabilities include cognitive strategies and skills such as learning, memory, decision making and creativity, which facilitate the performance of a particular behavior or task. On an organizational level, capabilities relate to the infrastructures available to support communication, innovation, planning and decision making between members of the organization.

These other levels of process are shaped by *values and beliefs,* which provide the motivation and guidelines behind the strategies and capabilities used to accomplish behavioral outcomes in the environment—i.e., *why* people do things the way they do them in a particular time and place. Our values and beliefs provide the reinforcement (*motivation* and *permission*) that supports or inhibits particular capabilities and behaviors. Values and beliefs determine how events are given meaning, and are at the core of judgment and culture.

Values and beliefs support the individual's or organization's sense of *identity*—i.e., the *who* behind the why, how, what, where and when. Identity level processes involve people's sense of role and mission with respect to their vision and the larger systems of which they are members.

Typically, a mission is defined in terms of the service performed by people in a particular role with respect to others within a larger system. A particular identity or role is expressed in terms of several key values and beliefs, which determine the priorities to be followed by individuals within the role. These, in turn, are supported by a larger range of skills and capabilities, which are required to manifest particular values and beliefs. Effective capabilities produce an even wider set of specific behaviors and actions, which express and adapt values with respect to many particular environmental contexts and conditions.

There is another level, that can best be referred to as a *spiritual* level. This level has to do with people's perceptions of the larger systems to which they belong and within which they participate. These perceptions relate to a person's sense of *for whom* or *for what* their actions are directed, providing a sense of meaning and purpose for their actions, capabilities, beliefs and role identity.

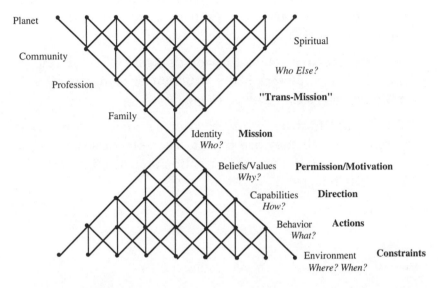

Levels of Processes Within Individuals and Organizations

In summary, coaching and modeling must address several levels of factors:

- **Environmental factors** determine the external opportunities or constraints which individuals and organizations must recognize and react to. They involve considering *where* and *when* success occurs.

- **Behavioral factors** are the specific action steps taken in order to reach success. They involve *what*, specifically, must be done or accomplished in order to succeed.

- **Capabilities** relate to the mental maps, plans or strategies that lead to success. They direct *how* actions are selected and monitored.

- **Beliefs and values** provide the reinforcement that supports or inhibits particular capabilities and actions. They relate to *why* a particular path is taken and the deeper motivations which drive people to act or persevere.

- **Identity factors** relate to people's sense of their role or mission. These factors are a function of *who* a person or group perceives themselves to be.

- **"Spiritual" factors** relate to people's view of the larger system of which they are a part. These factors involve *for whom* or *for what* a particular action step or path has been taken (the purpose).

Levels of Support for Learning and Change —A Roadmap for Large "C" Coaching

The task of the capital "C" Coach is to provide the necessary support and "guardianship" which help clients to successfully develop, grow and evolve at all these levels of learning and change. Depending on the situation and needs of the client, the coach may be called upon to provide support at one or all of these levels, requiring that he or she take on one of several possible roles (Dilts, 1998, 1999, 2000).

Guiding and Caretaking

Guiding and caretaking have to do with providing support with respect to the *environment* in which change takes place. Guiding is the process of directing a person or group along the path leading from some present state to a desired state. It presupposes that the 'guide' has been there before, and knows the best way (or at least a way) to reach the desired state. Being a caretaker, or "custodian," involves providing a safe and supportive environment. It has to do with attending to the external context and making sure that what is needed is available, and that there are no unnecessary distractions or interferences from the outside.

Coaching

Traditional coaching (i.e., small "c" coaching) is focused at a behavioral level, involving the process of helping another person to achieve or improve a particular *behavioral* performance. Coaching methods at this level derive primarily from a sports training model, promoting conscious awareness of resources and abilities, and the development of conscious competence. They involve drawing out and strengthening people's abilities through careful observation and feedback, and facilitating them to act in coordination with other team members. An effective coach of this type observes people's behavior and gives them tips and guidance about how to improve in specific contexts and situations.

Teaching

Teaching relates to helping a person develop *cognitive skills and capabilities*. The goal of teaching is generally to assist people to increase competencies and "thinking skills" relevant to an area of learning. Teaching focuses on the acquisition of general cognitive abilities, rather than on particular performances in specific situations. A teacher helps a person to develop new strategies for thinking and acting. The emphasis of teaching is more on new learning than on refining one's previous performance.

Mentoring

Mentoring involves guiding someone to discover his or her own unconscious competencies and overcome internal resistances and interferences, through believing in the person and validating his or her positive intentions. Mentors help to shape or influence a person's *beliefs and values* in a positive way by "resonating" with, releasing, or unveiling that person's inner wisdom, frequently through the mentor's own example. This type of mentoring often becomes internalized as part of a person, so that the external presence of the mentor is no longer necessary. People are able to carry "inner mentors" as counselors and guides for their lives in many situations.

Sponsoring

"Sponsorship" is the process of recognizing and acknowledging ("seeing and blessing") the essence or *identity* of another person. Sponsorship involves seeking and safeguarding potential within others, focusing on the development of identity and core values. Effective sponsorship results from the commitment to the promotion of something that is already within a person or group, but which is not being manifested to its fullest capacity. This is accomplished through constantly sending messages such as: *You exist. I see you. You are valuable. You are important / special / unique. You are welcome. You belong here. You have something to contribute.* A good "sponsor" creates a context in which others can act, grow and excel. Sponsors provide the conditions, contacts and resources that allow the group or individual being sponsored to focus on, develop and use their own abilities and skills.

Awakening

Awakening goes beyond coaching, teaching, mentoring and sponsorship to include the level of *vision, mission and spirit.* An awakener supports another person by providing contexts and experiences which bring out the best of that person's understanding of love, self, and spirit. An awakener "awakens" others through his or her own integrity and congruence. An awakener puts other people in touch with their own missions and visions by being in full contact with his or her own vision and mission.

As an illustration of these various levels of support at a very simple and practical level, consider the example of a little league baseball team.

In order for a group of young people to become an effective team, coaches need to organize essential environmental resources such as a field, uniforms, equipment and refreshments. These would be provided by various "caretakers." The players also need guidance relating to how to get to the field and regarding the timing of practice sessions and games (i.e., where and when activities will occur).

To utilize these opportunities and resources properly, the youngsters will need to develop behavioral competence with the fundamental actions which make up the game. This would come through traditional (small "c") coaching. Pitching and batting coaches, for instance, need to observe the players throwing the ball and swinging the bat, and provide specific feedback and tips to individual players. Coaches also have to help the players coordinate these activities (along with fielding and base running) in order to act as a team.

Behavioral competence is useless, however, if the players do not understand the game. Thus, coaches also have to teach players the rules of the game and explain to them how to adjust their actions in different situations. This involves cognitive understanding and judgment based upon knowledge of possible contingencies and outcomes. Players also need to learn to focus their attention properly and keep their "head in the game." These are elements of the so called "inner game" of a particular sport. It is this knowledge and understanding that form the basis for the skill and capability to play the game.

To work together effectively and develop the "will to win," players also need to believe in themselves and their teammates, and to share common values. A key job of a coach is to help instill values and beliefs that will help players to grow and succeed. The coach must motivate players to exhibit crucial values such as respect, reliability, discipline, team work, etc., demonstrating them by his or her own example. In addition, a good coach will need to provide inspiration and motivation for players to stay focused and get through challenging situations. Players can sometimes enter a "slump," in which they are not performing well. This will challenge their self-confidence and belief in themselves. In such situations the coach will need to act as a mentor to help players regain a positive frame of mind.

If a player is struggling at the pitcher's mound or while batting at the plate, for example, the coach might call a "time out" and have a brief talk with the player. During that talk, the coach is typically not offering specific behavioral feedback or explaining the game to the player. Rather, the coach is usually saying something like, "Come on. You know you can do this. We are all behind you. Just relax and give it your best." The purpose of these messages of encouragement is to help strengthen and bolster the player's belief in himself or herself.

The best coaches are also "sponsors" for their players, recognizing them as unique and special individuals, seeing that each player is a "winner" at an identity level, and welcoming each one to the team as an important and valued contributor. It is this recognition and acknowledgment that deeply inspires each player to give his or her very best. A good indication of the power of this type of sponsorship is shown by the results of attempts to elicit states of excellence and peak performance from athletes. When asked to, "think of a time when you were really playing your best and performing with excellence," athletes will typically recall certain events, but frequently have some difficulty recovering the full affect of the peak state. On the other hand, when asked to, "think of your best coach," many athletes immediately enter a strong, resourceful state. It was through the recognition and acknowledgment of their coach that they came to see themselves as a "ballplayer" and a "winner."

People often speak of learning important life lessons through their involvement with sports. This occurs when a coach is able to help awaken in them the experience of the game as a deeper metaphor for life. No doubt, the reason that some people end up dedicating their lives to a sport is because they feel connected to something larger through the sport. Certainly, a core outcome for a coach is to work to create a type of "team spirit" such that players feel a sense of purpose and belonging. This is a key success factor for every championship team, and something that can last the rest of the person's life.

This complementary group of competencies—caretaking, guiding, coaching, teaching, mentoring, sponsoring and awakening—define the skill set of large "C" coaching. These are essential skills, regardless of whether one is coaching a little league baseball team, a coworker trying to improve his or her ability to communicate, a project group in a company, a person making a life transition, or the Chief Executive Officer of a multinational organization. Each of the different levels of support requires a different quality of relationship on the part of the coach and a different tool set. The tools of mentoring, for instance, are distinct from those of teaching, guiding or awakening.

As the little league analogy illustrates, many situations will require a combination or sequence of tools, skills and types of support. The purpose of this book is to define the types of contexts and situations which call upon the capital "C" coach to focus on a particular role—i.e., caretaker, guide, coach, teacher, mentor, sponsor, awakener—and to provide a specific tool set for each role. In other words to provide the tool set an effective coach needs to manage the entire scope of large "C" coaching activities—from caretaking to awakening.

Chapter 1

Caretaking and Guiding

Overview of Chapter 1

- **Caretaking and Guiding**
  - **Environmental Factors**
  - **Caretaking**
  - **Guiding**
  - **Assumptions and Style of the Caretaker or Guide**
- **Cartaker Toolbox: "Psychogeography"**
  - **Using Psychogeography in Groups and Teams**
  - **Using Psychogeography to Facilitate Different Types of Group Processes**
  - **Psychogeography as a Key Aspect of Coaching and "Caretaking"**
- **Cartaker Toolbox: Guardian Angel**
  - **Guardian Angel Checklist**

Overview of Chapter 1 (Continued)

- **Guide Toolbox: Mapping, Metaphor and Intervision**
  - **Mapping**
  - **Metaphor and Analogy**
  - **Intervision**
  - **Intervision Mapping Process**

- **Guide Toolbox: Self-Mapping and Causal Loops**
  - **Causal Loops**
  - **Making a Causal Loop Map**

- **Summary**

Caretaking and Guiding

You've got to know the territory. —The Music Man

Guiding and caretaking have to do with providing support with respect to the environment in which an individual or organizational change is taking place.

Environmental Factors

Our *environment* is the external context in which our behaviors and interactions occur. "Environment" is that which we perceive as being "outside" of us. A particular "environment" is made up of factors such as the type of room, weather conditions, food, noise level, etc., that surround an individual or group. External stimuli such as these will affect the responses and the state of individuals and group members, and need to be considered as part of any goal-oriented process. Environmental factors thus determine the external opportunities or constraints which individuals and organizations must recognize and to which they must react. Such environmental influences shape our experience of the *where* and the *when* of a particular "problem space" of change—i.e., the contextual factors, such as physical space and time constraints, that influence the way we approach a problem or goal.

In decision theory, *environmental variables* include all dimensions of a "problem space" which are perceived as beyond the control of the actors or decision makers. The weather, for example, is a classic environmental variable. It is something that we cannot directly control and must adapt to. Our choice of clothing, however, is a "decision variable" related to our behavioral reactions to particular environmental variables. To successfully achieve the outcome of staying warm and dry when we go outdoors, we must take into account both environmental and decision variables.

In order to reach a particular outcome or desired state, environmental opportunities and constraints need to be identified and addressed in some way. Thus, in addition to defining a present state and desired state, effective performance involves taking advantage of the opportunities and addressing the constraints within the environment in which one is operating. The decisions that people make and the resources that they choose to mobilize are often the result of the environment in which people perceive or assume they are acting. Environmental factors show up in planning as "contingencies"—factors which may or may not vary but which are not subject to arbitrary control of the individual or organization.

Caretakers and guides help us to create or take advantage of environmental opportunities and to identify and address environmental constraints.

Caretaking

Being a *caretaker*, or "custodian," involves providing a safe and supportive environment. It has to do with attending to the external context, making sure that what is needed is available, and taking steps to see that there are no unnecessary distractions or interferences from the outside.

Good parents, for instance, act as caretakers when they prepare a safe and stimulating play space for their children. Any potentially dangerous items are removed, and interesting toys, tools and other playthings are provided in case the children should become interested. Such an environment gives the children an opportunity to experiment and explore based on their individual interests and desires.

Another good example of caretaking is when a person goes to a hospital or a clinic. In such an environment, patients' physical needs are provided for and they are placed in a context that is free from the stresses, contaminations and temptations of their typical surroundings. This allows people to focus on themselves and the personal or internal changes they need to make in order to recover or heal.

Creating an effective "off-site" event for managers is another example of a type of "caretaking." The purpose of these events is to provide a supportive and enriching environment that is conducive to team building and personal growth.

As these analogies suggest, when a coach is acting as a caretaker, he or she will want to create a context that maximally supports his or her clients to be able to achieve their goals and to successfully develop personally. This involves considering questions such as:

- What external resources and support do clients need in order to reach their goals?

- Where can clients get these resources and who will provide them?

- To achieve their outcomes, what actions and behaviors do clients need to explore or experiment with?

- Where and when and with whom would clients be able to try out these actions and behaviors?

- What kind of environment, support and protection would clients need from others to be able to do this?

- What tools and physical resources (e.g., chair, refreshments, writing instruments, journal, white board, flip chart, markers, etc.) do clients need in order to reach their goals?

- What steps can I take to physically ensure that clients are safe, uninterrupted, easily heard, clear about time frames and time limits, etc.?

Guiding

Merriam Webster's dictionary defines a *guide* as "one that leads or directs another's way," and "a person who exhibits and explains points of interest." Thus, *guiding* relates to the process of helping to direct another person along the path leading from some present state to a desired state, and helping that person to be aware of key opportunities and constraints along the way. The term can be traced to the Old English *witen*, which meant "to know." The implication is that the "guide" has been there before, and knows the best way (or at least a way) to reach the desired state—i.e., that the guide has "been there, done that, got the T-shirt."

When we arrive in some unfamiliar location or environment (such as a new city, museum, airport, shopping mall, etc.) we immediately look for some type of guidance—either in the form of a map or an actual guide—to help us find our way around. Guides help us to learn and recognize key landmarks and know what to look for as we seek a particular destination. In well-planned environments and events, guides are often stationed at various points along a route so that people do not get lost.

Guides also help us to understand something of the background and history relating to the environment we are in and to familiarize us with important patterns and customs.

Thus, when acting as a guide, a coach helps to orient his or her clients to the terrain that they will be traveling by providing direction, tips and other knowledge based upon the guide's experience. This involves considering questions such as:

• What is the new territory that the client is going into in order to reach his or her desired state?

• What information is the client likely to need to successfully navigate that new environment?

• When will the client need that information?

- What are the most important contextual cues the client will need to be aware of?

- What personal experiences do I have that I can share with the client to make his or her journey easier?

- What sort of "road map" can I provide for the client?

- What level of detail does that map need to include?

- What types of "milestones" or reference points can I provide for the client?

Assumptions and Style of the Caretaker or Guide

When assisting and supporting others, the beliefs of the guide or caretaker include:

People have the capabilities that they need to succeed.

In an environment of sufficient safety people will discover and apply the resources that they need in order to reach their outcomes.

If given the appropriate guidance, maps and tools, clients will be able to use their own resources to find their way and work things out.

The typical leadership style used when caretaking or guiding is known as "management by exception." Management by exception is a leadership style in which the coach intervenes only when problems arise, or when clients need something specific. As long as people are "making progress," and things are going in the right direction, the guide or caretaker does not try to change anything. If the client needs something or begins to get lost or off track, then the caretaker or guide will provide support in the form of some type of environmental adjustment or information.

As a leadership style, management by exception has the effect of transferring leadership to others. Guiding and caretaking give people a lot of freedom to act according to their own discretion in a context of relative safety. The guide or caretaker is always available to help or problem solve if there is a crisis or some other difficulty (like a seminar leader monitoring students during an exercise or parents monitoring children at play).

Caretaker Toolbox: "Psychogeography"

One of the goals of effective caretaking is to ensure that the environment helps support the client in reaching desired outcomes. *Psychogeography* refers to the influence that micro-geographical arrangements and relationships exert on people's psychological processes and interpersonal interactions. "Psychogeography" relates to the fact that the geographical relationship between the members of a group has an important non-verbal influence upon the group's process and interactions with one another. The spatial relationships and orientation between people exert both a physical and symbolic inluence on the interaction between group members. Psychogeography creates a type of relational "circuitry" between people, determining the type and quality of interaction. Thus, psychogeography is an important "caretaking" tool.

Consider the simplest case of two individuals interacting with one another. If they stand face-to-face at a close distance, this psychogeography will create and support a direct, and likely intense, interaction between the two of them (either positive or negative). If the two move farther away from one another, the intensity of the interaction is likely to diminish. If the two stand side-by-side, the essential nature of their relationship and interaction will most likely shift a bit. They become more like partners or members of a team, focused on a common direction or task rather than on each other. If one person stands slightly behind and to the side of the other, he or she will most likely begin to enter the role of a supporter, coach or mentor to the other.

It is important for coaches to consider the impact of their own physical relationship with their clients, and to help clients recognize how such physical relationships affect their interactions with others.

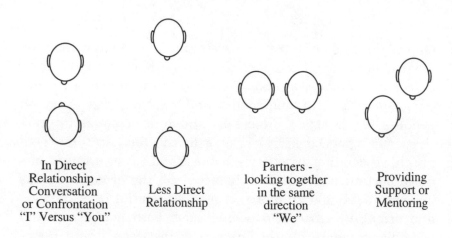

In Direct
Relationship -
Conversation
or Confrontation
"I" Versus "You"

Less Direct
Relationship

Partners -
looking together
in the same
direction
"We"

Providing
Support or
Mentoring

**"Psychogeography" Influences and Expresses the Quality
of Relationship and Interaction Between People**

Psychogeography in Groups and Teams

The same types of arrangements of "circuitry" influence, and
are reflected in, the behavior of larger groups. Consider the
constellation or "circuit" represented by the interaction dia-
gramed below. A lot can be inferred about the quality of the
interaction and the relationships between the various individuals involved by their psychogeography.

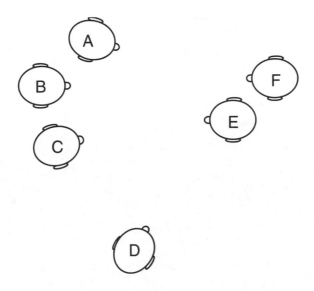

**The Psychogeography of a Group Reflects Their
Relationships and Interactions with One Another**

It seems evident that A, B and C make up one group, E and
F make up another group, and D seems to be more of an
observer. The attention of all the group members, however,
appears to be mostly focused on E. E appears to have more of
a leadership role with F as a supporter. A, B and C, on the
other hand, seem to be more equal in status.

Notice the difference between the previous grouping and
the following grouping, in which F has changed location.

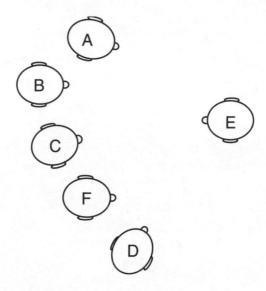

**Different Psychogeographies Reflect and Reinforce
Different Interactions and Relationships**

In this arrangement, all of the individuals appear to be one group, with E directing or leading the group in some way. The attention of F, however, appears to be directed somewhere other than on E.

Psychogeography has important implications for team coaching, leadership and group dynamics. Setting up a meeting room in a certain way, for instance, is a "meta message" about the kind of interaction in which people are expected to engage. As an example, sitting in a circle, as in a round table, encourages different types of feedback and interactions between group members than sitting at a rectangular table, or in a "theater style" arrangement. A round table also conveys a different kind of symbolic relationship between group members. For example, if someone enters a room that is set up with a blackboard at the front of the room, and chairs arranged facing the front of the room in "theater style," he or she is likely to interpret it as a context for a "presentation," and be prepared to sit passively and listen. If that person enters a room in which a small group of chairs is arranged facing each other in a "round table" format, he or she will most likely interpret it as a context for 'discussion' and be ready to be more proactive and participative.

A circular psychogeography will tend to focus people on their interpersonal relationships, distributing attention equally between all group members and implying an equal status between them all. Sitting around a rectangular table, on the other hand, creates a sense of hierarchy. Focus is typically directed toward the head of the table, and the person sitting at the "head of the table" is usually the person with highest status, followed by the person sitting closest to his or her "right hand" side, and then the "left hand."

Sitting in a semicircle would tend to focus the attention of the group members toward whatever is at the front of the semicircle. It tends to imply equality of status among the individuals in the semicircle, working to take action or reach a consensus with respect to whatever is at the center of their common focus. A group sitting side-by-side in a straight line, would also imply a common focus for all group members, but would greatly reduce the interaction between members with one another. They would be acting but not "interacting" as a group.

Using Psychogeography to Facilitate Different Types of Group Processes

Different psychogeographies can be constructed and utilized to promote different types of group processes. A circle, for instance, is an effective psychogeography for "dreaming" or brainstorming because it intensifies the interaction between group members. It implies that all members, and thus all ideas, are of equal value, and people can "bounce" ideas off one another rapidly, and quickly add to the ideas of others, without becoming overly focused on any one individual or idea.

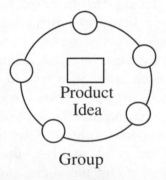

Group

Effective "Psychogeography" for "Dreaming" or Brainstorming

A semicircle is a more effective psychogeography for "realizing," or planning how to implement a particular goal or dream. In a semicircle, people would still be considered peers, but their focus is much more directed to a particular point. The idea or plan has become disconnected from any specific group member, and is the common focus of everyone in the group. The implication is that the group members are much more focused on their task than their relationship, and that they are moving toward consensus.

Effective "Psychogeography" for "Realizing" or Planning

A psychogeography in which the group members are all in a line, sitting next to one another, as if they were a panel, looking at the goal or idea, is a more effective psychogeography for criticizing or evaluating. The proximity of group members to one another presupposes that each person is part of the same group. Individuals, however, will be much more inclined to respond in accordance with their own perspective, as opposed to checking out the reactions of other group members.

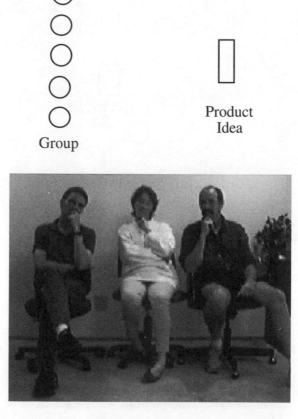

Effective "Psychogeography" for "Criticizing" or Evaluating

Psychogeography as a Key Aspect of Coaching and "Caretaking"

One key and very pragmatic aspect of coaching is arranging the psychogeography for your coaching sessions with your clients. It is important that your external environment support the types of activities your client will be engaged in. Before beginning each session with your clients, consider the following questions:

- What sort of environment do I want to create for my client(s) for this session?

- What type of interactive dynamic will the client(s) need to have for the session? (i.e., exploratory, brainstorming, open, focused, reflective, etc.)

- What type of physical arrangement of the room will best facilitate that dynamic? (i.e., presence and position of tables, chairs, flip chart, white board, projector, etc.)

- Given my client's goals for this particular session, what type of psychogeography will most support the individual or team to successfully reach the desired state?

- How will I physically position my client(s) with respect to:
  - myself?
  - the flip chart, white board, projector, etc.?
  - other participants (if any)?

Caretaker Toolbox: Guardian Angel

The role of caretaker can be likened in some ways to that of a "guardian angel"—someone who watches over and protects another person from a distance. *Guardian Angel* is a term used in some NLP exercises to denote a type of 'Meta Person' whose task is to give support and encouragement to particular group members. A common role for such "Guardian Angels" is as a supporter for a person preparing to perform in an interactive situation. The Guardian Angel supports the performer in a variety of ways including:

- providing for the performer's physical needs (i.e., making sure he or she has a chair, water, writing instruments, white board, flip charts, etc.).

- physically ensuring that the performer is safe, uninterrupted, easily heard, the time limits of the performance are clear, etc.

- non-verbally encouraging the words and ideas of the performer by nodding, smiling and laughing, etc.

- verbally encouraging the performer by authentically saying things like, "Please, tell us more," "Fascinating" and "Yes," etc.

The Guardian Angel provides his or her "client" ongoing support during the performance from a distance, helping the client to stay in a resourceful state by giving encouraging feedback and establishing resource anchors.

The following is an example of some common steps taken by the Guardian Angel to ensure that all appropriate external support is being provided for the client.

Guardian Angel Checklist

1. Ask the client what internal "resource state" he or she would like to be in during his or her performance.

2. Have the client identify past example(s) of the state, and reexperience them as fully as possible.

3. Notice the observable physical cues associated with the resource state (i.e., the client's posture, gestures, voice tone, facial expression, etc.). This is so that the Guardian Angel can tell when the client is in (or out) of the desired state.

4. Together with the client, select a signal or "anchor" to use to remind the client of these resourceful memories (e.g., a "thumbs up," wink, head nod, smile, etc.).

5. Ask the client to identify possible problem areas that may arise during the performance. These will be areas in which it is important for the Guardian Angel to be sure to provide the reminder signal and give encouragement.

6. Determine the psychogeography to be used by the Guardian Angel (i.e., where the Guardian Angel should position him/herself with respect to the client).

7. Establish S.O.S. signal to be used by the client—i.e., a signal for the client to use to request greater encouragement from the Guardian Angel.

8. Rehearse the way you will use the signal during performance by role playing some of the performance.

This process can be applied in a variety of contexts and situations, ranging from making a presentation to leading a team, or communicating with a difficult person.

Guide Toolbox: Mapping, Metaphor and Intervision

An important function of good guides is to provide us with helpful maps to follow. Maps aid us to more successfully navigate new territory. Thus, a key tool for effective guiding is to create maps that can offer guidance to others in order to better deal with a particular 'territory' or terrain.

Mapping

Mapping refers to the process of making a representation of some experiential 'territory'. Mapping involves the identification and encoding of key elements which make up some particular phenomenon or process—such as making a map of the streets in a particular city, the veins and arteries in the human circulatory system, the movement of a weather front, or the geographical features of a certain state or country. Webster's Dictionary, for instance, defines mapping as, "a function such that for every element of one set there is a unique element of another set." Thus, while there are many different forms of 'maps'—symbolic, schematic, metaphorical, etc.—the most important feature of a map is the degree of correspondence between the elements in the map and the elements of the territory they represent.

The value of mapping is that it allows us to understand, plan, and communicate about some experience or phenomenon without having to actually "be there." Prominent points of interest can be coded into a structure to be analyzed, contrasted and changed. Mapping also makes it possible to project and predict potential future responses and occurrences to some degree. A building inspector, for instance, might notice the prominence of water under a house, check the high and low spots in the immediate area, notice the ways in which the water is collecting or moving, and create a drainage system to handle the problem of the water.

Similarly, from the NLP perspective, the features of a personal "landscape" can be mapped and used to create effective plans for change and improvement. The NLP process of modeling, for example, involves making a map of a person's patterns of behavior, which may then be applied in various ways.

It is important to keep in mind, however, that "the map is not the territory." A key feature of all maps is that, to some degree, they must delete, distort or generalize aspects of the territory they were created to represent. It is also important to remember that territories change. Even a very detailed and precise map of a particular territory can become obsolete if the territory it represents changes.

From the NLP point of view, humans are avid map makers; and our maps of the world serve as our primary guide for interpreting and responding to the world around us. Our mental maps can either aid us or limit us, depending on the degree to which their elements correspond to the territory they are intended to represent, and on the choices that they make available.

Metaphor and Analogy

A dilemma that sometimes confronts coaches when they are called upon to be guides is that they do not have previous direct experience with the specific context or environment to be faced by their clients. One way to address this type of challenge is for the coach to create maps for his or her client using metaphor or analogy. Metaphors and analogies allow us to draw parallels between one environment or experience and another.

According to anthropologist and communication theorist Gregory Bateson, the ability to find analogies is a function of *abductive thinking*, which he contrasted with inductive and deductive thinking processes. Bateson argued that abductive or analogical thinking leads to more creativity, and was the source of art and genius. Bateson believed that analogies lead us to focus on the deeper structure of our experience, rather than on superficial differences.

Thus, an additional advantage of using metaphors and analogies is that they can stimulate us to enrich our understanding of some process or phenomena, and also to discover and evaluate our assumptions. Shifting the metaphors we use to understand a situation or phenomenon often triggers creativity and leads to new perspectives. Metaphorical representation is a very common and powerful way of engaging new associations with respect to the understanding of an idea, situation or concept. It is also a useful tool to transfer learning between different contexts. It stimulates a type of thinking that leads to the level of abstraction necessary to transfer or apply particular learnings between contexts.

Making analogies between very different types of contexts (e.g., skiing and working in an office) can create new areas of "perceptual space." For example, you might find that, although skiing is something one does by oneself and an office context has lots of other people, there still might be a kind of a metaphorical or analogical relevance between skiing and working in an office. You might make the analogy that avoiding trees and potholes while skiing is like dealing with the potential interferences created by people in the office.

Intervision

The term "intervision" has been used for some years by European psychotherapists as a way to describe group sessions in which they discuss how to handle challenging situations or clients in their practices. Intervision can be contrasted with supervision. In "supervision" there is an implied hierarchical relationship between people; the supervisor provides the "right map" to the other person. In "intervision" it is assumed that people are peers and that there is no one right map.

Intervision has much to do with the influence of the way we represent and conceptualize our problems, ideas and outcomes. One of the goals of this intervision process is to apply visual and symbolic thinking strategies to help map out solutions. A powerful form of co-creativity arises out of the fact that people have different maps of the world. The way that somebody else represents a particular individual's problems or outcomes can automatically help to enrich that person's own perception of the situation. In the words of Albert Einstein, "Our thinking creates problems that the same type of thinking cannot solve." Getting new maps is a very powerful way of finding new solutions.

Intervision Mapping Process

The following is a description of a way to adapt the intervision process for acting as a guide in a coaching context.

1. The client describes a situation in which he or she would like guidance: i.e., "I need guidance in the following situation . . ."

2. The guide listens for the key elements and patterns of the situation (the "deeper structure"). When the client has finished describing the situation, the guide is to think of situations that he or she has been in which are similar to what the client has described. If the guide has not been in the same physical environment as the one described by the client, the guide can use the process of analogy to find situations that are parallel with respect to the key elements and patterns described by the client.

3. The guide is to then draw a symbolic or metaphoric picture representing his or her understanding of the client's situation and the guidance that he or she would offer to the client. The picture can be any kind of a

diagram or a sketch. For example, somebody might draw a tree or landscape; another person may just draw a group of symbols like rectangles, circles and stars and connect them with lines and arrows.

The guide is to draws his or her own individual picture of his or her understanding of the client's situation and potential solution the guide has to offer.

4. The guide then shows the client his or her picture, explaining the possible solution—i.e., the guide shows his or her map and says:

My understanding of your situation is . . .

I have been in a similar situation to the one you are describing. It was . . .

What I did was . . .

What I think you need is . . .

If you are working in a group or team, it is often useful to do this process with several people in the role of guides in order to get a wider range of diversity. Since "intervisible" literally means to be "mutually visible," group intervision generally takes place with group members sitting in a circle. Each guide draws his or her own individual picture of his or her understanding of the client's situation and potential solution he or she has to offer.

After the possible solutions have been presented to the client, it can be useful to discuss the assumptions behind the various drawings and interpretations. Contrasting different people's maps and assumptions about a particular environment is a way to enrich perceptions about that perceptual space and uncover other assumptions.

The presupposition of the exercise is that making external maps in the form of drawings is an effective method to 1) acknowledge the diversity of maps between people and 2) develop multiple perspectives of a particular situation.

At the end of the intervision process, the client should give feedback to the guide(s) in terms of how his or her own map of the situation has been enriched. The client restates the situation and describes in what ways his or her map has been enriched.

Guide Toolbox: Self-Mapping and Causal Loops

Another way that guides can support clients is to assist them in mapping their own past successes. This is a form of self-modeling and can help to clarify the client's understanding of his or her environment and solidify potential resources.

Different types of maps can unveil features of a particular territory that may not have been previously noticed. Causal loop maps are a particularly revealing form of mapping that help to uncover and clarify key systemic dynamics associated with a particular environment or situation.

Causal Loops

Conceptualizing processes and phenomena in terms of 'causal loops' is an essential part of systems thinking. In *The Fifth Discipline*, his classic book on systemic thinking, Peter Senge (1991) claims that the "essence" of the discipline of systems thinking is:

a) seeing relationships rather than linear cause-effect chains

b) seeing the entire process of change rather than snap-shots.

Senge asserts that, to think systemically, we must alter our ways of visualizing and mapping the structure of the situations we are attempting to understand or influence. As a starting point, Senge suggests the type of circular structure shown in the following diagram of the processes involved in filing a glass with water. The diagram depicts the basic elements involved in the activity as a simple feedback loop, connected by arrows indicating the "influence" the various elements have on one another. Senge emphasizes the use of circular arrows as a way to ensure that a person envisions the entire feedback loop and breaks the habit of linear and mechanical thinking.

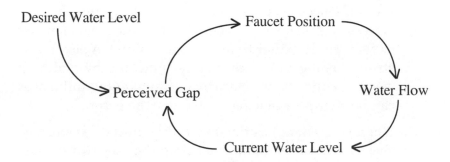

A "Causal Loop" Diagram for Filling a Glass with Water

Using causal loops to help clients to visualize the relationships between "environmental" and "decision" variables can provide valuable guidance and assist them in better understanding how to utilize opportunities and manage constraints. The following process provides a structure for using causal loop maps to help clients model key success factors from their own successful experiences.

Making a Causal Loop Map

Ask your client to recall a time that he or she was able to successfully manage a time of transition or change—a time that he or she was able to "bounce back" from adversity or "survive in a changing world." Together with your client, create a "causal loop map" of this 'story of change' by going through the following steps:

1. While the client is speaking, note down 7-10 key words from the story or example on a piece of paper. Key words may be of any type: behaviors, people, beliefs, values, phenomena, etc.

2. Draw arrows connecting the key words which illustrate the influences between key words and capture the flow of the story. (The arrows should be in the form of an arc or semi-circle rather than a straight line.) A positive or strengthening influence can be indicated by adding a (+) under the arrow. Negative or weakening influences can be shown by placing a (-) under the arrow.

3. When your client has finished telling his or her story, go over your initial map, checking the key words and giving him or her the chance to edit them, or add other key words you may have missed. Also review and check the links you have drawn between the key words.

4. Make sure that you have "closed" feedback loops (as a rule of thumb all key words should have at least one arrow going from them, and another arrow pointing to them).

5. Refine the map by considering the delays that may be involved between links, and searching for other missing links that may be an important part of the story.

6. Find out what beliefs are behind the map (what assumptions do these links presuppose?).

Frequently, you will find that managing change involves several loops relating to the *how* (the steps and strategies involve), the *why* (the beliefs, values and motivation related to the change) and *who* (the role and identity issues).

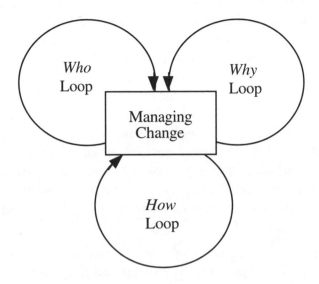

**Managing Change Frequently Involves a "How" Loop, a
"Why" Loop and a "Who" Loop**

As an example, consider the following description made by a client about a time he was able to deal effectively with a difficult situation.

Some years ago I was involved in a new business venture. Things went well at first, and we were very excited about what we were doing. We had a really innovative idea and seemed to be leading the marketplace. But then competition got stronger and the economy started slumping. This lead to a lot of internal challenges within our management team and conflicts about which direction to go. As one of the founding members, I was under a lot of pressure and it was starting to feel almost overwhelming.

Eventually, I had to step back, get some distance and set a few personal boundaries. This helped to relieve some of the pressure, and I was able to remember what our vision was and what we stood for. As a result, I was able to get clear about what our goals should be and what my role was in reaching them. We had a team meeting and talked about the importance of realigning with that original vision and the values it stood for. This allowed us to look at what we were doing and check for any areas of waste or distraction. A few people decided to leave the company, but the ones that stayed were really committed. So, we were leaner but more focused.

We also talked to some of our key customers who had been with us since the beginning, asking them about their needs and what we could do to provide an even better service.

As a result of this we ended up dropping some of what we were doing, repurposing some of our products and starting with a fresh focus. Not only did we get through the slump, but were even more ready than our competitors to provide what our customers needed and take advantage of new opportunities when things improved.

One way to map this "story of change" using a causal loop approach is shown in the following diagram.

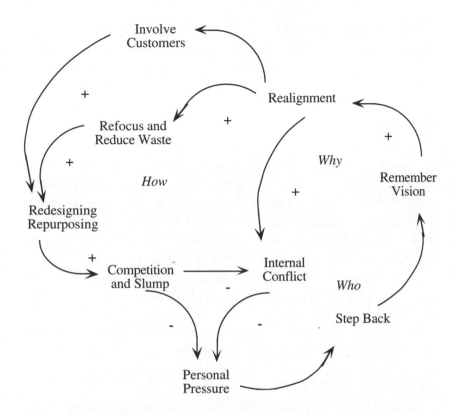

Example of a Causal Loop Map for a Client's Process of Change

The diagram illustrates that competition and the slumping economy was creating internal conflict among the management team. Both these factor were increasing the sense of personal pressure felt by the client. Through the loop of stepping back and remembering the vision (the *who* loop) a process of realignment took place, which reduced the internal conflict within the team (the *why* loop). This also triggered two parallel loops of refocusing and reducing waste, and involved customers (the *how* loop) which lead to the redesigning and repurposing of products and services, and ultimately helped to positively address the issues related to competition and economic slump.

Such maps can help clients "see" patterns in their own experiences that they can learn from and turn into effective strategies which can be used to deal with future challenges.

Summary

In summary, caretaking and guiding are processes which address the *environmental* surroundings of coaching clients.

Caretaking involves attending to the client's ongoing external context, making sure that what is needed is available, and taking steps to see that there are no unnecessary distractions or interferences from the outside.

Psychogeography is a caretaking tool that helps to optimize the spatial and interactive relationships within which the client is performing.

Acting as a *Guardian Angel* is another caretaking resource in which the coach provides key support for clients who are facing new performance hurdles or challenging environments.

Guiding involves orienting clients to unfamiliar environments by providing them with direction, tips and other useful knowledge, including the guide's personal experience.

The processes of mapping, metaphor and intervision are tools which provide ways for clients to get useful information and insights about environments that are new for them.

Causal loop maps help clients to become aware of significant systemic dynamics within their enviornments and more clearly recognize how to take advantage of opportunities and manage constraints.

Chapter 2

Coaching

Overview of Chapter 2

- Coaching
  - Behaviors
  - Behavioral Coaching
- Coaching Toolbox: Establishing Goals
  - Defining Goals
  - Goal Setting Questions
- Coaching Toolbox: Well-Formed Outcomes
  - Well-Formed Outcome Worksheet
- Parable of the Porpoise
  - Coaching Principles Illustrated by the Parable of the Porpoise
  - Relevance of the Parable of the Porpoise to Coaching
  - Applying the Parable of the Porpoise
- Coaching Toolbox: Feedback and Stretching

Overview of Chapter 2 (Continued)

Coaching

It's not the will to win that matters — everyone has that. It's the will to prepare to win that matters.
—Paul "Bear" Bryant

We all have dreams. But in order to make dreams into reality, it takes an awful lot of determination, dedication, self-discipline, and effort.
—Jesse Owens

Caretaking and guiding frequently evolve into more in-depth coaching, which brings with it a different relationship with the client and a distinct set of tools. In contrast with guides, coaches actively help clients develop specific behavioral competencies. The notion of coaching as we will use it in this chapter, is that of small "c" coaching or "performance coaching." As we established earlier, small "c" coaching is more focused at a behavioral level, referring to the process of helping another person to achieve or improve a particular behavioral performance.

Behaviors

Effective behavioral performance involves the ability to sense and coordinate your body's actions as you move through a particular external environment. This level of learning and change relates to the specific behavioral activities or results that occur within an environment—i.e., *what* happens or is supposed to happen at a particular where and by when. Thus, our *behaviors* are the explicit physical actions and reactions through which we interact with the people and environment around us. Behaviors are the product of the psychomotor system, a deeper level of neurology than the sense organs we use to perceive our environment.

The specific behaviors that people actively engage in, such as tasks, procedures and interpersonal interactions serve as the primary means for the successful achievement of desired goals and outcomes. Behavioral factors are the particular action steps taken in order to reach success. They encompass what, specifically, must be done or accomplished in order to succeed.

Behavioral Coaching

As we have mentioned before, small "c" coaching methods derive primarily from a sports training model, promoting conscious awareness of resources and abilities, and the development of conscious competence. These methods involve drawing out and strengthening people's abilities through careful observation and feedback, and facilitating individuals to act in coordination with other team members. Effective performance coaches carefully observe their clients' behaviors and give them tips and guidance about how to improve in specific contexts and situations.

When supporting and working with others, some of the beliefs of the small "c" coach include:

People have the capabilities that they need to perform effectively. These capabilities can be drawn out with the appropriate rewards and input.

My client will improve his or her performance naturally if given the appropriate encouragement and feedback.

Everybody is the best in the world at something. With the appropriate encouragement and feedback from me, my client will become the best he or she can be.

If people know better what they are already doing well, they can easily extend it.

My clients will grow and improve through stretching themselves and getting positive feedback for trying.

The leadership style of the small "c" coach is that of contingent reward. *Contingent reward* is a fairly directive leadership style. It involves contracting an exchange of reward for effort. A good coach, at this level, tells people what to do if they want to succeed or be rewarded. The coach assures people that they can get what they want in exchange for effort, and gives special commendations and acknowledgment for good work. Effective small "c" coaches also provide specific, ongoing behavioral feedback for how to improve.

Coaching Toolbox: Establishing Goals

One of the most important skills of coaching is helping people to define and solidify goals. As was stated in the *Introduction* of this book, coaching methodologies are solution focused and outcome-oriented rather than problem-oriented. Certainly, without a goal, no system of rewards or feedback can be established.

Webster's Dictionary defines a *goal* as "the end toward which effort or ambition is directed," or "a condition or state to be brought about through a course of action." A goal, then, is essentially a person's or group's desired state or outcome. It is the answer to the question, "What do you want?" Goals are the source of motivation, and can stimulate powerful self-organizing processes that mobilize both conscious and unconscious resources.

Goals are a fundamental feature of all NLP techniques, strategies and interventions. They constitute the target and the central focus of all of the activity associated with any particular intervention or strategy. It has been said that "if you do not want anything, then NLP is of no value to you."

Because of their significance, it is important that coaches help clients to establish appropriate and meaningful goals. In this sense, being a good coach is a bit like being a taxi driver. What is the first question the driver asks when a client gets in the cab? The driver asks, "Where are you going?" You can say to the driver, "I hated it here. I've had a lot of problems. It has been just awful." However, after listening patiently and acknowledging your discomfort, the driver will eventually have to respectfully repeat the question, "So, where do you want to go?" You could respond with, "Well I don't want to go McDonald's, and I had a terrible time at the zoo the last time I went. And I certainly don't want to go anywhere cold." Once again, the driver can graciously acknowledge your concerns, but must still continue to ask, "So, where do you want to go then?"

Eliciting goals and outcomes from coaching clients can sometimes be as challenging as the taxi driver example described above. Often, when people come in for coaching, they know more about what they don't want than what they do want.

The following descriptions outline some common methods people use to define goals, each of which can offer different insights into the nature of a client's desired state.

Defining Goals

Goals are most often established *in relation to* a present state or problem state. For example, a person may have a problem state involving a *"fear of public speaking."* The simplest (although often the most problematic) form of goal setting is to define the goal as the *negation of the problem state*. If the problem state involves the "fear of public speaking," a person may initially define his or her goal as, *"I want to stop being afraid of talking in front of a group."*

While this is certainly a common way to identify goals, and can be a good starting point, the problem with this strategy is that it does not actually answer the question "What do you want?" It is a statement of what the person does *not* want, and thus is no real goal at all. In fact, negative statements such as this often focus people more on the problem state than the desired state. Consider the somewhat paradoxical challenge of the following instruction: "Do *not* think of a blue elephant for the next thirty seconds." In order to know what you are not supposed to think of, you have to think of it!

A second common goal setting method is to define the goal as the *polarity* or *opposite of the problem state*. In the case of "fear of public speaking," the person may say, *"I want to be confident while talking in front of a group."* Again, this is a logical strategy, and certainly helps the person to focus somewhere other than the problem situation; but it can also create inner polarities and conflict. It sets up a constant reference and comparison to the problem state. In the words of Albert Einstein, "You cannot solve a problem with the same level of thinking that is creating the problem." A polarity is defined at the same level of thinking as its opposite.

A third goal setting process involves using an external reference or role model as a means to define the desired state. In organizational planning and development, this is often referred to as "benchmarking." In the example of public speaking, a person might do this by saying, *"I want to talk to a group like Martin Luther King would."* This has certain advantages over simple negation and polarizing. It provides a concrete reference for comparison and helps direct attention away from the problem state. One of the challenges with it is that it is an "arm's length" outcome—it is an externalized reference. This can make it difficult to personally identify with. It can also, of course, lead people to build inappropriate expectations, or create the types of incongruence and insincerity that comes from imitation. This can bring out negative comparisons and a sense of failure. There is also the ecological danger of applying a behavior that is appropriate in one context (i.e., that of the role model) to situations in which it does not fit.

Another strategy for defining goals involves using key characteristics to define the structure of the desired state. These qualities can be drawn from either oneself or key role models. With respect to public speaking, this might involve something like reasoning, *"I want to embody the qualities of mastery when I am talking to a group: such as, flexibility, congruence, integrity, etc..."* This is essentially a deductive approach. It involves manifesting higher level characteristics and principles within concrete situations. While it opens the door to more flexibility of action and expression, it is also necessarily removed from specific personal experiences. Thus, it can lead to clarity of understanding about what is needed, but does not necessarily ensure that people will be able to do what they know is required.

A fifth goal setting method involves establishing a "generative" outcome. Rather than being defined with respect to a problem state or according to external or abstract references, a generative outcome involves extending existing resourceful qualities. Generative goals are statements of what one wants "more of," and are characterized by the word "more." For example, in a public speaking situation, a person may say, *"I want to be more balanced and creative."* An important aspect of this generative method for defining outcomes is that it presuppose that a person already possesses and is able to behaviorally execute at least some of the desired qualities or characteristics. With this approach, the outcome is viewed as simply a matter of having more of what one already has.

This brings up a final goal setting strategy, that of acting "as if" one had already reached the desired state. It is more difficult to define goals while one is still associated in the problem state. In fact, that is often part of the problem itself; when one is stuck in the problem state, it is much harder to be creative and think of alternatives. With the "as if" strategy, one removes oneself from the problem state and moves in time to the desired state by imagining what it would be like if one had already reached his or her desired state. In relation to public speaking, a person might say, *"If I had already reached my desired state, I would be relaxed and comfortable in front of people right now."*

All of the different strategies for defining goals have their advantages and help both client and coach to have a richer understanding of the client's desired state. In fact, the most effective goal setting strategy is to use all of them as part of the process of defining goals. Taken together, they form a powerful sequence for exploring and building achievable goals from a number of perspectives.

Goal Setting Questions

You can use the following set of questions with clients to help them shift attention from their problem state to their desired state and develop a rich and robust representation of their goals.

Identify the problem state.

What is the problem state you want to change?

My problem is that I _____.

Define your goal using each of the goal setting strategies:

1. Negating the problem state. *What do you want to stop or avoid?*

I want to stop _____.

2. Identifying the polarity of the problem state. *What is the opposite of the problem state?*

I want to _____ instead.

3. Defining the desired state with respect to an external reference. *Who else is already able to achieve a desired state similar to the one you want?*

I want to act or be like _____.

4. Using key characteristics to define the structure of the desired state. *What are some important characteristics (embodied by the role model whom you selected in your previous answer) that you would like to manifest in the desired state?*

I want to embody the characteristics of _____.

5. Establishing a "generative" outcome - Extending existing resourceful qualities. *What qualities, associated with your desired state, do you already have that you need or would like to have more of?*

I want to be more _____.

6. Acting "as if." *If you had already reached your desired state, what would you be doing, or doing more of?*

If I had already reached my desired state I would be

_____.

Once you have defined a goal, it is important to check it to be sure that it is "well-formed." NLP has established a number of "well-formedness conditions" for outcomes, which help to ensure that goals are realistic, motivating and achievable.

Coaching Toolbox: Well-Formed Outcomes

Well-formedness conditions are the set of conditions an outcome must satisfy in order to produce an effective and ecological result.   In NLP, a particular goal is considered "well-formed" if it can be:

1. stated in positive terms.

2. defined and evaluated according to sensory based evidence.

3. initiated and maintained by the person or group who desires the goal.

4. made to preserve the positive by-products of the present state.

5. appropriately contextualized to fit the ecology of the surrounding system.

In summary, an outcome is considered "well-formed" when it has met the following conditions:

1. *The outcome must be stated in positive terms.* In many respects, it is practically and logically impossible to give someone the negation of an experience. Thus if a client says, "I want to not feel so anxious anymore," or "I don't want to be so critical of myself," or "I want to be less upset at my co-workers," the coach's first task is to find out what the client, in fact, does want in place of the negative experience (like the taxi driver mentioned earlier). The coach might ask, for example, "If you weren't anxious, what would you be feeling instead?" or "What would you like to be doing to yourself in place of being critical?" or "What would things be like if you were able to be less upset with your co-workers?" It is in general much easier to

coach a client to operate toward a positive outcome than away from a negative one.

2. *The outcome must be testable and demonstrable in sensory experience.* The only way in which setting an outcome is going to be useful to anyone is if you are explicitly able to perceive and evaluate progress towards it, as you attempt to achieve it. In our analogy of the taxi driver, this means we have to provide the driver with a location that is actually reachable. If one were to say something like "I want to go somewhere nice," the driver would not have specific enough information to get there. Similarly, coaches need to help clients identify and define behavioral demonstrations of their desired states. An effective coach will minimally want to establish two sets of criteria, or tests, for the client's outcome: a) one set for the ongoing coaching context; and b) one set for the client to use outside the coaching environment. For example, the coach may ask, "What will be a demonstration to you and me, here, today, that you can achieve the outcome(s) that you want for yourself?" and "What will be a demonstration to you that you have achieved (or are achieving) your outcome(s) with your co-workers (spouse, children, family, boss, or others)?" The coach then has an explicit way of knowing when he or she has been successful with the client.

3. *The desired state must be initiated and maintained by the client.* One of the major goals of a good coach is to put the locus of control, with respect to achieving the outcome, with the client. Thus, if a client states, "I want my supervisor to stop ignoring me," the statement does not yet satisfy any of the criteria listed so far for a well-formed outcome. In this case the coach would want to first ask "What would your supervisor be doing if he or she weren't ignoring you?" (getting a positive statement of the outcome). The coach would then want to get a sensory-based

description of how the supervisor would be paying attention to the client. Some satisfactory answers might be, "He (or she) would *talk* to me more about the projects I am working on," or "He (or she) would *notice* and *comment* on the quality of my work more often." The coach would then want to put the control of the outcome in the client's hands by asking, "What could you do (have you done, are you doing) to get your supervisor to want to talk to you about your projects and comment on your work more often?" The coach could then help the client develop the appropriate flexibility of behavior to achieve the outcome.

4. *The desired state must preserve any positive by-products of the present state.* The positive by-products of seemingly negative behaviors are best illustrated in what are referred to as habits (smoking, overeating, heavy drinking, etc.) Many smokers, for instance, smoke to calm themselves down when they are nervous. A surprising number of smokers smoke to remind themselves, and compel themselves, to breathe deeply. If a smoker quits, and no substitute or alternative has been installed by which the smoker may relax and remember to breathe deeply, he or she will experience a great amount of difficulty and discomfort. When the positive by-product is not explicitly accounted for in the desired state, people will often take on substitute behaviors that become just as problematic. For example, people may take to overeating or drinking, instead of smoking, when they are nervous, or manifest some other form of "symptom substitution." Many people procrastinate in order to avoid potentially uncomfortable consequences of taking action. Especially in companies and organizations, the repercussions of any desired outcome should be explored in detail so they may be prepared for and handled appropriately. The coach will want to explore what the client, as well as the client's system, will stand to lose, as well as gain, upon the achievement of any

outcome. Sometimes the shockwave through a system that results from a change in one member's behavior may create an outcome that is more problematic than the initial presenting problem.

5. *The outcome must be appropriately contextualized and ecologically sound.* Many times people state their outcomes in the form of absolutes or "universal quantifiers." In such cases, it is implied that the outcome is wanted in all contexts and for all circumstances, when in actuality the old behavior may be quite useful and appropriate in some situations, and conversely, the desired behavior may be inappropriate and problematic in other situations. Therefore, if someone says, "I want to stop being so hesitant about sharing my ideas," the coach would want to ask, "Are there any times in which being hesitant about sharing your ideas would be appropriate?" or "Are there any times when you would *want* to be hesitant about sharing your ideas?" Likewise, if someone says, "I want to be more assertive with my team members when they are uncooperative," the coach would respond, "Are there situations where your team members are uncooperative but you would not want to be assertive?" In each case, the coach is specifying the appropriate boundaries and limits for desired and undesirable outcomes. The goal of effective coaching is not to take away responses or behaviors or to simply substitute one behavior for another, but to *give the client more choices*. To ensure that the choices available to the client are going to be the best ones, the coach will often have to contextualized desired outcomes to specific times, persons, places, activities, etc.

Well-Formed Outcome Worksheet

1. **Outcome**—Stated in Positive Terms. *What do you want?*

2. **Sensory Evidence**—Observable Behavioral Demonstration of the Outcome. *How, specifically, will you know when you achieve this goal? What are the performance criteria? How will they be tested?*

3. **Self-Achievable**—Goal Can Be Initiated and Maintained by the Person or Group Desiring It. *What specifically will you do to achieve this goal?*

4. **Positive 'By-Products' Preserved**—Positive Intentions and Secondary Gains of the Problem State. *What positive things, in any way, do you get from your present way of doing things? How will you maintain those things in your new goal?*

5. **Appropriately Contextualized**—Outcome Is Appropriately Contextualized and Ecologically Sound. *Who and what else could reaching this goal affect? Under what conditions would you and would you NOT want to have this outcome?*

• Contexts in which the Outcome Is Wanted:

• Contexts in which the Outcome Is Not Wanted:

Parable of the Porpoise

The most important role of the small "c" coach is to provide feedback and encouragement to clients so that they can recognize and optimize key actions and behaviors. The following "parable of the porpoise" provides a powerful analogy and set of principles for coaches of all types.

Anthropologist Gregory Bateson spent a number of years studying the communication patterns of dolphins and porpoises. In order to supplement their research, the research center he was involved with often used the animals under study to put on shows for live audiences—sometimes as often as three times a day. The researchers decided to demonstrate to the audience the process of training a porpoise to do a trick. A porpoise would be led from a holding tank into the performing tank in front of the audience. The trainer would wait until the porpoise did some conspicuous behavior (conspicuous to humans, that is)—say, lifting its head out of the water in a certain way. The trainer would then blow a whistle and give the porpoise a fish. The trainer would then wait until the porpoise eventually repeated the behavior, blow the whistle again and give it a fish. Soon the porpoise had learned what to do to get the fish and was lifting its head quite often, providing a successful demonstration of its ability to learn.

A couple of hours later, however, the porpoise was brought back to the exhibition tank for a second show. Naturally, it began lifting its head out of the water as it did in the first show, and waited for the expected whistle and fish. The trainer, of course, didn't want the porpoise to do the same old trick, but rather to demonstrate to the audience how to learn a new one. After spending roughly two-thirds of the show period repeating the old trick over and over, the porpoise finally became frustrated and flipped its tail. The trainer immediately blew the whistle and threw it a fish. The surprised and somewhat confused porpoise cautiously flipped its tail again, and again got the whistle and fish. Soon it was merrily flipping its tail, successfully demonstrating again its ability to learn and was returned to its home tank.

At the third session, after being led to the exhibition tank, the porpoise began dutifully flipping its tail as it had learned in the previous session. However, since the trainer wanted it to learn something new, it was not rewarded. Once more, for roughly two thirds of the training session the porpoise repeated the tail flip with growing frustration, until finally, out of exasperation, it did something different, such as spinning itself around. The trainer immediately sounded the whistle and gave the porpoise a fish. After a while it successfully learned to spin itself for the audience and was led back to its home tank.

For fourteen straight shows the porpoise repeated this pattern—it spent the first two-thirds of the show in futile repetitions of the behavior that had been reinforced in the previous show until, seemingly by "accident," it engaged in a new piece of conspicuous behavior and was able to complete the training demonstration successfully.

With each show, however, the porpoise became increasingly disturbed and frustrated at being "wrong" and the trainer found it necessary to break the rules of the training context and periodically give the porpoise "unearned fish" in order to preserve his relationship with the porpoise. If the porpoise became too frustrated with the trainer it would refuse to cooperate at all with him, which would create a severe setback in the research as well as the shows.

Finally, in between the fourteenth and fifteenth session, the porpoise seemed to become almost wild with excitement, as if it had suddenly discovered a gold mine. And when it was let into the exhibition tank for the fifteenth show it put on an elaborate performance including eight completely distinct new behaviors—four of which had never been observed in its species before.

Coaching Principles Illustrated by the Parable of the Porpoise

The important elements of the story are:

1) The porpoise had to learn a class of behavior as opposed to a particular behavior.

2) The specifics of the behavior was determined by the porpoise not the trainer. Rather, the main task of the trainer was to manage the context in such a way as to draw new behavior out of the porpoise.

3) The learning problem was context specific (the exhibition tank).

4) The whistle was not a specific stimulus to trigger a specific response but rather a message to the porpoise about something it had already done.

5) The fish given to the porpoise was less a reinforcement for the particular behavior the porpoise had performed than it was a message about its relationship with the trainer. The fish is a meta-message.

6) Had the trainer not been sensitive to the relationship and not taken actions to preserve it, the experiment would have been a failure.

7) Both porpoise and trainer were being observed by an audience. It was pleasing the audience, in fact, that defined the purpose of the whole training context.

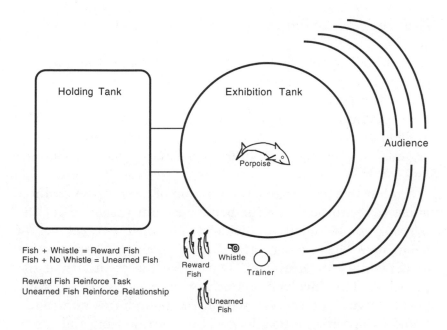

Fish + Whistle = Reward Fish
Fish + No Whistle = Unearned Fish

Reward Fish Reinforce Task
Unearned Fish Reinforce Relationship

Whistle

Reward Fish

Trainer

Unearned Fish

An Effective Porpoise Trainer Must Give Both Feedback (Earned Fish) and Encouragement ("Unearned" Fish)

According to Bateson, the stimuli used in such learning experiments are not so much triggers for reflexes, but are context markers that give the animal a clue to interpret the context - a kind of meta-message. The whistle-fish combination makes up a context marker that says, "Repeat the behavior you just did." The exhibition tank is a context marker which surrounds the whistle-fish context that says, "Do something different than what you did for the previous shows." The relationship to the trainer, as Bateson points out, is the context of the context of the context. That is, the relationship with the trainer is a context which surrounds both of the other contexts. The relationship with the trainer spans the holding tank, exhibition tank, the whistle and the fish. And the context defined by the trainer's implicit responsibility to the audience influences his relationship to the porpoise.

Relevance of the Parable of the Porpoise to Coaching

In the analogy of Bateson's porpoise parable, the porpoise trainer is like a coach; the porpoise is like the performer or client; the performance tank is like the office, classroom or other environment in which the performer must act; and the audience observing the trainer and porpoise represents the organization or social system surrounding both performer and coach.

Similar to a good coach, the mission of the porpoise trainer is not to "condition" specific behaviors, but rather to get the porpoise to be creative inside of its own natural set of behaviors. The success of the porpoise trainer is based on his or her ability to "draw out" or release the creativity of the porpoise. This involves reinforcing the porpoise to generate new behaviors on its own within the boundaries and conditions of a specific context defined by a certain time and space.

The porpoise trainer is not some unaccounted for, disembodied, objective observer (as most animal researchers like to perceive themselves) but rather is in an intense relationship with the porpoise—and the trainer's success depends on maintaining the quality of that relationship. Relational communication is not conducted through "stimuli" and objectified "reinforcements" but rather through messages and meta-messages about (1) the state and status of the beings involved in the relationship; (2) the set of contexts in which both the task and the relationship are occurring and (3) the level of messages being sent. The medium in which the message is being sent is a higher level message about the message being sent.

Applying the Parable of the Porpoise

The parable of the porpoise emphasizes some important principles for coaching and learning, including:

1. The relevance of both task and relationship in performance enhancement.
2. The relevance and difficulties of learning to learn as a part of effective performance.
3. The influence of others (the audience) on the activities and relationship between the coach and the performer.
4. The relevance of different kinds of feedback (the whistle and the fish) with respect to learning.
5. The fact that effective feedback is related to both information (whistle) and motivation (fish).
6. Higher level learning involves self-motivated activity on the part of the performer.
7. Lack of positive feedback can damage the performer-coach relationship and cause performers to "give up."

A person attempting to learn to be a more effective performer is like the porpoise in the training tank. He or she must make self-initiated changes in behavior, depending upon the nature of the context, and respond to multiple types of feedback.

The NLP approach to effective coaching involves the implementation of feedback and rewards similar to that described in the Parable of the Porpoise. Individuals engage in activities, involving interactions with others, which are related to defining and implementing particular objectives. At various points in these activities, people are provided with two types of feedback: "whistles" and "fish". "Whistles" are given in the form of observations about particular behaviors. "Fish" are provided in the form of personal comments reflecting something that the observer liked about that behavior. This type of feedback is not only provided by "official" trainers and coaches, but by all of the members of the group or learning team. On one level, the purpose of this type of feedback is to identify what someone is doing well and encourage him or her to do more of it. On a deeper level, the purpose is to encourage people to be more proactive, continually searching for ways to improve and become more flexible.

To be effective in giving this type of feedback, people must first learn how to distinguish observations from interpretations. The "whistle" must be based on concrete observable behaviors. The "fish" reflects interpretations related to that behavior. The rule in this form of feedback is that if you make an observation, you must also provide a "fish" (a comment on what you liked about what you observed). Observations without any accompanying interpretations or responses are just data. They contain no motivation or meaning. It would be like the porpoise trainer blowing the whistle but never offering any fish to the porpoise. Feedback provides information when it contains specific data relevant to the task to be performed (like the porpoise trainer's whistle). Feedback provides motivation when the information or the task are made more "meaningful" (as when the porpoise trainer connects the task to the giving of the fish).

Similarly, if you make a comment about something you liked, you must also provide a description of the specific behavior to which your response relates. If a person is given praise or some other reward but no information about what he or she has done to elicit such a reaction, the person will ask, "What did I do? What is this for?" This is because the individual has no idea what to repeat or how to improve.

For example, let's say a person has made a presentation about his or her vision and mission. When that person has finished the interaction, a group member might say, "I observed that you continually made eye contact with the members of the group (whistle), and that made it easier to feel that we were all part of the same team (fish)."

Thus, the basic form of feedback always contains two key elements:

What I observed:_____

What I liked about it: _____

People are also invited to give "gifts" or "unearned fish" in the form of encouragement or positive comments that are not task related. For instance, a person may say to another, "I appreciate your commitment to congruence and integrity." Or, "Thank you for your support and encouragement." This type of message is primarily focused upon the individual and the relationship. Its purpose is to bolster the sense of rapport between group members.

Notice that this process does not include any negative or 'corrective' feedback. The focus is on what a person is doing that is working well. Just as in our example of the porpoise, the porpoise trainer never threw any 'rotten fish' to the porpoise if he or she did not like what the porpoise was doing. Nor did the trainer impose any other form of punishment or negative conditioning. Rather than giving negative feedback, the porpoise simply received an absence of whistle or fish unless it did something new.

Sometimes people think that this type of feedback eventually becomes ineffective because people build the illusion that they are always successful and are not making any mistakes. And this might be true if it were not for the other elements of the process. A wise business executive once said that in order to "grow as a leader" a person must feel "a strong will to modify the environment to make it better, then create challenging situations that (he or she) can't get out of except by changing." This is where the learner participates in creating the challenge that will lead to his or her growth. The "illusion" of success is avoided because the performer is encouraged to create "challenging situations" for him or herself. Because the environment is not hostile, the learner is able to monitor his or her own self-managed learning path.

The presuppositions of this method of feedback are, *"You are in a context in which it is safe to learn. You can be curious and creative, and challenge yourself. The amount that you are able to learn and grow depends upon your own initiative. It's okay to try new things and make mistakes. Nothing bad will happen to you if you don't perform perfectly at first. You will be guided by concrete and supportive feedback. What is most important is that you do your personal best. You won't be criticized if you don't do it the "right way"; because there is no one correct way to behave. Rather, the effectiveness of your actions shifts depending upon the context and the type of "audience"—which you can determine by becoming more aware of certain cues. Thus, it is important to continually explore new behaviors and develop your own awareness, flexibility and self-mastery."*

Keep in mind that the purpose of this type of feedback is to encourage the development of flexibility and the ability to produce new behaviors as an adaptation to a changing context. If a person needed to follow a particular procedure in a stable or threatening context, a process that involved supervision and corrective feedback may be more appropriate. The objective of this method of learning is to draw out, "reveal" and maximize natural abilities through a process of encouragement and effective feedback.

Coaching Toolbox: Feedback and Stretching

One objective of coaching is to help people develop a wider range of flexibility in their behavior. The following coaching exercise applies a number of principles derived from the Parable of the Porpoise to help encourage and reward effective performance.

1. The performer (client) is to select a context in which to enact a well-formed performance goal that he or she has defined.

2. With the assistance of the coach, the performer enacts a simple role play for approximately 5 minutes (simulating the context selected by the performer) in order for the performer to behaviorally practice achieving his or her goals.

3. When the performer is through with the role play, the coach gives the performer feedback in the following form:

   What I observed:_____

   What I liked about it: _____

   The feedback may be given orally and in written form. Providing written "whistles and fish" allows people to take their feedback home with them and reread it later on.

4. The coach is then to write suggestions of specific behaviors that would challenge, "stretch," or increase the flexibility of the performer in relation to his or her goals, such as:

Move your hands more (or less)

Change your physical position with respect to the other person

Keep constant eye contact with the other person

Speak in analogies and metaphors

5. The performer chooses one of the suggestions and continues or repeats the role play for 2-3 more minutes, incorporating it as he or she attempts to achieve the defined goal(s).

6. At the end of 2-3 minutes, the performer stops and again is given feedback by the coach, in the form:

What I observed:_____

What I liked about it: _____

The process may be repeated as many times as the coach and performer decide is appropriate.

When working with a group or team, several people can offer the performer "whistles and fish" and "stretches" in order to increase the amount of feedback and options he or she receives.

At the end of the process, the performer may share what he or she has learned with respect to his or her conscious and unconscious competencies.

Coaching Toolbox: Contrastive Analysis and "Mapping Across"

Once well-formed outcomes have been established and performance criteria established, one of the major tasks of a coach is to help clients identify and activate the key resources necessary to achieve the outcomes and meet the criteria. One simple and powerful set of tools to accomplish this is that of contrastive analysis and "mapping across."

Contrastive analysis and mapping across are a good example of the pragmatic application of the coaching-modeling loop. *Contrastive analysis* refers to the process of comparing different states, representations, maps, performances or descriptions, for the purpose of discovering the "differences that make a difference." By comparing and contrasting, a person can discover information that allows that person to have a better understanding of the structure of the experience. For example, if a person has an experience of creativity in one context, and an experience of being uncreative in another. These two situations can be analytically contrasted with respect to the key differences involved. The person can notice how the feelings, body posture, focus of attention, beliefs and values, thinking strategies, and environmental conditions differ. Knowledge of these differences may then be used to make strategic changes to allow the person to become more creative in the situation where he or she has previously been stuck.

Mapping across is a term used to describe the process of transferring features or elements from one strategy, state or situation to another. The process of "mapping across" is a basic *utilization* technique in which certain characteristics of one state, strategy or situation (such as a resource state) are transferred to another state or situation (such as a problem state), in order to precipitate change or produce a solution. Mapping across is typically done in conjunction with a Contrastive Analysis, in which processes and features of two experiences or situations are compared for similarities and differences. Certain characteristics of one state or strategy are then transferred to the other through verbal guidance, or other behavioral strategies.

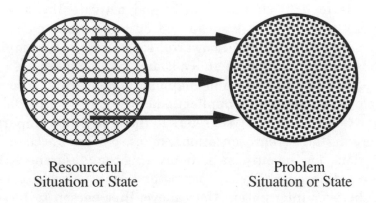

Resourceful   Problem
Situation or State   Situation or State

**In "Mapping Across," Features and Elements of One State
or Situation Are Transferred to Another, in Order to
Create Change or Find a Solution**

Thus, the mapping across process involves several steps:

1. The identification of the states or situations to be contrasted.

2. Comparing and contrasting the states or situations in order to elicit and identify key differences.

3. Altering the characteristics of one of the states or situations (a stuck state, for example) to incorporate key features of the other (resourceful) state or situation. This can be accomplished though verbal suggestion, role playing, planning or acting "as if."

The following is a simple coaching/modeling format in which a coach can apply the mapping across process with an individual or team to bring resources into a challenging situation. This is done by contrasting currently challenging situations with past examples of success in order to identify (model) key success factors and transfer them into other contexts.

Contrastive Analysis Format

1. Ask the individual or team member to think of a challenging situation.

   "What is the challenging situation you are facing?"

2. Coach the individual and other team members to think of times when they were able to perform effectively.

   "Can you think of a similar situation in which you were able to remain resourceful or be successful?"

3. Reflect together upon the key success factors and learning.

   "What did you do?" "What did you learn?"

4. Explore how significant success factors and learnings can be transferred or "mapped" into the currently challenging situation.

   "How can you apply what you did or learned in that situation to the challenge you are facing now?"

Body Posture and Performance

As an adjunct to the contrastive analysis process, the following pictures can be used to help clients identify key behavioral characteristics associated with resourceful states. A client can be instructed to circle the pictures that most represent his or her posture when in an effective performance state. Clients can be instructed to put a square around the pictures that most represent their posture when they are stuck, distracted or in doubt. (Clients should choose both a front and a side view).

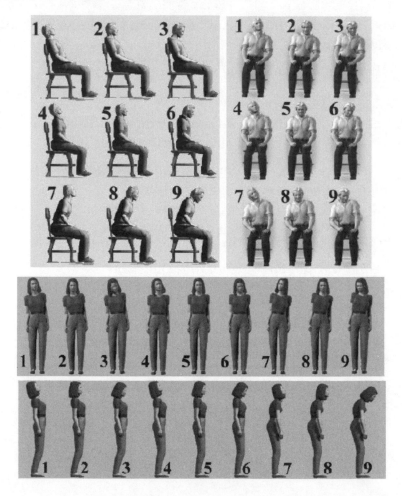

Gestures and Performance

Recalling the contrasting states identified in the first comparison, clients can be instructed to circle the picture that most represents the gestures they most often use in an effective performance state, or draw the gestures on the picture provided to the right.

Effective Performance State

The client may then circle the picture that most represents the gestures characterizing a stuck or distracted state, or draw the gestures on the picture provided on the right.

Stuck or Distracted State

Coaching Toolbox: Anchoring

Another simple but powerful tool that coaches can use to help clients access and transfer resources to contexts and situations in which they are needed is that of anchoring. In NLP, *anchoring* refers to the process of associating a behavioral response with some environmental or mental trigger, so that the response may be quickly reaccessed. Anchoring is a process that on the surface is similar to the "conditioning" technique used by Pavlov to create a link between the hearing of a bell and salivation in dogs. By associating the sound of a bell with the act of giving food to his dogs, Pavlov found he could eventually just ring the bell and the dogs would start salivating, even though no food was given. In the behaviorist's stimulus-response conditioning formula, however, the stimulus is always an environmental cue and the response is always a specific behavioral action.

In NLP this type of associative conditioning has been expanded to include links between aspects of experience other than purely environmental cues and behavioral responses. A remembered picture may become an anchor for a particular internal feeling, for instance. A touch on the leg may become an anchor for a visual fantasy or even a belief. A voice tone may become an anchor for a state of excitement or confidence. A person may consciously choose to establish and retrigger these associations for him or herself. Rather than being a mindless knee-jerk reflex, an anchor becomes a tool for self-empowerment. Anchoring can be a very useful tool for helping to establish and reactivate the mental processes associated with creativity, learning, concentration and other important resources.

Anchoring Your Inner Resources

Coaches can help clients use anchors or triggers to assist them to quickly get in touch with inner resources when they need them. Anchoring uses the natural process of association to help clients recall positive experiences through the following steps.

1. Identify an inner resource that would help you improve your performance (e.g., determination, motivation, confidence, calm, etc.).

2. Remember a time when you experienced that resource strongly.

3. Find something to use as an anchor to trigger that resource (object, mental picture, key word, gesture, etc.).

4. Put yourself back into the resourceful experience. See what you saw, hear what you heard and feel what you felt as vividly as you can. Connect the memory of this experience to your anchor by shifting your attention momentarily to the cue or trigger.

5. Clear your mind for a moment. Do something to distract yourself.

6. Put your attention on your anchor. You should immediately get the resourceful feeling. If you don't, repeat step 4 a few more times.

Summary

Performance coaching, or small "c" coaching, is directed toward helping clients develop specific behavioral competencies. Performance coaching methods involve drawing out and strengthening people's abilities through observation, encouragement and feedback. Effective performance coaches carefully observe their clients' behaviors, giving them tips and guidance about how to improve in specific contexts and situations, and helping them gain fuller access to their own inner resources.

Establishing goals and well-formed outcomes is a primary tool of effective performance coaching. Clear goals provide the direction and focus for all coaching activities.

Providing positive feedback and encouragement, through explicit messages directed toward both task and relationship, is an effective way to help people stretch and develop the behavioral flexibility to more effectively reach desired outcomes.

The tools of contrastive analysis and mapping across help clients to become more aware of the physical and mental factors that produce effective behavior and to apply those success factors more consciously to produce effective results in other contexts.

Anchoring is a useful tool to help clients access and transfer their own inner resources between different contexts and situations.

Chapter 3

Teaching

Overview of Chapter 3

- **Teaching**
  - **Developing Capabilities**
  - **Teaching and the "Inner Game" of Performance**
- **Representational Channels**
  - **Representational Channels and Learning Styles**
- **Teaching Toolbox: Learning Style Assessment Questions**
  - **Applying the Results of the Learning Style Assessment Questions**
- **Teaching Toolbox: Visualizing Success and "Mental Rehearsal"**
- **Teaching Toolbox: State Management**
  - **The Circle of Excellence**
- **Modeling Capabilities**
  - **The T.O.T.E.: Minimum Requirements for Modeling Effecitve Skills and Behaviors**

Overview of Chapter 3 (continued)

- **Teaching Toolbox: T.O.T.E. Modeling Questions**
- **Teaching Toolbox: Mapping Across Effective T.O.T.E.s**
- **Teaching Toolbox: Cooperative Learning**
  - **Cooperative Learning Process**
- **Teaching Toolbox: Focusing on Feedback Instead of Failure**
- **Basic Perceptual Positions in Communication and Relationships**
  - **Second Position**
- **Teaching Toolbox: Building a "Second Position" Perspective**
- **Teaching Toolbox: Meta Mapping**
  - **Basic Meta Map Format**
- **Teaching Toolbox: Imagineering**
  - **Imagineering Coaching Format**
- **Summary**

Teaching

Learning is finding out that you already know. Doing is demonstrating that you know it. Teaching is reminding others that they know just as well as you.
—Richard Bach

Teaching is the process of helping people to develop cognitive skills and capabilities. The goal of teaching is to assist people in increasing competencies and "thinking skills" relevant to an area of learning. Teaching focuses on the acquisition of general cognitive abilities, rather than on particular performances in specific situations. An effective teacher helps a person to develop new strategies for thinking and acting. The emphasis of teaching is more on new learning than on refining one's previous performance.

Developing Capabilities

Our cognitive *capabilities* relate to the mental maps, plans or strategies that lead to success. They direct *how* actions are selected and monitored. Capabilities involve mastery over entire classes of behavior—i.e., knowing *how to* do something. While some behaviors are simply reflexive responses to environmental stimuli, most of our actions are not. Many of our behaviors come from "mental maps" and other internal processes whose source is within our minds. This is a level of experience that goes beyond our perceptions of the immediate environment. We can make pictures of things that do not relate to the particular room we are in, for instance. We can remember conversations and events that took place years ago. We can imagine events that may happen years from now.

Capabilities come from the development of a mental map that allows us to select and organize groups of individual behaviors. Capabilities have to do with the mental strategies and maps people develop to guide their specific behaviors. Simply engaging in behaviors does not ensure that learning will take place. It is our cognitive strategies that determine how to select and guide these behaviors. It is these strategies which determine whether a learner actually develops the capabilities necessary to continuously and elegantly perform the behavioral skill he or she has been practicing. The degree to which people are able to generalize something to new situations outside of the context in which they initially learned it is a consequence of their mental capabilities. The function of capabilities is to provide the *perception* and *direction* necessary to achieve particular objectives.

Developing capabilities involves establishing cognitive maps and strategies. According to the NeuroLogical Levels model, capabilities stand in between our beliefs and our behaviors. Our capabilities are what allow us to turn our beliefs and values into tangible behaviors.

Teaching and the "Inner Game" of Performance

The notions of teaching and developing capabilities with respect to coaching are related to what can be referred to as the *inner game* of performance. The concept of the "inner game" was developed by Timothy Gallwey (1974, 2000) as a way of helping people to achieve excellence in various sports (e.g., tennis, golf, skiing, etc.), music and also business and management training. Success in any area of performance involves using your mind as well as your body. Preparing yourself mentally to perform well is the essence of your "inner game."

The "outer game" has to do with physical skills. In a sport like baseball, for example, this would have to do with how to hold and swing the bat, pitch, throw, field, run bases, etc. The "inner game," on the other hand, has to do with your mental approach to what you are doing. This includes your attitude, confidence in yourself and your team, your ability to concentrate effectively, deal with mistakes and pressure, and so on.

Athletes and coaches often talk about the importance of focusing and "getting your head into the game." When your outer game and inner game are working together, actions flow with a kind of effortless excellence that is called, "playing in the zone." Some indicators that your inner game is in order and that you are in "the zone" are:

- A feeling of confidence and the absence of anxiety and self-doubt
- No fear of failure or self-consciousness about achieving your goals
- A focus on performing beautifully and excellently
- Performance comes without effort and without having to think about it

Small "c" coaching, or performance coaching, is clearly more focused on the "outer game" of a particular performance. When teaching, the focus of the coach is on helping the client develop his or her "inner game."

Some of the beliefs of an effective teacher include:

Everyone is capable of learning.

I have questions and ideas that are exciting and stimulating that I can share with others.

I will be enriched by this person's ideas and questions.

The process of expanding one's capabilities in the world is inherently motivating.

People will learn easily if they are given praise and acknowledgment for their own ideas.

People learn in their own way and at their own speed, and that is the best way for them.

*This person is intelligent. He or she deserves to have
my knowledge and attention.*

*He or she will make good use of whatever knowledge or
information I provide, and in the way that is best for
him or her.*

The most common leadership style of a teacher is that of
intellectual stimulation. *Intellectual stimulation* involves
encouraging people to find new perspectives and rethink
their own ideas. As a result, old situations and issues are
thought of in new ways. Intellectual simulation stresses
intelligence, rationality and careful problem-solving. Teachers frequently give praise for new ideas and clear thinking.

When acting as teachers, coaches focus on helping people
to develop clarity, new understanding and a wider map of the
world. Teachers stimulate both new cognitive maps and help
to provide the reference experiences that give those maps
meaning. The emphasis of the teacher is on how to learn. As
Gallwey describes it:

> *Coaching [at the capability level — R.D.] is
> eavesdropping in on someone's thinking process. The
> most important part of the job of a coach is to listen
> well. Effective coaching in the workplace holds a
> mirror up for clients, so they can see their own thinking
> process. As a coach, I am not listening for the content
> of what is being said as much as I am listening to the
> way they are thinking, including how their attention is
> focused and how they define the key elements of the
> situation.* (p. 182)

Thus, an effective teacher helps people develop new strategies for learning, as opposed to simply presenting new
contents. Good teachers also acknowledge and adapt to the
individual learning styles (e.g., visual, auditory, kinesthetic)
of students.

Representational Channels

According to NLP, we build our mental maps of a particular environment or behavior out of information from the five senses or "representational systems": sight, sound, feeling, taste, and smell. Our senses constitute the form or structure of thinking, as opposed to its content. Every thought that you have, regardless of its content, is going to be a function of pictures, sounds, feelings, smells or tastes, and how those representations relate to one another. We are constantly linking together sensory representations to build and update our maps of reality. We make these maps based on feedback from our sensory experience.

Representational channels relate to the senses and the type of sensory modality or representation a person is employing in order to learn or communicate. When someone is speaking out loud he or she is using a *verbal* channel of external representation. *Writing* is a more visual channel of representation. A pictorial or symbolic channel of representation would involve drawing or displaying *symbols* and *diagrams*. Behavioral demonstrations or enactments constitute a more *physical* channel of representation.

The representational channel a client uses in order to learn, develop or refine his or her capabilities is a significant aspect of helping the client to be successful at his or her "inner game." From the NLP perspective, it is important for coaches to be aware of the way that they and their clients use these different representational channels internally and externally when communicating or learning. Does the client, for example, tend to be primarily verbal, preferring discussion and spoken interactions? Maybe a client's preferred mode of communication and learning is reading and writing. Perhaps the client has a preference for pictures and imagery, or likes to physically act out ideas through role plays or "micro demonstrations."

Which senses an individual uses to cognitively represent information, such as desired future events and potential consequences, is not simply a trivial detail. For example, some people run into problems accomplishing tasks because they have great visions but no comprehension of the feelings of effort that it might take to accomplish the vision, or no realization of the logical sequence of activities leading to the goal.

Different modalities of representation have different strengths. The verbal channel of representation, for instance, is strong in terms of sequencing information. The visual channel is often the best way to synthesize information into a whole or "gestalt." Acting out an idea or concept physically brings out its concrete aspects.

Representational Channels and Learning Styles

The notion of "learning style" is an acknowledgment that people learn in different ways. Different people develop their sensory capabilities to differing degrees. Some people are naturally very visual. Other people have a very difficult time forming visual images, or thinking visually at all. Some people are more verbal, and can speak and articulate experience very easily, while others struggle with words. Words confuse them. And some people are very feeling oriented, and learn by doing.

We often make assumptions that others have the same cognitive capabilities that we do. But this frequently is not the case. In communicating with others, matching their channel of representation is an important method of establishing rapport and ensuring that they will understand a communication.

Learning can be enhanced by either strengthening somebody's weakness or utilizing their strengths. If somebody does not typically use visualization, encouraging him or her to think in terms of pictures could be very transformational for that person.   If somebody is already good at visualizing, emphasizing and enriching the use of that capability can also increase learning abilities in certain situations.

Emphasizing different channels of communication and representation can lead people into different kinds of thinking styles. For example, the visual channel helps to stimulate imaginative thinking. The verbal channel is often most effective for logical or critical thinking. Focusing on physical channels influences people toward a more realistic, action orientation.

In summary, different representational channels may be used to enhance learning and communication in a number of ways:

1) matching the channel that is most used and valued by the type of learners or receivers (appealing to a strength)

2) using a channel that is not often used in order to stimulate new ways of thinking or perceiving (strengthening a weakness)

3) emphasizing the representational channel most appropriate or most suited to a particular cognitive process or type of learning task

4) enhancing overlaps or connections between different representational channels

Teaching Toolbox: Learning Style Assessment Questions

Understanding the learning style of one's clients is essential to the success of an effective coach, especially when in the role of teacher. To help determine the learning style of a client, you can present him or her with the following questions. Have the client indicate the answer that best explains his or her preference. If a single answer does not match, the client may indicate two or more choices. On a piece of paper, keep track of how many of the client's answers are a V, A or K.

1. Recall a time in your life when you learned how to do something like playing a new board game. How did you learn best? By

   V) visual clues—pictures, diagrams, written instructions?

   A) listening to somebody explaining it?

   K) experimenting, trying it out?

2. You are having difficulty finding your way to your hotel in city where you have stayed only a few days. Do you

   K) drive around and try to find a familiar landmark?

   A) ask directions?

   V) look at a map?

3. You need to learn to use a new program on a computer. Would you

   K) ask a friend to walk you through it?

   V) look at the manual that comes with the program?

   A) telephone a friend and ask questions about it?

4. You are not sure whether a word should be spelled "dependent" or "dependant." Do you

   V) picture the word in your mind and choose the one that looks right?

   A) sound it out in your mind?

   K) write both versions down and pick the one that feels right?

5. Do you prefer a lecturer/teacher who likes to use

   V) flow diagrams, handouts, slides?

   K) field trips, labs, practical sessions?

   A) discussion, guest speakers?

6. You have purchased an item that requires assembly. Would the easiest way for you to figure out how to put it together be to

   A) listen to a tape describing the steps you need to take?

   K) start putting it together and assemble it through trial and error?

   V) watch a video of it or read printed instructions?

7. You are taking care of a friend's house while he or she is on vacation. You need to quickly learn how to take care of your friend's yard and/or pets. Is it best for you to

   V) watch someone do it?

   A) get instructions and discuss it thoroughly?

   K) have someone walk you through it?

8. A person gives you a very important number (such as a phone number, code, or serial number) to remember. To be sure that you will remember it, would you

A) repeat it to yourself or someone else?

V) make a mental picture of it?

K) write or type it several times?

9. You have to make an oral presentation to a small group. Are you most comfortable that you will be able to make this presentation when you have

A) a good sense of the basic tone and words you want to communicate?

V) diagrams and notes that you can look at during the presentation?

K) rehearsed the presentation a number of times?

10. Which of the following hobbies do you most enjoy?

K) Walking outdoors/gardening/dancing

V) Drawing/painting/sightseeing/photography

A) Music/singing/storytelling

11. To acquire a new skill, do you most prefer to

A) hear a description and ask questions?

V) see diagrams and watch demonstrations?

K) do exercises?

12. When you really want to teach something to others, do you

V) create a picture for them?

A) logically explain it to them?

K) physically lead them through it?

Applying the Results of the Learning Style Assessment Questions

To determine your client's learning preference, add up the number of individual Vs, As, and Ks he or she has indicated. Match the letter your client has recorded most frequently to the same letter in the learning styles categories below. Each category contains suggestions that will help you adapt to your client's learning style and to facilitate his or her learning process.

V)isual

Visual learners tend to learn by watching or reading. When you are coaching or teaching a more visually oriented client, you will want to provide your client with plenty of pictures, charts and reading materials. Use pictures and photos to illustrate key points and ideas, and remind the client to make mental pictures and use visualization to remember significant information.

When learning new behaviors, demonstrate the key elements to your client, or have the client watch demonstrations by role models, either live or on videos.

When discussing ideas, draw them out in the form of symbols, charts and diagrams. Make sure you have paper and different colored pencils or markers. Highlite key points with colors and encourage your client to redraw and reconstruct images in different ways, replacing words with symbols and initials. It is also a good idea to have your client practice turning visuals back into words.

A)uditory

A person with an *auditory* learning style will learn best through listening and discussion. When you are coaching or teaching a client with an auditory learning preference, you will want to explain things carefully, repeat key points and encourage the client to ask lots of questions. It will be crucial to provide the client with clear definitions. If the client is trying to understand visually oriented information, it is helpful to organize diagrams into statements and describe or talk about images and pictures.

It will be important to be a good "sounding board" for your client and encourage him or her to think outloud. It will also be important for you to reflect back what the client has said, so that the client can hear it in another voice. Auditory clients can benefit from the use of a tape recorder, putting key ideas on tapes and relistening to them again later. It is also often useful to let the client know that you can be available by phone, so the client can call with any questions or to discuss ideas or decisions.

Clients who have an auditory learning style should be encouraged to discuss topics with friends, explain new ideas to other people and restate key points into other words.

K)inesthetic

Kinesthetic learners need to become physically involved, moving around and trying things out. When you are coaching or teaching a kinesthetic client, you will want to use a hands-on approach, applying trial-and-error methods in which the client can physically explore and experiment. Kinesthetic learners thrive on practice, exercises and real life examples of key ideas.

To help with verbal recollection, kinesthetic clients can be encouraged to write out words again and again, drafting out lists and practice answers. They should also be encouraged to act out key points and ideas in order to "get them in the muscle."

When teaching new behaviors, it is important to walk kinesthetically oriented clients through key parts of the performance. When planning and preparing for a future performance, kinesthetically oriented clients should be encouraged to use all their senses, putting themselves into particular situations in their imagination and role-playing or rehearsing what they will do in particular situations.

If you are coaching a group or team of people with a variety of different learning styles, you will want to take a multi-sensory approach. For each key idea or significant aspect of the performance, you will want to ask yourself, "How do I demonstrate this visually? How do I demonstrate it so the people get a feel for it? How do I demonstrate this so they hear it?"

Teaching Toolbox: Visualizing Success and "Mental Rehearsal"

Physical practice is what builds the skills of your "outer game" and puts them into "muscle memory" so you don't have to think about it during the performance. Similarly, certain mental exercises can help you to improve your "inner game." Regardless of the learning style or preferred representational channel of your clients, practicing strategies modeled from others can be quite useful and can help clients to expand their cognitive abilities.

Visualization, for instance, is often used by athletes and sports psychologists to help refine capabilities and improve performance. Many examples exist of how visualizing has been used to promote and enhance physical performance. In one study, for instance, gymnasts who were to learn a new move were divided into two groups. One group was instructed to visualize themselves being able to do this particular move, while the other group was given no instructions. A couple of weeks later, when the time came for them to do this particular move, without the benefit of any previous physical practice, the group who visualized had a 50%-60% success rate, whereas the group that had not visualized had only about 10% success initially.

In another example, a basketball team was split into two groups in order to practice "free throws." One group physically practiced making the shots. The other group was instructed to sit in the bleachers and mentally practice by visualizing that they were making the shots. When the two groups competed with each other to see who performed better, those players who visualized made more shots successfully than the group who had actually practiced.

Visualization is a form of "mental rehearsal." Mental rehearsal refers to our ability to practice a process or activity in our minds. The following instructions can be used by the coach to guide clients through the basic mental rehearsal process:

1. Choose the skill you want to improve.

2. Think of a good role model for that skill. Picture how it is done in your mind as if you are an observer watching it on a video.

3. Put yourself into your mental picture, as if you are the player, and imagine you are doing the action exactly as you pictured it. See, hear and feel the whole thing.

Teaching Toolbox: State Management

A person's internal state is an important influence on his or her ability to interact with others and perform effectively. Knowing how to manage one's internal state is an important skill for success in practically every area of human competence. According to the great psychologist William James:

> *The greatest revolution of our generation is the discovery that human beings, by changing the inner attitudes of their minds, can change the outer aspects of their lives.*

Athletes getting ready to compete in a sports event, for instance, prepare their internal states as much as they prepare themselves physically. They talk about the importance of maintaining a calm, relaxed and focused internal state, even for events that require intense effort and expenditure of physical energy.

As another example, in a study of effective leadership, mangers were asked, "How do you deal with challenging situations involving uncertainty, conflict and/or complexity?" The most common reaction to this question went something like:

> *I gather as much information as I can; looking at the situation from every angle and gathering the relevant data. But when I actually am in that situation I do not really think about what I am going to do or say or how I should react or respond. There are too many things that could come up that I haven't thought of. At that time there is only one thing on my mind: "What state do I want to be in?" Because if I am in the wrong state, I will struggle no matter how well prepared I am. But if I am in right state, even if I don't know the answer, the inspiration will come.*

Some internal states, such as "test anxiety," inhibit us from using our resources effectively, and actually block us from using what we know. Resourceful states, on the other hand, help us to optimize our mental and physical competence and perform with excellence.

From the NLP perspective, internal states are a synthesis of both mental and physiological attributes that influence performance and stimulate unconscious processes. Having methods for selecting and managing one's internal state is a key part of successful performance. Different types of internal states are more effective for handling different situations and environments. Learning various strategies for establishing and shifting internal states can help make clients more effective in all aspects of their personal and professional lives.

The Circle of Excellence

One of the most important parts of the "inner game" is the ability to manage our internal states. This involves the capacity to select and maintain the types of internal states that will promote and sustain effective performance. The Circle of Excellence is a fundamental NLP process to help people more intentionally and effectively manage their internal states. Its purpose is to help people anchor, enrich and recover states of optimal performance.

The goals of the Circle of Excellence format are to 1) discover something about your own internal and behavioral cues for an effective state, 2) establish an internal anchor to be able to more easily reaccess that state, and 3) learn to observe and read other people's cues more effectively.

The coach can guide the client through the Circle of Excellence procedure using the following instructions:

1. Choose a resourceful state you would like to experience more often (e.g., creativity, confidence, etc.).

2. Identify a specific time in which you fully experienced that state.

3. Imagine a circle on the ground in front of you, or select a specific color, symbol or some other visual cue or sound that you would associate with that state.

4. When you are ready, step forward into the circle (or other symbol that you have chosen). Relive the experience, by associating into the state fully. See through your own eyes, hear through your own ears, and feel the sensations, breathing patterns, etc.

Stepping into the 'Circle of Excellence'

5. Take an inventory of the cognitive and behavioral patterns, both obvious and subtle, associated with the state. Focus your attention internally and notice any inner representations, sensory characteristics, breathing patterns, muscle tension, etc.

6. Enhance your experience of the state by amplifying any sensory qualities (color, movement, brightness, etc.) associated with the state, including all representational modalities (sight, sound, feeling, movement, smell and taste).

7. Step back and shake off the state.

8. Test your "circle of excellence" by stepping forward and noticing how quickly and fully you can reaccess the state.

9. Repeat steps 1 to 7 until you can achieve an easy, clean access to the state.

10. Identify some of the situations in which you would like to have this state. Imagine you can take your "circle of excellence" into each situation and "future pace" your experience.

The Circle of Excellence allows clients to discover the key cognitive and physical patterns associated with personal states of optimal performance. It also helps both clients and coaches to develop awareness about the types of cues that might be valuable in terms of recognizing and managing the states of other people.

Even very subtle behaviors can make a difference in performance. If you can find some of these cues, you can help to reaccess that state in a more conscious and purposeful way. The more you know about both the cognitive and physiological aspects associated with your own peak performances, the more chance that you have of being able to reaccess it at will.

Modeling Capabilities

Visualization, mental rehearsal and state management are examples of cognitive capabilities. Such capabilities are the deeper structures behind specific tasks or procedures. Procedures are typically a sequence of actions or steps that lead to the accomplishment of a particular task. A particular skill or capability, however, (such as the ability to think creatively, or to communicate effectively) may serve as a support for many different kinds of tasks, situations and contexts. Instead of a linear sequence of steps, skills are organized around a T.O.T.E. (Miller, Gallanter and Pribram, 1960)—a feedback loop between (a) goals (b) the choice of means used to accomplish those goals and (c) the evidence used to assess progress towards the goals.

The T.O.T.E.: Minimum Requirements for Modeling Effective Skills and Behaviors

The letters T.O.T.E. stand for *Test-Operate-Test-Exit*. The T.O.T.E. concept maintains that all effective performances revolve around having a fixed goal and a variable means to achieve that goal.

This model indicates that, as we think, we set goals in our mind (consciously or unconsciously) and develop a TEST for when that goal has been achieved. If that goal is not achieved we OPERATE to change something or do something to get closer to our goal. When our TEST criteria have been satisfied we then EXIT on to the next step. So the function of any particular part of a behavioral program could be to (T)est information from the senses in order to check progress towards the goal or to (O)perate to change some part of the ongoing experience so that it can satisfy the (T)est and (E)xit on to the next part of the program.

As an example, a TEST for effective "coaching" might be that a client is able to achieve a particular performance standard. If the client has not yet reached that standard, the coach will need to OPERATE or go through procedures (such as setting well-formed outcomes, shifting psychogeography, mapping across resources, anchoring, etc.) to attempt to help the client improve to the point that he or she is able to reach the desired level of performance. When the standard is met, coach and client can EXIT on to another activity.

According to NLP, in order to effectively model a particular skill or performance we must identify each of the key elements of the T.O.T.E. related to that skill or performance:

1) The performer's goals.

2) The evidence and evidence procedures used by the performer(s) to determine progress toward the goal.

3) The sets of choices used by the performer(s) to get to the goal and the specific behaviors used to implement these choices.

4) The way the performer(s) respond(s) if the goal is not initially achieved.

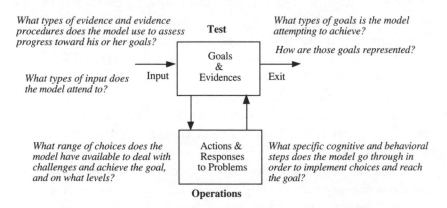

Modeling Involves Defining the Various Elements of the Performer's T.O.T.E.

The T.O.T.E. is a useful and powerful tool that can be used as part of the coaching-modeling loop. The following questions can be used by coaches to help clients self-model key success factors from their own past performances which can then be applied to help clients achieve better quality and consistency in the future.

Teaching Toolbox: T.O.T.E. Modeling Questions

1. What is a context in which you commonly use the skill to be modeled?

2. What are the goals or objectives that guide your actions as you apply the skill in this context? (List them in short sentences or key words.)

3. What do you use as evidence to know that you were accomplishing those goals?

    a. What criteria do you use to evaluate results?

        1) How, specifically, do you know when to continue with what you are doing versus try something different? What are your go/no go points?

        2) How do you sort good results from bad ones?

    b. When do you want feedback?

        1) What kind?

        2) From whom?

4. What do you do to get to the goals—what are some specific steps and activities that you use to achieve your goals in this context?

    a. What parts of your experience or environment do you utilize in order to get to your goal?

    b. What is the necessary sequence of mental activity you need to go through in order to be successful?

5. When you experience unexpected problems or difficulties in achieving your goals in this context, what specific activities or steps do you take to correct them?

    a. What steps do you take to avoid these disruptions?

    b. How do you respond if you run into these problems?

    c. Think of a time you were stuck and were able to break out of it. What did you do?

Teaching Toolbox: Mapping Across Effective T.O.T.E.s

Once information about a client's T.O.T.E. or strategy has been elicited, it may then be *utilized* in order to help the person improve in several ways. As we explored in the previous chapter, one of the most common NLP utilization methods is known as *mapping across*. Mapping across is a type of 'self-modeling' in which the steps or elements of a strategy that are effective for one situation or task are analyzed and then applied in a completely different context. Because strategies are content independent, a strategy for creative cooking, for instance, could be utilized or "mapped across" to help a person be more creative in some other area, such as composing music, solving organizational problems or new product development. Mapping across is typically done in conjunction with a Contrastive Analysis, in which processes and features of two cognitive strategies (or T.O.T.E.s) which produce different results are compared for similarities and differences. Certain characteristics of the effective strategy are then transferred to the other context in order to help produce more effective results.

One of the most basic NLP utilization procedures is to elicit the four elements of the T.O.T.E. loop for both the effective and ineffective strategies and contrast them for the key differences (*Tools for Dreamers*, Dilts, Epstein and Dilts, 1991). The effective strategy may then be utilized to enrich the ineffective strategy in two ways:

1) by replacing the elements of the ineffective T.O.T.E. with the corresponding elements of the effective T.O.T.E.

2) by adding the elements of the effective T.O.T.E. to those of the ineffective T.O.T.E.

The following figure shows an example of two contrasting T.O.T.E.s for contexts involving communication. The chart has been filled out a client who is an effective teacher but gets stuck and inflexible when he or she has to delegate a specific task to someone. As you can see, the two strategies differ in some important and significant ways.

Example:	*e.g., Teaching* **Effective Context**	*e.g., Delegating* **Ineffective Context**
What are your goals?	Sharing knowledge with others and having fun	Getting the task done the right way
How do you know you are achieving your goals?	The look on peoples' faces and my inner feelings	The end result of the task
What do you do in order to reach your goals? *What do you do if you are not satisfactorily reaching your goals?*	Use many examples and pictures Say the same thing in different words Try to get the audience into a more open state	Explain instructions clearly Become angry

Example of Contrasting Two T.O.T.E.s

Rather than judge the limiting strategy as "bad" or "wrong" and something that the client shouldn't do, the effective strategy can be utilized by coaching the person whose T.O.T.E.s are described above to simply add the elements of his or her teaching T.O.T.E. to his or her delegation process. That is, the person can be asked:

When you are delegating, can you make your goals include both getting the task done correctly *and* sharing knowledge in a fun way with others?

Can you use both the end result of the task *and* the looks on peoples' faces and your own feelings while the task is being carried as evidence to know you are achieving your goals for the delegation?

Can you both explain instructions clearly *and* use examples and pictures as you are explaining them?

If the delegation goals are not being satisfactorily achieved, can you *add the choices* of saying the same instructions in different words and trying to get the person you are delegating to into a more open state of mind as other alternatives to getting angry?

Notice that there are a few adjustments that need to be made to adapt the effective strategy to the new context. Sometimes this requires a little creativity. But often it can be done fairly simply.

Teaching Toolbox: Cooperative Learning

The T.O.T.E. structure can also be used by coaches as a means to help client's compare and contrast performance strategies with others, as a form of "intervision." This facilitates a type of "cooperative learning" between the coach and his or her client, or between groups of clients.

Cooperative learning is a process in which effective strategies may be transferred between two or more people. For example two managers, or two musicians, or two salespeople may have different strategies for accomplishing the same kind of task in the same context. Eliciting and sharing goals, evidence procedures and operations can help to widen and enrich the range and scope of creativity, flexibility and learning.

Cooperative Learning Process

This process can be done with a coach and his or her client, or with several clients if the coach is working with a group. Each person fills in the T.O.T.E. information on the chart below. Different individuals then compare their answers, noting the similarities and differences.

Clients are then encouraged to imagine what it would be like to add the operations, evidence procedures, goals or responses to problems, of other people's processes to their own strategy, and consider how it might change or enrich the way they approach the task or context.

Context: _____

	Person #1	Person #2
What are your goals?		
How do you know you are achieving your goals?		
What do you do in order to reach your goals? What do you do if you are not satisfactorily reaching your goals?		

Cooperative Learning Template

Teaching Toolbox: Focusing on Feedback Instead of "Failure"

A key aspect of the T.O.T.E. model relates to how clients responds if they experience unexpected problems or difficulties achieving their goals—in essence, how clients responds to "failure" in reaching their outcomes This response is fundamental to successful performance. Effective performers learn from their mistakes, but don't obsess about them.

There was an enlightening study done with good and mediocre athletes that illustrates this point. When good athletes were interviewed about their successes, they became very active and involved, and could remember every detail. When asked about their failures, however, they were more distant, vague and uninvolved.

When mediocre athletes were asked about their successes, on the other hand, they became distant, vague and uninvolved. When asked about their failures, however, they were active and involved, remembering and reliving each excruciating detail.

There is a saying which states, "Energy flows where attention goes." A key to learning from mistakes is to get some emotional distance from them, see what you can learn, and staying connected to your successes. The following simple two-step process can be used by coaches to help their clients to accomplish this.

1. Think of your mistakes like you are watching yourself on a video, looking at yourself as if you are a good coach giving yourself constructive feedback.

2. When you remember your good performances, put yourself "into the picture" and relive the experience as if you are right there doing it.

Basic Perceptual Positions in Communication and Relationships

As the previous exercise demonstrates, our perceptions of situations and experiences are greatly influenced by the point of view or perspective from which we consider them. Being able to take different perspectives of a situation is a key element of our "inner game" with respect to a particular situation or performance. In fact, there are several basic "perceptual positions" from which any situation or interaction may be viewed.

A "perceptual position" is essentially a particular perspective, or point of view from which one is perceiving a situation or relationship. NLP defines several basic positions one can take in perceiving a particular experience. *First position* involves experiencing something through our own eyes, associated in a "first person" point of view. *Second position* involves experiencing something as if we were in "another person's shoes." *Third position* involves standing back and perceiving the relationship between ourselves and others from an "observer" perspective. The notion of *fourth position* relates to the sense of the whole system or "relational field" (sense of a collective "we") derived from a synthesis of the other three positions.

Like all other NLP distinctions, perceptual positions are characterized by specific physical, cognitive and linguistic patterns. These patterns are summarized in the following descriptions:

First position is you, standing in your own physical space, in your own habitual body posture. When fully associated in first position, you will use words like "me," "I," and "myself" when referring to your own feelings, perceptions and ideas. In first position, you are going through the experience of the communication from your own perspective: seeing, hearing, feeling, tasting and smelling everything that is going on around you and inside of you in that experience from an associated perspective. If you are truly in first position, you will not see yourself, but will be yourself, looking out at the world through your own eyes, ears, etc. You will be fully associated in your own body and map of the world.

Second position is being able to assume another person's perspective within the interaction. (If there is more than one other person in the interaction, there may be multiple "second positions"). This is a temporary, information gathering position in which you shift to another person's perceptual position, taking on his or her physical posture and world view, as though you were that person. You see, hear, feel, taste, and smell what the communication loop is like from that person's point of view, i.e., "walk a mile in his or her shoes," "sit on the other side of the desk," etc. In second position, you will be experiencing the world through another person's eyes, thoughts, feelings, beliefs, etc.   In this position, you will be dissociated from yourself and associated into another person. You will address your "first position" self as "you" (as opposed to "I" or "me"), using "second person" language. Temporarily assuming another person's position is a wonderful way of evaluating how effective you are on your side of the communication loop. (After you have stepped into another person's perspective, it is important to make sure you return to yourself fully, cleanly, and with the information which will aid you in your communication.)

Third position, or "observer" position, puts you temporarily outside of the communication loop in order to gather information, as though you were a witness to, and not a participant in, the interaction. Your posture will be symmetrical and relaxed. In this position, you will see, hear, feel, taste, and smell what the communication loop is like from the position of an interested but neutral observer. You will use "third person" language, such as "she" and "he," when referring to the persons you are observing (including the one that looks, sounds and acts like you). You will be disassociated from the interaction, and in a type of "meta" position.

This position gives you valuable information about the balance of behaviors in the loop. The information gathered from this perspective can be taken back to your own first position and used, along with the information gathered in second position, to assist in enhancing the quality of your state, interaction and relationship within the communication loop.

Fourth position involves a synthesis of the other three perspectives, creating the sense of "being the whole system." It involves an identification with the system or relationship itself, producing the experience of being part of a collective, characterized by language such as "we" (first person plural). Fourth position is essential for producing a "group mind" or "team spirit."

In summary, perceptual positions refer to the fundamental points of view you can take concerning a relationship between yourself and another person:

1st Position: Associated in your own point of view, beliefs and assumptions, seeing the external world through your own eyes—an *"I"* position.

2nd Position: Associated in another person's point of view, beliefs and assumptions, seeing the external world through his or her eyes—a *"you"* position.

3rd Position: Associated in a point of view outside of the relationship between yourself and the other person—a *"they"* position.

4th Position: Associated in the perspective of the whole system—a *"we"* position.

As the descriptions above indicate, perceptual positions are characterized and expressed by key words—"I," "you," "they," and "we." In a way, these key words are a type of meta message that can help you to recognize and direct the perceptual positions people are assuming during a particular interaction. For instance, someone who frequently uses the word "I" is more likely to be speaking from his or her point of view than a person who is using the word "we" when talking about ideas or suggestions. A person who is stuck in one perspective can be encouraged to shift perceptual positions through the subtle use of such language cues.

For example, let's say a person is coaching a project team, and one of the members of that team is being overly critical of an idea or plan and says something like, "I don't think this will ever work," indicating a strong "first position" reaction. The coach could help shift the individual to a more "systemic" position by saying, "I understand you have some big concerns about this plan. How do you think we can approach it in a way that will work?"

To guide the person to an observer position, the coach could suggest, "Imagine you were a consultant for this team. What ways would you suggest for them to work together more effectively?" To encourage the critical individual to go to "second position" the coach could say, "Put yourself in my shoes (or one of the other team members) for a moment. What reactions do you think I would have to your concern?"

The ability to switch points of view and take multiple perspectives of a situation or experience is a key element of one's "inner game" of performance, and one of the most important communication and relational skills a coach can help clients to use and develop.

Second Position

As we established in the previous section, taking *second position* involves the ability to step into another person's point of view, or "perceptual position," within a particular situation or interaction. It involves shifting perspectives and viewing the situation as though you were another individual. From second position, you see, hear, feel, taste and smell what the interaction is like from the other person's perspective; to "be in his or her skin," "walk a mile in his or her shoes," "sit on the other side of the desk," etc.

Second position involves being associated in another person's point of view, beliefs and assumptions, and seeing the external world through his or her eyes. In this position, you are disassociated from yourself and associated into the experience of another person. When in second position, you use words such as, "You are," "You look," etc., when you refer to your first position self.

The ability to take second position with others and experience their map of the world is the basis for compassion and empathy. It is the essence of the "Golden Rule" to "Do unto others as you would have them do unto you." Second position of some kind is also necessary for all effective modeling. Temporarily assuming another person's position is also a wonderful way of evaluating how effective you are on your side of an interaction or communication loop.

Second position is an important skill for many professions. Effective managers and leaders, for instance, often talk about the need to put themselves "into the head" of their collaborators, or to "enter the feeling space" of others. In a 1998 interview in *Speak* magazine, criminal lawyer Tony Serra commented:

> *[W]hen you represent the criminal defendant . . . you become him, you feel like him, you walk in his shoes, and you see with his eyes and hear with his ears.*

You've got to know him completely to know that nature of his behavior. But you have "the word." That is, you can translate his feeling, his meaning and his intellect as components that are relevant to his behavior into legalese, into the words of the law, or into persuasive metaphors. You take the clay of a person's behavior and you embellish it, you make a piece of art. And that is the lawyer's creativity.

The ability to take second position is an important skill for both coaches and their clients.

Teaching Toolbox: Building a "Second Position" Perspective

The process of taking second position involves committing your sensory experience and mental maps to the perspective of another. This can be done fully or only partially. For instance, if someone says, "If I were you I would . . . ," the person really has no second position at all. The person making this statement is not taking on the world view of the other, but rather projecting his or her own world view into the other's situation.

Saying, "From the perspective of this other person, I see myself standing over there," is also indicative that one is not fully in "second position." The reference to "myself standing over there" shows that the speaker is still more identified with his or her own first position. This statement reflects a second position that is more theoretical than felt. To be fully in second position requires that you see, hear, feel and verbalize from the other person's point of view (saying, "I see that other person over there" when talking about yourself).

Thus, it is possible to be in "mixed" or "contaminated" perceptual positions. That is, a person may be seeing and feeling a situation from his or her own first position, but talking to him/herself using second position language (i.e., saying to oneself, "Be careful that *you* don't make a mistake."). Being able to consciously assume a complete second position, or select particular aspects of second position is a skill that can be developed through the appropriate coaching and practice.

There are different levels and degrees of taking second position. Being in someone's home or workplace is a way to get a second position on an environmental level. Imitating a person's actions is taking second position on a behavioral level. Learning about a person's thinking strategies and mental maps is a way to develop second position on a capability level. Taking on a person's values and beliefs is a way of getting a second position at an even deeper level. Identifying with another person and taking on his or her personality would involve second position at a very deep identity level.

The following process can be used to help clients build a rich second position perspective on a number of these levels.

Ask your client to select a person whom he or she would like to model or understand better. Create two physical locations: one for the client and one for the other person.

Have the client start from his or her own "first position." Standing in the "self location," have your client make an inventory of his or her own experience of his or her environment, physical being, thoughts, beliefs, values, sense of self, and his or her own sense of vision and purpose. Create an anchor or "life line" to this "first position" location.

Then coach the client to begin to enter the perspective of the other person in stages by stepping into the location for the other person and going through the following steps:

1. Imagine being in the environment of the other. *Where and when do you operate?*

2. Imagine being "in the shoes" of the other. *What behaviors and actions do you engage in within that environment?*

3. Imagine being in the mind of the other. *What skills and capabilities do you need to effectively act or operate in that environment?*

4. Imagine being in the belief system and value system of the other. *What priorities and assumptions do you have about your work?*

5. Imagine being in the identity or role of the other. *What is your perception of your mission and yourself as that other person?*

6. Imagine being in the larger system of the other. *Who and what else is critical to your purpose or mission?*

When you are finished, have the client return to his or her own first position by stepping out of the location representing the other person, shifting his or her physiology and inner state, then stepping back into the "self location" and using the anchor or "life line" to bring the client fully back into his or her own perceptual position.

It is often helpful to establish a neutral "meta position" or "third position" between the locations for "self" and "other." You can use this third location as a transition state between the client's own perspective and that of the other individual to help ensure that there is a good separation between the two perceptual positions.

Teaching Toolbox: Meta Mapping

The Meta Map is a process that applies the different perceptual positions in order to help clients map and more effectively address challenging interactions, situations and relationships. The purpose of the Meta Map is to assist a person to identify and then alter characteristics of the communication loops that are producing or maintaining a problematic interaction.

Often, when we experience difficulties in communicating with others, we become entrenched in our own point of view. The Meta Map begins by acknowledging that perspective, but then provides us with the opportunity to see the interaction from other points of view. In addition to identifying "invisible" (i.e., internal and non-physical) influences on the situation, the Meta Map allows us to see and modify some of the ways in which we may be contributing to our own difficulties.

A number of the specific steps of the Meta Map were derived from modeling effective leaders in companies and organizations. As part of the modeling process, leaders would be placed in challenging, and largely unpredictable, interactive situations. The leaders were then questioned about how they prepared themselves mentally to meet the challenges.

A good example of a common response was:

> *I would think about the people involved in the situation, and imagine the possible actions they could take that would create problems. I would then look at myself and try to see what I could do in response, and whether I felt comfortable with that. I also tried to see the situation from the other person's perspective, and get a sense of what motives might be behind their actions. I would then view the situation from the company's perspective to see what was going to be the*

best way to handle the situation for all concerned. Having done my "homework," I would finally think about what internal state I wanted to be in, and what state would help me respond most creatively and appropriately. I figured that if I was in the wrong state, I wouldn't be able to respond well no matter what happened; but if I was in the right state, the inspiration would be there, even if something happened that I hadn't prepared for.

By taking multiple perceptual positions, leaders were able to fine tune their "inner game" so that they could most effectively manage the situation. Reflecting upon such examples of success, we can conclude that the basic elements of an effective Meta Map include: (a) identifying a difficult or challenging communication situation; (b) mapping the dynamics occurring between oneself, the other person in the interaction, and one's inner observer; (c) taking the perspective of the other person, and viewing the situation from his or her point of view; (d) establishing a "meta position" from which to examine both mental and physical patterns occurring within the interaction that may be contributing to the problem; and (e) exploring possible changes in communication, attitude and internal state that could make the interaction more comfortable and productive.

The following is the basic Meta Mapping format, based on the strategies of effective leaders, that can be taught to clients as an effective strategy for reflecting upon, or planning for, a challenging situation or interaction.

Basic Meta Map Format

This process is best done in a type of role playing format, in which the client is instructed to physically move to different locations and act out the various perceptual positions. Before beginning, lay out three locations in the "psychogeography" shown below.

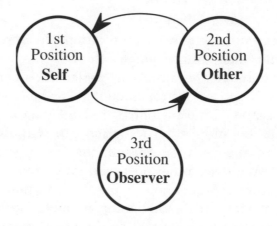

The Three Physical Locations for the Meta Map Format

Lead the client through the following set of instructions:

1. Think about a particular situation you have been in, or are expecting to be in, involving a challenging other person.

2. Physically put yourself into the first position location, taking your own perspective in the interaction as if the challenging other person were there right now and you were looking at him or her through your own eyes. Run through some of the things the other person does that makes him or her challenging to deal with. Notice the

internal response that you have—i.e., what is currently going on in your "inner game"?

3. Now, physically step away from your first position location and step into the second position location. Imagine you are "in the shoes" of the other person, looking at yourself through his or her eyes. Take on the perspective, thinking style, beliefs and assumptions of the individual as if you were that person for a moment. What is that person's perspective of the interaction? What do you learn about this other person's map of the world? How is it different from your own?

4. Physically move to the third position location and view the relationship between yourself and the other person as if you were an observer watching a video of two people interacting. What do observe about the "outer" and "inner" games of the two people involved in that communication loop? What internal state and resources would you like to transfer to the first position you to enhance your inner game? (You may use the Circle of Excellence, anchoring or mapping across formats to bring in these resources.)

5. As an optional step, take the perspective of the whole system and consider what would be in the best interest of the system.

Notice how taking the different perceptual positions changes your experience of the interaction.

What new awareness did you get about yourself, the other person or the situation?

(For a more advanced Meta Mapping format, see *The Encyclopedia of Systemic NLP,* Dilts & DeLozier, 2000.)

Imagineering

Another very useful set of perceptual positions are embodied within the "imagineering" process. *Imagineering* is a term coined by Walt Disney to describe the process he used to "create the future" by forming dreams and then turning them into realities. A powerful insight into the imagineering process is provided by one of Disney's co-workers who pointed out, ". . . there were actually three different Walts: the *dreamer*, the *realist*, and the *spoiler*. You never knew which one was coming into your meeting." Imagineering involves the coordination of these three subprocesses: Dreamer, Realist and Critic, all of which are key components to be successful in the "inner game" of reaching future goals.

A Dreamer without a Realist cannot turn ideas into tangible expressions. A Critic and a Dreamer without a Realist just become stuck in a perpetual conflict. A Dreamer and a Realist might create things, but they might not be very good ideas without a Critic. The Critic helps to evaluate and refine the products of creativity (when destructive, a Critic is a "spoiler;" when constructive, a Critic is an "advisor"). There is a humorous example of an entrepreneur who prided himself on his innovative thinking abilities but lacked some of the Realist and Critic perspective. The people who worked in the company used to say, "He has an idea a minute . . . and some of them are good."

In summary:

- A Dreamer without a Realist and Critic is just that: only a Dreamer.

- A Realist without a Dreamer and Critic is a Robot.

- A Critic without a Dreamer and a Realist is a Spoiler.

- A Dreamer and a Realist without a Critic are a research & development department—they make a lot of prototypes but lack the quality standards for success.

- A Realist and a Critic without a Dreamer are a Bureaucracy.

- A Dreamer and a Critic without a Realist are a roller coaster of Manic-Depression.

Effective innovation and problem solving involve a synthesis of these different processes or phases. The Dreamer is necessary in order to form new ideas and goals. The Realist is necessary as a means to transform ideas into concrete expressions. The Critic is necessary as a filter for refining ideas and avoiding possible problems.

The following is a summary of the basic cognitive and physical patterns associated with each of these key thinking styles.

Dreamer

The Dreamer phase of a process is oriented towards the longer term future. It involves thinking in terms of the bigger picture and the larger chunks in order to generate new alternatives and choices. The emphasis of the Dreamer stage of a process is on representing and widening the perception of a particular plan or idea. Its primary level of focus is on generating the content or the "what" of the plan or idea. According to Disney, the function of a Dreamer is to "see clearly in his own mind how every piece of business in a story [or project] will be put." Dreamer objectives include: Stating the goal in positive terms and establishing the purpose and payoffs of the desired state.

To think like a Dreamer it is helpful to keep your head and eyes up, and get into a comfortable posture that is symmetrical and relaxed.

Realist

The purpose of the Realist is to turn the dream into a workable plan or product. As a Realist, you want to act "as if" the dream is possible, and focus on the steps or actions required to actually reach the dream. Your primary focus should be on "how" to implement the plan or idea.

The Realist phase of a process is more action oriented to moving towards the future, operating with respect to a shorter term time frame than the Dreamer. The Realist is often more focused on procedures or operations. His or her primary level of focus is on "how" to implement the plan or idea.

To think like a Realist it helps to sit with your head and eyes straight ahead or slightly forward with a posture that is symmetrical and slightly forward. Your cognitive focus should be to act "as if" the dream is achievable and consider how the idea or plan can be implemented; emphasizing specific actions and defining short-term steps. It also helps to put oneself into the "shoes" of the other people involved in the plan and perceive it from several points of view.

Critic

The Critic phase of creativity follows the Dreamer and Realist. The purpose of being a Critic is to evaluate the plan or project that has been proposed, and look for potential problems and "missing links." To be an effective Critic, it is important to take the perspectives of people who might influence, or be influenced by, the plan or project (either positively or negatively), and consider their needs and reactions. The primary purpose of the Critic is to find potential problems and missing links in a particular plan or potential solution. The strategy of the Critic is to help avoid problems by taking different perspectives and finding missing links by logically considering "what would happen if" problems occur.

Thinking like a Critic involves taking on an angular posture, in which the eyes and head are down and slightly tilted, and touching your chin or face with one of your hands.

Teaching Toolbox: Imagineering Coaching Format

The imagineering process essentially involves chunking the dream into all of the steps that were necessary to manifest it.

The following procedure uses both physiology and key questions to help draw out the client's ability to be Dreamer, Realist and Critic during a creative planning process.

The questions have been formulated to stimulate the thinking patterns associated with Dreamer, Realist and Critic. It is important to keep in mind, however, that a Dreamer question, answered from a Critic's physiology, is not likely to produce a congruent Dreamer answer. Similarly, a Critic or Realist question answered from a Dreamer physiology will not yield a good answer. It will be very important, then, for the coach to carefully observe the client during the procedure in order to ensure that the client does not "contaminate" his or her answers by unconsciously shifting to an inappropriate physiology while answering the questions asked by the coach.

1. For each phase of the creative cycle (Dreamer, Realist and Critic), the coach is to ask the questions relevant for that phase (listed on the following worksheets) and help the client keep track of his or her answers.

2. While answering the questions, the client is to assume and maintain the appropriate physiology and thinking style defined in the guidelines below.

3. The coach is to watch and ensure that the client maintains the appropriate state and does not 'contaminate' it.

4. Keep cycling through the phases to make successive approximations of the plan.

Use the following worksheets to record the answers to the various questions posed at each stage of the imagineering cycle.

"WANT TO" PHASE—Dreamer

Objectives: State the Specific Goal in Positive Terms; Establish the Payoffs of the Idea.

Answer the following questions from the Dreamer posture.

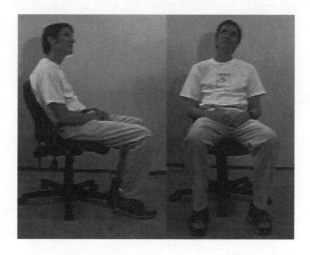

Dreamer State Physiology

1. What do you want to do? (As opposed to what you want to avoid or not do.)

   The goal is to _____

2. Why do you want to do it? What is the purpose?

   The purpose is to _____

3. What are the benefits?

The beneficial effects of this will be _____

4. How will you know that you have them?

An evidence of these benefits will be _____

5. When can you expect to get them?

The benefits can be expected when _____

6. Where do you want this idea to get you in the future?

This idea will lead to _____

7. Who do you want to be or be like in relation to manifesting this idea?

I/We want to be _____

"HOW TO" PHASE—Realist

Objectives: Establish Time Frames and Milestones for Progress. Make Sure the Idea Can Be Initiated and Maintained by the Appropriate Person or Group and that Progress Is Testable through Sensory Experience.

Answer the following questions from the Realist posture.

Realist State Physiology

1. When will the overall goal be completed?

   The overall time frame for reaching the goal is _____

2. Who will be involved? (Assign responsibility and secure commitment from the people who will be carrying out the plan.)

   The chief actors include _____

3. How specifically will the idea be implemented? What will be the first step?

The steps to reach the goal involve

(a) _____

What will be the second step?

(b) _____

What will be the third step?

(c) _____

4. What will be your ongoing feedback that you are moving toward or away from the goal?

An effective ongoing feedback will be _____

5. How will you know that the goal is achieved?

I will know that the goal has been reached when _____

Create a pictorial "storyboard" for your plan by finding or drawing simple images to represent the steps required for reaching your goal or vision. This can help to "anchor" your own map of your plan and make it easier to communicate to others. Use the following frames to draw pictures representing the three key steps of the path that you have identified as being necessary to reach the goal or dream. Write any titles or comments in the spaces below the frames.

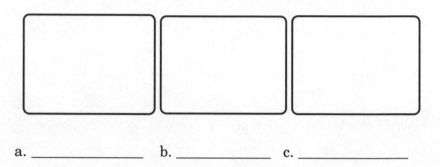

a. _____   b. _____   c. _____

Refer to this storyboard as you proceed to the next phase of the process—the Critic.

"CHANCE TO" PHASE—Critic

Objectives: Make Sure the Plan Preserves Any Positive By-Products of the Current Way(s) of Achieving the Goal.

Answer the following questions from the Critic posture.

Critic State Physiology

1. Who will this new idea affect and who will make or break the effectiveness of the idea?

    The people most affected by this plan are _____

2. What are their needs and payoffs?

    Their needs are _____

3. Why might someone object to this plan or idea?

    Someone might object to this plan if _____

4. What positive gains are there in the present way(s) of doing things?

The present way of doing things _____

5. How can you keep those things when you implement the new idea?

These positive gains will be preserved by _____

6. When and where would you NOT want to implement this plan or idea?

I would not want to implement this plan if _____

7. What is currently needed or missing from the plan?

What is currently needed or missing from the plan is

_____

Note: I have developed a software program, for both Macintosh and Windows operating systems, which guides individuals and groups through Disney's *Imagineering* process. The software is available through:

Journey to Genius
P.O. Box 67448
Scotts Valley, California 95067-7448
E-Mail: info@journeytogenius.com
Homepage: http://www.journeytogenius.com

Summary

In summary, teaching involves helping clients develop cognitive capabilities that will lead them to improvements in performance. When in the role of teacher, a coach focuses his or her attention on the client's "inner game," supporting the client to be mentally prepared to do his or her best.

Effective teachers understand that individuals have different learning styles, founded upon their preferred representational channel (sight, hearing, feeling, etc.). Learning Style Assessment Questions help coaches to better recognize and adapt to the learning styles of clients, supporting their strengths and bolstering areas that can be improved.

Good teachers also help people develop new strategies for "learning to learn." Visualizing success and mental rehearsal are teaching tools that allow clients to practice and refine a process or activity in their minds before entering the performance context, which greatly increases their chance of success.

State management is a key element of a person's inner game of performance. Processes such as the Circle of Excellence teach clients to recognize and reaccess states of excellence that can enhance their performance in a variety of different situations and contexts.

The T.O.T.E. Model is a basic framework for the coaching-modeling loop that provides a simple structure and set of questions which can be used by teachers to help clients become aware of key success factors behind effective performance, within themselves and others, and then transfer those factors to other contexts and environments.

Effective performers learn from their mistakes, but don't obsess about them. Good coaches encourage clients to perceive mistakes as feedback rather than failures and help clients to learn from mistakes by getting emotional distance from them while staying connected to their successes.

The capacity to take different perceptual positions is another key element of a person's inner game. The ability to view a situation from first (self), second (other) and third (observer) position can help clients to greatly improve their ability to communicate and interact with others. Second position is particularly important to succeed in the inner game of working effectively with others. The Meta Map applies the different perceptual positions to help clients better understand and handle challenging individuals.

Imagineering strategy uses Walt Disney's cycle of Dreamer, Realist and Critic to help clients create a positive and satisfying future and building the path to reach that desired state.

Chapter 4

Mentoring

Overview of Chapter 4

- **Mentoring**
  - Values
  - Values and Beliefs
  - The Power of Beliefs
  - Mentoring Values and Beliefs
- **Role Modeling**
- **Mentoring Toolbox: Establishing Inner Mentors**
- **Mentoring Toolbox: Values Audit**
  - Values Audit Worksheet
- **Aligning Values with Vision and Actions**
- **Mentoring Toolbox: Creating Alignment for Change**
- **Mentoring Toolbox: Putting Values Into Action**
- **Mentoring Toolbox: Values Planning**
- **Mentoring Toolbox: Establishing Practices**
- **Belief Systems and Change**

Overview of Chapter 4 (continued)

- **Mentoring Toolbox: Belief Assessment**
  - Belief Assessment Worksheet
- **Mentoring Toolbox: Using Inner Mentors to Build Confidence and Strengthen Belief**
- **Mentoring Toolbox: The "As If" Frame**
- **Reframing**
  - One-Word Reframing
- **Mentoring Toolbox: Applying One-Word Reframes**
- **Mentoring Toolbox: Values Bridging**
- **Reframing Critics and Criticism**
  - Getting Positive Statements of Positive Intentions
  - Turning Criticisms Into Questons
- **Mentoring Toolbox: Helping Critics to Be Advisors**
- **Summary**

Mentoring

Knowledge speaks, but wisdom listens. —Jimi Hendrix

In Greek Mythology, Mentor was the wise and faithful counselor to the hero Odysseus. Under the guise of Mentor, the goddess Athena became the guardian and teacher of Odysseus' son Telemachus, while Odysseus was away on his journeys. Thus, the notion of being a "mentor" has come to mean one who engages in the process of both (a) advising or counseling, and (b) serving as a guide or teacher. Mentoring (especially in an occupational setting) emphasizes the informal relational aspect of learning and performance as much as it does the mastery of the task.

A mentor has overlaps with, but is distinct from, either a teacher or coach. A teacher instructs, and a coach provides specific behavioral feedback, in order to help a person learn or grow. As advisors and counselors, mentors frequently help others to establish, clarify or strengthen key *values and beliefs*, often through their own example.

Values and beliefs provide the reinforcement that supports or inhibits particular capabilities and actions. While values and beliefs are clearly a key part of a person's inner game, they are on a different level than cognitive capabilities. Values and beliefs relate to *why* a particular path is taken and the deeper motivations which drive people to act or persevere. Our values and beliefs transcend any particular thoughts or behaviors and serve to encourage, inhibit or generalize particular strategies, plans and ways of thinking. They have to do with why we think what we think and do what we do. Why, for instance, should a person consider changing his or her thoughts or actions?

A person's degree of motivation will determine how much of his or her own inner resources he or she is willing to mobilize. Motivation is what stimulates and activates how people think and what they will do in a particular situation.

Values

According to Webster's Dictionary, *values* are "principles, qualities or entities that are intrinsically valuable or desirable." Because they are associated with worth, meaning and desire, values are a primary source of a client's internal motivation. When people's values are met or matched, they feel a sense of satisfaction, harmony, or rapport. When their values are not met or matched, people often feel dissatisfied, incongruent, or violated.

To help a client explore his or her own values, ask him or her consider the following questions: "In general, what motivates you?" "What is most important to you?" "What moves you to action, or 'gets you out of bed in the morning'?"

Some possible answers might be:

Success
Praise
Recognition
Responsibility
Pleasure
Love and Acceptance
Achievement
Creativity

Values such as these greatly influence and direct the outcomes that clients establish and the choices that they make. The goals that clients set for themselves are, in fact, the tangible expression of their values. A client who has a goal to "build an effective team," for instance, most likely values "working together with others." A person whose goal is to "increase income" probably values "financial success." Similarly, a person who has a value of "stability" will set goals related to achieving stability in his or her personal or professional life. Such a person will seek different outcomes than a person who values "flexibility," for example. A person who values stability may be content with a 9-to-5 job that has consistent pay and involves well established tasks. A person who values flexibility, on the other hand, may try to find work involving a range of tasks and a variable time schedule.

Values and Beliefs

Values are intimately connected to beliefs. According to the NeuroLogical Levels model, beliefs and values occupy the same level of learning and change. Together, beliefs and values form the answer to the question *"Why?"* Values are characterized by a felt sense of meaning or desirability. Beliefs are cognitive structures which connect values to other aspects of our experiences.

Beliefs are essentially judgments and evaluations about ourselves, others and the world around us. According to the NeuroLogical Levels model, in order for deeper structures such as values (which are more abstract and subjective) to reach the tangible environment in the form of concrete behaviors, they must be linked to more specific cognitive processes and capabilities through beliefs. Beliefs are the answers to questions such as, "How, specifically, do you define the quality or entity you value?" "What causes or creates this quality?" "What consequences or outcomes result from that value?" "How, specifically, do you know if some behavior or experience fits a particular value?"

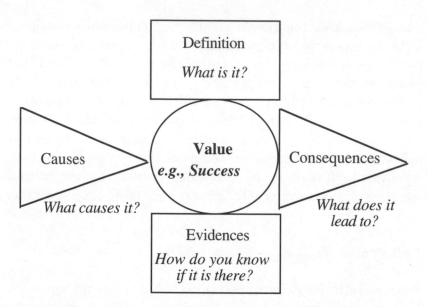

**Beliefs Connect Values to Various Aspects of Our
Experience**

In order for a particular value to become operational, this system of beliefs must be specified to a certain degree. For a value such as "professionalism" to be enacted behaviorally, for example, one must build beliefs about what professionalism is (the definition professionalism); how you know it is being enacted (the evidences); what causes it; and what it leads to (its consequences). These beliefs are as significant as the value itself in determining how people will act.

Two people can share the same value of "safety," for example. One person, however, may believe that safety is caused by "being stronger than one's enemies and striking them before they strike you." The other person may believe that safety is caused by "understanding and responding to the positive intentions of those who threaten us." These two will seek safety in quite different ways. Their approaches may even appear to contradict one another. The first one will seek safety by building power (having "a bigger stick" than those he or she perceives as an "enemy"). The other will seek safety through communication, gathering information and looking for options.

Clearly, an individual's beliefs relating to his or her core values will determine the person's "mental map" with respect to those values; and thus, how the person approaches manifesting those values. In order to adequately teach or establish values, all of these belief issues must be appropriately addressed. For people in a system to act coherently with core values, they must all share certain beliefs, as well as values, to some degree.

Values and beliefs form a type of non-physical framework which surrounds all of the interactions of the people within a system, such as a family, team or organization. They are the key to motivation and culture in organizations and social systems. Shared values and beliefs are the "glue" which holds an effective organization or team together. Conflicts of values and beliefs, on the other hand, are the source of disharmony and dissension.

The Power of Beliefs

Beliefs are a powerful influence on our lives. It is common wisdom that if someone really believes he can do something he will do it, and if he believes something is impossible no amount of effort will convince him that it can be accomplished. The power of beliefs was demonstrated in an enlightening study in which a group of children who were tested to have average intelligence was divided at random into two equal groups. One of the groups was assigned to a teacher who was told that the children were "gifted." The other group was given to a teacher who was told that the children were "slow learners." A year later the two groups were retested for intelligence. Not surprisingly, the majority of the group that was arbitrarily identified as "gifted" scored higher than they had previously, while the majority of the group that was labeled "slow" scored lower! The teacher's beliefs about the students affected their ability to learn.

Another good example of the power of beliefs to both limit us and empower us is that of the "four minute mile." Before May 6, 1954, it was believed that four minutes was an unbreakable barrier to the speed with which a human being could run a mile. In the nine years prior to the historic day in which Roger Bannister broke the four minute ceiling, no runners had even come close. Within six weeks after Bannister's feat, the Australian runner John Lundy lowered the record by another second. Within the next nine years nearly two hundred people had broken the once seemingly impenetrable barrier.

Certainly, these examples seem to demonstrate that our beliefs can shape, effect or even determine our degree of intelligence, health, relationships, creativity, even our degree of happiness and personal success. NLP has developed a wealth of belief change techniques and methodologies. A number of them, however, (such as reimprinting, belief outframing, integrating conflicting beliefs, etc.) are more therapeutic in their application. In this book, we will concentrate on approaches that can be done easily in a conversational, solution-focused coaching context.

[For more in-depth information on NLP belief change techniques see *Changing Beliefs with NLP* (Dilts, 1990), *Beliefs: Pathways to Health and Well-Being* (Dilts, Hallbom & Smith, 1990), and the *Encyclopedia of Systemic NLP* (Dilts &DeLozier, 2000).]

Mentoring Values and Beliefs

Mentors guide us to establish, strengthen and align empowering values and beliefs, often through their own example. As the example of the mythological Mentor suggests, mentoring includes the possibility of counseling and guidance from a deeper level than cognitive understanding. This type of mentoring often becomes internalized as part of the individual, so that the external presence of the mentor is no longer necessary. People are able to carry "inner mentors" as counselors and guides for their lives in many situations.

In NLP, the term *mentor* is used to refer to individuals who have helped to shape or influence your life in a positive way by "resonating" with, releasing, or unveiling something deeply within you. Mentors can include children, teachers, pets, people you've never met but have read about, phenomena in nature (such as the ocean, mountains, etc.), and even parts of yourself.

When supporting and advising others, mentors operate from the following beliefs:

When people want something and believe in it enough, they will find the way to make it happen.

The most important thing I can do is to help people believe in themselves and value what they are doing.

At their core, all people are positively intended. Having the appropriate values and beliefs is the foundation for being able to express our positive intentions in the most effective and ecological manner.

This person will be able to naturally establish empowering beliefs and appropriate values with advice and attention from me.

One of the best ways to advise others is by being an effective role model.

The leadership style of mentoring is that of inspirational leadership. Inspiring others involves motivating and encouraging them to do their best or to give a little extra. Mentoring and inspirational leadership emphasize values, and empowering beliefs in future possibilities.

Role Modeling

A primary personal quality of effective mentoring is being a good example and role model for others. A *role model* is a person who serves as an exemplar for a particular task or set of values. Typically, a role model is a person whose behavior in a particular role is imitated, or "modeled," by others in order to produce a similar performance or to reach similar results.

In their life times, people need to assume many role identities, such as parent, student, supervisor, leader, partner, etc. Many times, however, a void in a person's past experience or personal history leaves a deficit or impoverishment with respect to the capabilities, strategies, beliefs, etc., that would support a particular role. It is important for people to find others who can serve as mentors, guides and "models" for enriching their maps of particular role identities.

Role modeling is based on the assumption that if someone has been able to achieve a goal, others can model that person and learn to attain similar results. It is possible to discover the thinking patterns, beliefs and behaviors etc., that will allow other individuals to perform successfully, drawing from the patterns of that role model. Because we are members of the same species, a person who has achieved a particular result can be used as a role model for achieving a similar goal. As members of the human race, we all share a common structure for our nervous system and biological make-up, allowing us to learn and 'borrow' abilities from others without having to "reinvent the wheel."

Even fictitious characters can be effective role models.

Thus, role models, actual or fictional, can be rich and powerful sources of learning and inspiration.

Consider the following story about Mahatma Gandhi:

A mother was concerned about her son who had diabetes yet was eating sugar, which was bad for his health. So she took him to Gandhi and asked that he should tell him not to eat any sugar. Gandhi told the woman to return in three weeks. Three weeks later the woman returned and Gandhi told her son, "Do not eat any sugar." The lady asked Gandhi, "Gandhi-ji, it took me three days to get here from my village, and then three days to return and now another three days. Why couldn't you tell my son to stop eating sugar three weeks ago?" Gandhi replied, "Three weeks ago I loved sugar and would eat a lot. I had to stop eating it myself before I could advise your son."

This is a good illustration of a principle that Gandhi frequently pointed out: "You have got to *be* the change that you want see."

It is important for coaches and mentors to realize that they are role models and examples for others. Being an effective example or role model involves the abilities to be influential, to inspire emulation and to be trustworthy and credible.

Check your ability to be a good example as a coach by considering the following questions:

What am I a good example of?
What influence do I have?
What are the consequences of my actions?

To what degree am I able to:

• inspire emulation?
• be influential?
• be trustworthy?

Mentoring Toolbox: Establishing Inner Mentors

As was mentioned earlier, people frequently carry "inner mentors" as counselors and guides for their lives in many situations. Such inner mentors can be utilized to help draw knowledge, resources or unconscious competencies out of the clients in a natural and intuitive manner.

The basic way to use an inner "mentor" is to imagine the presence of the person or being, and then to take "second position," by stepping into the perspective or "shoes" of the mentor. This often allows clients to access qualities which are present within them, but not recognized or included by them as part of their map of the situation (or of themselves). By representing these qualities, the inner mentor helps clients to bring them alive in their ongoing behavior (as a consequence of the client taking on the perceptual position of the mentor). Once a person has experienced these qualities from second position with the mentor, that person is able to bring them back into his or her own first position within the situation, and enact them.

The following exercise demonstrates how the process of inner mentoring can be used to help a client deal more effectively with a challenging situation.

1. Identify a challenging situation that you would like to deal with more effectively.

2. Select three important mentors that can help you to respond more effectively at several levels. Choose (a) one as a guide or advisor with respect to your behavior, (b) one as a supporter for your ability to think and understand, and (c) one as a counselor for your beliefs and values. Imagine those three mentors were with you in the challenging situation.

3. Associate into (i.e., go to second position with) each of the mentors, one at a time. Experience being "in that person's shoes" and imagine how that individual would advise you to approach the situation. What resources would that mentor remind you that you have? What advice or message would that mentor have for you?

4. Return to your own perceptual position and notice how the mentors' advice and guidance changes your perception and understanding of the situation, and brings out more confidence in you.

5. Find a way that you can anchor and remind yourself of the lessons from each of these mentors in the actual situation that you have been exploring.

Mentoring Toolbox: Values Audit

A person's or group's *hierarchy of values* is essentially the order of priorities that they apply when deciding how to act in a particular situation. Hierarchies of values relate to the *degree* of importance or meaning which people attach to various actions and experiences.

An example of a "hierarchy of values" would be a person who values "health" more than "financial success." Such a person would tend to put his or her health "first." This person would probably structure his or her life more around physical activities than professional opportunities. A person whose hierarchy of values placed "financial success" over "health" would have a different lifestyle. He or she might sacrifice health and physical well-being in order to "get ahead" monetarily.

Helping clients to clarify their values and hierarchies of values is an important part of a mentor's job. The Values Audit is a mentoring tool that can be used to help people establish and strengthen important values by defining the needs, purposes, consequences and assumptions related to those values. One of the outcomes of the Values Audit is to address the following basic questions:

What is the value to be established or strengthened?

What is personally important to you?

What is the connection between the value and what is personally important to you?

The values "auditing" process uses verbal prompts and key words to help you make sure you have fully explored the supporting system of beliefs necessary to bring values into action.

Values Audit Worksheet

1. Identify a core value that is important for you to establish or strengthen. Write down the value you want to strengthen in the space marked Value below to complete the value statement.

2. For each of the prompt words, read your value statement, add the prompt word(s), and complete the sentence, answering the question listed below the blank space.

3. When you are finished, read your answers all together and notice what has changed and been strengthened.

Value: _____ is important and desirable.
What is a core value that is important for you to establish or strengthen?

because I _____
Why is it desirable and appropriate to have this as a value?

therefore I _____
What is a behavioral consequence of having this value?

whenever I _____
What is a key situation or condition relating to this value?

so that I _____
What is the positive purpose of this value?

if I _____
What constraints or results relate to this value?

*although I _____
What alternatives or constraints are there with respect to this value?

in the same way that I _____
What is a similar value that you already have?

For example, if a client wanted to strengthen his or her belief in and commitment to the value of "health," the process would start with the statement of that particular value: "Health is important and desirable." Holding this value statement constant, the individual would then go through each prompt, and its related question, to explore all of the supporting reasons.

In this case it would be important to begin each new sentence with the word "I." This helps to ensure that the client remains associated in the experience and avoids merely making "rationalizations."

An example of how someone would complete these sentences might be:

Health is important and desirable *because* I need strength and energy in order to create and survive.

Health is important and desirable *therefore* I will begin the appropriate steps to take care of myself.

Health is important and desirable *whenever* I want to be prepared for the future.

Health is important and desirable *so that* I can enjoy myself and be a good role model for others.

Health is important and desirable *if* I want to be happy and productive.

Health is important and desirable **although* I have other goals and responsibilities to be fulfilled.

Health is important and desirable *in the same way that* I need the necessary foundations and resources to reach my dreams.

After finishing the new statements, it is interesting to read each of the entries deleting the prompt words—with the exception of "although." (It is important to retain the word

"although" or that particular response will appear negative.)
The series of responses can form a surprisingly coherent and
valuable statement of reasons to commit to the core value
that you have selected:

> *Health is important and desirable. I need strength and*
> *energy in order to create and survive. I will begin the*
> *appropriate steps to take care of myself. I want to be*
> *prepared for the future. I can enjoy myself and be a*
> *good role model for others. I want to be happy and*
> *productive.* Although *I have other goals and*
> *responsibilities to be fulfilled, I need the necessary*
> *foundations and resources to reach my dreams.*

As you can see, this creates a coherent set of ideas and
affirmations that can help to strengthen a client's commitment to and belief in the value of health. The paragraph
defines elements of a pathway for expressing the value,
provides motivation, and even addresses possible objections.
Because the group of statements identify a multiplicity of
reasons (or causes) and puts them into words, it becomes a
powerful source of positive affirmations. It provides an overall explanation justifying commitment to the value. It also
provides a rich source of ideas for addressing doubts.

Aligning Values with Vision and Actions

In effective individuals, teams and organizations, behaviors and capabilities support key values. Those values, in turn, are aligned with the identity, mission and vision of the individual team or organization. Thus, in an effective team or organization, the actions of individuals within their micro environments are congruent with their higher level strategies and goals. These goals, in turn, are congruent with the system's culture and mission with respect to the larger environment. In other words, there is an internal alignment of the individual with his or her vision, and another level of alignment with the team or organization in which a person will attempt to achieve his or her vision.

There are three types of alignment: 1) personal alignment, in which there is a congruity between all parts of an individual, 2) alignment of supporting processes with respect to a goal or vision, 3) environmental alignment, in which the goals and actions of individuals or groups fit congruently and ecologically with the larger system (team, organization, community, culture, etc.).

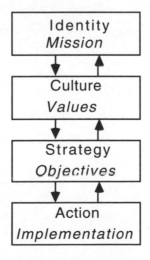

Alignment of Processes in a System

In a functional system, values and beliefs are aligned with the organization's identity and the environment. Goals and actions on an individual level support the functional objectives and strategy related to roles, which in turn are congruent with the organization's culture and identity, and mission with respect to its larger environment.

In a dysfunctional system, values and beliefs which are in conflict with basic values can take on a life of their own and begin to operate like a "thought virus" with a destructive capability similar to that of a computer virus or biological virus.

Thus, alignment is a key to the success and longevity of effective individuals, teams and organizations. *Building trust* and *growing team spirit* are a result of the coach's ability to mentor and strengthen alignment within the individuals and teams with whom he or she is working.

Mentoring Toolbox: Creating Alignment for Change

The following is a simple format that coaches can apply to mentor alignment within individuals and teams. It involves a series of questions that help clients to identify the larger purpose which serves as the focal point for their activities and then to identify and organize the individual capabilities, actions and resources they will need to mobilize in order to achieve it.

The questions may be directed toward an individual or a team as a whole.

1. What is your vision?

2. What is your role (mission) with respect to that vision? What role models will you follow as an example?

3. What values and beliefs motivate you to take on that role and vision?

4. What capabilities are necessary to reach the vision and stay consistent with your beliefs and values? Which ones do you already have? Which ones do you need?

5. What action steps will you take in order to reach your vision?

6. What environmental opportunities and constraints will you have to take advantage of or contend with in order to reach the vision?

Mentoring Toolbox: Putting Values Into Action

The purpose of this mentoring tool is to build upon the alignment process by taking clients to a greater degree of detail in defining the other levels of processes needed to effectively express their core values. To authentically and congruently express values, a person must have the supporting skills and capabilities necessary to assess situations and make decisions about which actions are in line with stated values. Higher level strategies and skills are needed to be able to define and implement the consequent behaviors, which express particular values, in widely differing environments.

Rather than prescriptions, values are usually represented by a portfolio of behaviors to be selected and enacted in key environments. The following questionnaire helps clients to define in detail the other levels of processes necessary to bring values congruently and consistently into action.

1. What is the *value* to be implemented (e.g., "health," "professionalism," "integrity," etc.)?

   _____

2. What are the key *capabilities* necessary to establish and implement that value (e.g., self-control, communication, creativity, alignment, etc.)?

   _____   _____

   _____   _____

   _____   _____

3. What 'portfolio' of activities (consequent *behaviors*) best
   expresses and manifests this value (e.g., healthy eating,
   listening, acknowledging contributions, rewarding new
   ideas, etc.)?

_____ _____

_____ _____

_____ _____

4. What are the significant *environments* or contexts in
   which it is most important to express this value (e.g.,
   home, office, team meetings, factory floor, interactions
   with customers, etc.)?

_____ _____

_____ _____

_____ _____

Mentoring Toolbox: Values Planning

The portfolio of activities which expresses particular values cannot be enacted mechanically or reactively in response to changing circumstances. Rather it must be put into action consistently through time. Time must be allocated to the ongoing "practice" of those activities. Time allocation is where "the rubber meets the road" with respect to values. In a very real way, what a person spends his or her time doing is the most direct expression of his or her values (even if the person is not consciously aware of those values).

The purpose of the following mentoring tool is to assist clients to determine the amount of time to be allocated for each item in the portfolio of activities which expresses their chosen values. Ask your client to list the mix of activities that best expresses the values to be implemented in the spaces on the left. On the pie chart, represent the amount of time to be allocated to each activity, if the values are to be successfully established.

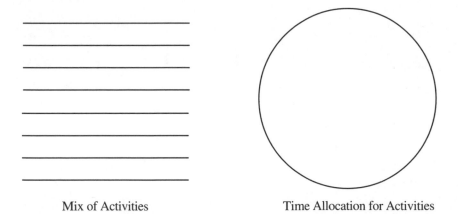

Mix of Activities   Time Allocation for Activities

**Values Planning Involves Determining the Desired Mix of
Activities and the Time to Be Allocated to Them**

Mentoring Toolbox: Establishing Practices

Practices are a means to establish and reinforce core values and beliefs. Values and beliefs cannot be established by temporary, one time actions or techniques. We do not simply give "lip service" to values or "fix problems in values," we "live values" and *practice* values." *Practices* are repetitive activities that have both (1) a practical purpose and (2) a symbolic value. Practices differ from rituals in that the emphasis of a ritual is more on its symbolic aspects. A team ritual might be "giving an award for the best idea." While giving an award has some indirect pragmatic value as a potential reinforcement, it is essentially a symbolic act. A more pragmatic, as well as symbolic activity, would be taking 10 minutes to reflect on the team's process at the end of each meeting, having each team member say what he or she liked and what he or she feels could be improved upon.

Practices can be either professional or personal. Common examples of personal practices include getting a certain amount of exercise every day, writing or practicing a musical instrument for a certain time period every day, spending a certain minimum amount of time with one's children, attending a particular meeting every week, etc. A "morning constitutional" walk each day is a classic example of a practice. The activity of walking has direct benefits for physical health and endurance, and it is also symbolic of a commitment to health and fitness. Some people have a practice of setting specific goals for the day each morning, or reviewing their vision, mission, values, beliefs and capabilities before going to a meeting or starting work each day.

On a professional level, the practice of getting together with team members and backtracking each person's contributions at the end of each meeting, or "touching base" before the beginning of each meeting, exemplifies a similar combination of pragmatic and symbolic functions. A weekly lunch meeting, open to all company employees and attended by top

management, in which there is an open agenda, is another
example of a "professional" practice.

Helping clients to establish values involves helping them
to create practices that reflect and affirm those values. Doing
so involves designing activities that they will be establishing
as a pattern. Each activity should be defined in terms of
what the client will do, where and when he or she will do it,
and with whom. Then specify *why* it is being done. What
values does this practice represent? Also determine what
pragmatic purpose the activity serves? For example:

Activity: *What, Where, When and With Whom*	Value: *Why*
Listening non-critically to ideas of collaborators for 10 minutes at the beginning of each meeting	Respecting others
Taking one hour each day to ask customers what they like or would want improved	Customer service and satisfaction
Hold a meeting every two weeks to survey best practices and successes of other companies	Quality

Activity: *What, Where, When and With Whom*	Value: *Why*
_____	_____
_____	_____
_____	_____
_____	_____

Belief Systems and Change

Believe that you will succeed. Believe it firmly, and you will then do what is necessary to bring success about.
—Dale Carnegie

One of the most important tasks of a mentor is to help clients to believe in themselves and in their ability to achieve desired outcomes. The basic belief issues that arise in regard to reaching outcomes relate to several fundamental components of the overall process of change:

1. The desirability of the outcome.

2. Confidence that the specified actions will produce the outcome.

3. The evaluation of the appropriateness and difficulty of the behavior (regardless of whether it is believed that it will produce the desired result).

4. The belief that one is capable of producing the required behaviors necessary to complete the plan leading to the outcome.

5. The sense of responsibility, self-worth and permission one has in relation to the required behaviors and outcome.

Belief Issues Related to Change

For example, consider a client who is attempting to become healthy, learn something new or be successful in a business project. Belief issues may arise with respect to any one of the elements of change identified above.

A first issue relates to the desirability of the outcome. How much does the client *really* want to be be healthy, learn, or succeed? All things being equal, everyone no doubt wants all of these things. But it is rarely the case that all things are equal, and the fact is that health, learning or success may not always be at the top of a person's hierarchy of values. Someone might argue, "Health is not really a priority for me right now." "I have so many things demanding my attention, learning something new is not that important". "Other people need me. It would be selfish to be concerned with my own success."

Even if a client desires health, learning or success very highly, he or she may question whether it is possible to achieve them. A client might say, "It is not possible to get well no matter what I do." "Old dogs can't learn new tricks." " I shouldn't build false hope about succeeding. There is nothing I can do that will make any difference."

A client may deeply desire an outcome and believe it is possible to achieve, but be in doubt as to whether a particular behavioral path is the most appropriate way to achieve the outcome. He or she might contend, "I believe it is possible to achieve my outcome, but not by using this (plan/technique/ program/etc.)." Another client might think that a particular pathway is effective, but object to the efforts or sacrifices required by a particular path, or worry about the consequences it will have on other areas of his or her life. A client may believe, for instance, that exercising or eating a better diet will help him or her become healthier, but not want to go through the hassle of changing his or her life style. Other clients might believe that a particular course will help them learn something important, but not feel that they have the time to do it. Similarly, a client may believe that a new job may lead to success, but be concerned about the impact it would have on his or her family.

It is also possible that clients can desire the outcome, think it is possible, and believe that the proposed behavioral path is appropriate to achieve the result, yet doubt their abilities to perform the required actions. They might think, "I am not (skilled/consistent/intelligent/focused/etc.) enough to successfully do what I have to do in order to complete the path necessary to reach my desired outcome."

Even when clients want an outcome, trust that it is possible, believe in the actions that have been defined in order to reach that outcome, and have confidence in their own abilities to perform the necessary skills and actions, they may question whether it is their responsibility to perform the required actions or reach the outcome. A client may complain, "It is not my responsibility to make myself healthy, learn or become successful. That is the job of the experts. I want to be able to rely on someone else." Clients may also doubt whether they deserve to be healthy, learn or succeed. This is an issue of self esteem. Sometimes clients feel unworthy of health, intelligence or success. If a client does not believe that he or she deserves to reach a goal or is responsible to do what needs to be done in order to achieve it, then it doesn't matter if he or she is capable, knows the appropriate path or desires it.

Mentoring Toolbox: Belief Assessment

It is important for mentors to be able to assess and address this whole system of beliefs in order to help people achieve their goals. Plans and actions cannot be effectively carried out if there is too much conflict or doubt. On the other hand, as the placebo effect demonstrates, empowering beliefs and assumptions can release capabilities and "unconscious competencies" that are inherent in a particular person or group, but which have not yet been mobilized.

One way to determine the motivation of a person or group is to make an assessment of the five key beliefs we have identified as relevant to the process of change. The beliefs can be assessed by making a specific statement of the belief as illustrated in the following examples:

1. The desirability of the outcome.
   Statement: *"The goal is desirable and worth it."*

2. Confidence that the outcome is attainable.
   Statement: *"It is possible to achieve the goal."*

3. The evaluation of the appropriateness or difficulty of the behaviors needed to reach the outcome (regardless of whether it is believed they will produce the desired result).
   Statement: *"What has to be done in order to achieve the goal is appropriate and ecological."*

4. The belief that one is capable of producing the required behaviors.
   Statement: *"I/we have the capabilities necessary to achieve the goal."*

5. The sense of self-worth or permission one has in relation to the required behaviors and outcome.
   Statement: *"I/we have the responsibility and deserve to achieve the goal."*

After the beliefs have been stated, clients may rate their degree of confidence in relation to each of the statements on a scale of 1 to 5, with 1 being the lowest and 5 being the highest degree of belief. This can provide an immediate and interesting profile of potential problem areas of motivation or confidence. Any statements which are given a low rating indicate possible areas of resistance or interference which will need to be addressed in some way.

The following Belief Assessment Worsheet provides a simple but effective instrument for quickly assessing the relevant areas of a client's belief system in relation to a goal or plan.

Belief Assessment Worksheet

Write down a one-sentence description of the goal or outcome to be achieved.

Goal / Outcome: _____

Then write down a short description of the current plan or solution, if any, to be enacted in order to reach the goal.

Plan / Solution: _____

In the spaces provided below, rate your degree of belief in the outcome in relation to each of the statements on a scale of 1 to 5, with 1 being the lowest and 5 being the highest degree of belief.

a. *The goal is desirable and worth it.*

| 1 | 2 | 3 | 4 | 5 |

b. *It is possible to achieve the goal.*

| 1 | 2 | 3 | 4 | 5 |

c. *What has to be done in order to achieve the goal is appropriate and ecological.*

| 1 | 2 | 3 | 4 | 5 |

d. *I (You / We) have the capabilities necessary to achieve the goal.*

| 1 | 2 | 3 | 4 | 5 |

e. *I (You / We) have the responsibility and deserve to achieve the goal.*

| 1 | 2 | 3 | 4 | 5 |

As an example of how one might use this sheet, let's say a client had a goal to "better balance personal and professional life." To assess the client's degree of belief in this outcome, the mentor would ask the client to make the following statements and rate his or her level of confidence in each one:

The goal to balance personal and professional life is desirable and worth it.

It is possible to achieve the goal to balance personal and professional life.

What has to be done in order to achieve the goal to balance personal and professional life is appropriate and ecological.

I have the capabilities necessary to achieve the goal to balance personal and professional life.

I have the responsibility and deserve to achieve the goal to balance personal and professional life.

Let's suppose that the client has ranked his or her own belief in each statement in the following way:

Desirable and Worth It = 5
Possible = 2
Appropriate and Ecological = 4
Capable = 4
Responsible and Deserving = 5

Obviously, the belief that, "It is possible to achieve the goal to balance personal and professional life," is the area of greatest concern. It is here that the mentor would first want to focus the client's attention to find the types of experiences that would help to strengthen his or her beliefs and expectations.

Mentoring Toolbox: Using Inner Mentors to Build Confidence and Strengthen Belief

The following steps can be used to help clients to build confidence and strengthen belief through the use of inner mentors.

1. What else would you need to know, add to your goal, or to believe in order to be more congruent or confident?

2. Who would be your mentor for that knowledge or belief? Imagine where that mentor would be located physically around you in order to best support you.

3. Put yourself into the shoes of your mentor and look at yourself through your mentor's eyes (second position). What message or advice would that mentor have for you?

4. Return to your own perspective (first position) and receive the message. How does it affect your degree of confidence and congruence?

Beliefs, both empowering and limiting, are often built in relation to feedback and reinforcement from significant others. Our sense of identity and mission, for instance, is usually defined in relation to significant others who serve as reference points for the larger systems of which we perceive ourselves as a part. Because identity and mission form the larger framework which surrounds our beliefs and values, establishing or remembering significant relationships can exert a strong influence on beliefs. Thus, clarifying key relationships, and messages received in the context of those relationships, often spontaneously facilitates changes in beliefs.

Mentors are generally significant others who have helped us to discover our own unconscious competencies, and strengthen beliefs and values—often through their own example. Mentors are typically individuals who have helped to shape or influence our lives in a positive way by "resonating" with, releasing, or unveiling something deeply within us. Identifying such mentors with respect to the beliefs in the Belief Assessment process can help to spontaneously strengthen our confidence and congruence.

When working with a group or team, it is useful to assess the beliefs of all of the group members with respect to the goal. Identifying common areas of doubt between individuals would point to key areas of concern for the team as a whole. And, if there are differences in the rankings of the various beliefs, the individuals who have greater confidence may have information or experiences that can help to raise the confidence of others. These individuals can become internal mentors to the rest of the team, helping to increase their sense of assurance and conviction.

Mentoring Toolbox: The "As If" Frame

The "as if" frame is one of the simplest but most useful tools in the mentor's toolbox. The *"as if" frame* is a process by which an individual or group is instructed to act "as if" the desired goal or outcome has already been achieved. The "as if" frame is a powerful way to help people identify and enrich their perception of the world, and/or their future desired states. It is also a useful way to help people overcome resistances and limitations within their current map of the world.

The "as if" frame is often used to challenge limiting beliefs by creating counter examples or alternatives. For example, if a person says, "I can't do X" or "It is impossible to do X," the "as if" frame would be applied by asking, "What would happen if you could do X?" or "Act as if you could do X. What would it be like?" or "If you were (already) able to do X, what would you be doing?" For instance, if a company executive were unable to describe what his or her desired state for a particular project is going to be, a mentor might say, *"Imagine it is five years from now. What is going on that is different?"*

Acting "as if" allows us to drop our current perception of the constraints of reality and use our imagination more fully. It utilizes our innate ability to imagine and pretend. It also allows us to drop the boundaries of our personal history, belief systems, and "ego."

In the process of reaching goals, outcomes, and visions, for instance, we first act "as if" they are possibilities. We create pictures of them visually in our minds' eyes, and give those pictures the qualities we desire. We then begin to bring them to life by acting "as if" we were experiencing the feelings and practicing the specific behaviors that fit those dreams and goals.

Acting "as if" is also an important component of the coaching-modeling loop. The "as if" frame is one of the key tools for mentors and advisors. The following format applies the "as if" frame as a means to help clients bypass doubts and limiting beliefs.

1. The mentor asks the client to think of some goal or situation about which he or she has doubt. The client is to express the limiting belief verbally to the mentor— i.e., "It is not possible for me to . . .," "I am not capable of . . .," "I don't deserve . . .," etc.

2. The mentor respectfully encourages the client by saying things like:

   "What would happen if (it was possible/you were capable/you did deserve it)?"

   "Act 'as if' (it was possible/you were capable/you did deserve it). What would it be like?"

   "Imagine that you had already dealt with all of the issues relating to your belief that (it is not possible/you are not capable/you do not deserve it). What would you be thinking, doing or believing differently?"

3. If other objections or interferences arise from the client, the mentor is to continue asking:

   "Act 'as if' you have already dealt with that interference or objection. How would you be responding differently?"

Reframing

Another way that mentors can help clients bypass perceived limitations and boundaries is through the process of reframing. *Reframing* literally means to put a new or different frame around some image or experience. Psychologically, to "reframe" something means to transform its meaning by putting it into a different framework or context than it has previously been perceived. Psychological "frames" relate to the cognitive context surrounding a particular event or experience. Such a "frame" establishes the borders and constraints surrounding a situation. Frames greatly influence the way that specific experiences and events are interpreted and responded to because of how they serve to "punctuate" those experiences and direct attention. A painful memory, for example, may loom as an all-consuming event when perceived within the short term frame of the five minutes surrounding the event. That same painful experience may seem almost trivial when "reframed" to be perceived with respect to the background of one's lifetime. "Reframing" in this manner is one of the most profound and powerful ways to help a client shift perspectives and widen his or her map of the world.

Reframing has to do with the fact that our experiences and interpretations of events are influenced by our perspective and context. The fact that it is likely to rain, for example, is a blessing to someone who has been living in drought, a good excuse for someone who has been looking for a reason to stay home from a company picnic, an inconvenience for someone who had planned to go shopping, and a curse for someone who has been planning an outdoor wedding. Sometimes we get stuck looking at only one side of a situation, event or consequence, and become caught in a single point of view. It is important to realize that there are multiple ways to look at anything.

The frame around a picture is a good metaphor for understanding the concept and process of reframing. Depending on what is framed in a picture, we will have different information about the content of the picture, and thus a difference perception of what the picture represents. A photographer or painter who is recording a particular landscape, for example, might only "frame" a tree, or choose to include an entire meadow with many trees, animals and perhaps a stream or pond. This determines what an observer of the picture later on will see of the original scene. Furthermore, a person who has purchased a particular picture might subsequently decide to change the frame so that it fits more esthetically in a particular room of the house.

Similarly, because they determine what we "see" and perceive with respect to a certain experience or event, psychological frames influence the way we experience and interpret a situation. As an illustration, consider for a moment the following picture.

Frame Number One

Notice how your experience and understanding of the situation being pictured is widened to include more of the situation.

Frame Number Two

The first picture does not have much "meaning" per se. It is simply of a "fish" of some type. When the frame is widened to produce the second picture, we suddenly see a different situation. The first fish is not simply a "fish," it is a "little fish about to be eaten by a big fish." The little fish seems unaware of the situation that we can see easily due to our perspective and our "larger frame." We can either feel alarmed and concerned for the little fish, or accept that the big fish must eat in order to survive.

Notice what happens when we "reframe" the situation again by widening our perspective even more.

Frame Number Three

Now we have another perspective and a new meaning altogether. We see that it is not only the little fish who is in danger. The big fish is also about to be eaten by an even bigger fish. In his quest to survive, the big fish has become so focused on eating the little fish that it is oblivious to the fact that its own survival is threatened by the even bigger fish.

The situation depicted here, and the new level of awareness that comes from reframing our perspective of the situation, is a good metaphor for both the process and purpose of reframing. People frequently end up in the situation of the little fish, or of the fish in the middle. They are either unaware of some impending challenge in their larger surroundings like the little fish, or so focused on achieving some outcome, like the fish in the middle, that they do not notice an approaching crisis. The paradox for the fish in the middle is that it has focused its attention so much on one particular behavior related to survival that it has put its survival at risk in another way. Reframing allows us to see the "bigger picture" so that more appropriate choices and actions can be implemented.

In NLP, reframing involves putting a new mental frame around the content of an experience or situation so that these perceptions may be more wisely considered and resourcefully handled.

One-Word Reframing

A simple and fundamental way that mentors can apply the process of reframing with clients conversationally is with "one-word reframes" of other words. This is done by taking a word expressing a particular idea or concept and finding another word for that idea or concept that puts a different slant on the concept. As the philosopher Bertrand Russell humorously pointed out, "I am firm; you are obstinate; he is a pig-headed fool." Borrowing Russell's formula, we could generate some other examples, such as:

> I am righteously indignant; you are annoyed; he is making a fuss about nothing.
>
> I have reconsidered it; you have changed your mind; he has gone back on his word.
>
> I made a genuine mistake; you twisted the facts; he is a damned liar.
>
> I am compassionate, you are soft, he is a "pushover."

Each of these statements takes a particular concept or experience and places it in several different perspectives by "re-framing" it with different words. Consider the word "money," for example. "Success," "tool," "responsibility," "corruption," "green energy," etc., are all words or phrases that put different "frames" around the notion of "money," bringing out different potential perspectives. Try finding some of your own one-word reframes for some of the following concepts:

responsible (e.g., stable, rigid)
playful (e.g., flexible, insincere)
frugal (e.g., wise, stingy)
friendly (e.g., nice, naive)
assertive (e.g., confident, nasty)
respectful (considerate, compromising)

Mentoring Toolbox: Applying One-Word Reframes

A simple way to apply one-word reframing to help clients move past perceived boundaries and limitations is to rephrase key words or phrases that they use when describing those boundaries or limitations. This can be accomplished in the following way:

1. Identify a key word or phrase used by the client to describe a perceived limitation or boundary. You can do this by having the client complete the following statement:

I stop myself because I _____
  .

e.g., Client:

"**I stop myself because** I am *not sure I am competent to* do this."

"**I stop myself because** I am afraid I will be *criticized* by others."

"**I stop myself because** I am concerned I will *lose* something."

2. Reframe the key word or phrase by rephrasing it with a new word or phrase that presents a different or wider perspective, leading to a more positive connotation.

Word or phrase that has a negative or limiting connotation. ⟶ *New word or phrase that presents a different or wider perspective, leading to a more positive connotation.*

e.g., Mentor:
"I am confident your learning curve will be a short one."
(*unsure of competence*————▶ *phase of learning curve*)

"All feedback has some value."
(*criticism*————▶ *feedback*)

"Change does sometimes involve letting go of what you are
    familiar with."
(*lose*————▶ *let go of the familiar*)

Mentoring Toolbox: Values Bridging

One-word reframes can also be used to help clients resolve conflicts or incongruences with respect their values or beliefs. Situations often arise in which there seem to be clashes in the core values of individuals or groups. A client, for example, may desire both "growth" and "security." The client may believe that the steps necessary to promote growth, however, threaten his or her sense of security. These types of seemingly fundamental incompatibilities can create conflict and resistance if not properly addressed.

One way to deal with seeming values conflicts is to use verbal reframing to create a "chain" linking the differing values. As an example, "growth" can be easily reframed to "expanding possibilities and choices." "Security" can be reframed to "not having all your eggs in one basket." In many ways, "expanding possibilities and options" and "not putting all your eggs in one basket" are quite similar. Thus, the simple verbal reframes have closed the gap between the two seemingly incompatible values.

As another example, let's say a client has a core value of "quality;" but is also keen on "creativity." These two values might initially seem at odds with one another ("quality" is about "keeping to standards" but "creativity" is about "changing things"). "Quality," however, could be reframed as "continual improvement." "Creativity" could be reframed as "producing better alternatives." Again, the simple reframes can help clients to create a bridge and see the connection between the two seemingly disparate values.

To try this with clients, use the following format.

1. Identify an area in which your client seems incongruent or in conflict.

2. Specify the seemingly incompatible values related to the conflict or incongruence. Write the two values in the spaces titled Value #1 and Value #2.

3. Reframe each value using a word or phrase that overlaps with the value but offers a different perspective. See if you can find two reframes that "chain" the seemingly incompatible values together in a way that makes them more harmonious or complementary.

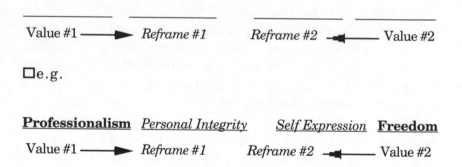

Value #1 ⟶ *Reframe #1*   *Reframe #2* ◄— Value #2

☐e.g.

Professionalism *Personal Integrity*   *Self Expression* **Freedom**

Value #1 ⟶ *Reframe #1*   *Reframe #2* ◄— Value #2

Reframing Critics and Criticism

In the previous chapter, we examined Walt Disney's Imagineering Strategy as a tool for coaching clients to define and create an effective path to future goals and dreams. We established that the ability to manage and balance Dreamer, Realist and Critic, was a key element for success in one's "inner game" for successful performance. A major challenge of accomplishing this is dealing with the potentially negative effects of criticism.

"Critic" is often considered the most challenging perspective to manage because of the seemingly negative focus associated with that perspective and the tendency for Critics to find problems with the ideas and suggestions of others. Critics are frequently perceived as "spoilers," because they operate from a "problem frame" or "failure frame."

A major problem with criticisms, on a linguistic level, is that they are typically asserted in the form of generalized judgments, such as: "This proposal is too costly," "That idea will never work," "That's not a realistic plan," "This project requires too much effort," etc. One problem with such verbal generalizations is that, given the way they are stated, one can only agree or disagree with them. If a person says, "That idea will never work," or, "It is too expensive," the only way one can respond directly is to say, either "I guess you are right," or "No, you are wrong, the idea will work," or, "No, it is not too expensive." Thus, criticism usually leads to polarization, mismatching and ultimately conflict, if one does not agree with the criticism.

The most challenging problems occur when a Critic doesn't merely criticize a dream or a plan, but begins to criticize the Dreamer or Realist on a personal level. This would be the difference between saying, "That *idea* is stupid," and, "*You* are stupid for having that idea." When a Critic attacks a person at the identity level then the Critic is not only a "spoiler," but also a "killer."

It is important to keep in mind, however, that criticism, like all other behavior, is positively intended. The purpose of the Critic is to evaluate the output of the Dreamer and Realist. An effective Critic makes an analysis of the proposed plan or path in order to find out what could go wrong and what should be avoided. Critics find missing links by logically considering "what would happen if" problems occur. Good Critics often take the perspective of people not directly involved in the plan or activity being presented, but who may be affected by it, or influence the implementation of the plan or activity (either positively or negatively).

Getting Positive Statements of Positive Intentions

One of the problems with many criticisms is that, in addition to being "negative" judgments, they are stated in negative terms linguistically—that is, they are stated in the form of a verbal negation. "Avoiding stress," and "becoming more relaxed and comfortable," for example, are two ways of verbally describing a similar internal state, even though they use quite different words. One statement ("avoiding stress") describes what is not wanted. The other statement ("becoming more relaxed and comfortable") describes what is wanted. We explored some of the implications of this in the Well-Formed Outcome section in the Coaching chapter.

Many criticisms are framed in terms of what is not wanted, rather than what *is* wanted. This can create complications in determining how to most appropriately respond to the positive intention or purpose of the criticism. As an example, the positive intent (or value) behind the criticism, "this is a waste of time," is probably the desire to "use available resources wisely and efficiently." This intention is not easy to ascertain from the "surface structure" of the criticism however, because it has been stated in terms of what is to be avoided. Thus, a key linguistic skill in addressing criticisms, and transforming problem frames to outcome frames, is the ability to recognize and elicit positive statements of positive intentions.

This can be challenging at times, because Critics operate so much from a problem frame. For example, if you ask a Critic for the positive intention behind a criticism such as, "This proposal is too expensive," you are likely to get initially a response like, "The intention is to avoid excessive costs." Notice that, while this is a "positive intention," it is linguistically stated or framed negatively—i.e., it states what is to be "avoided" rather than the state to be achieved. The positive statement of this intention would be something like, "To make sure it is affordable" or "To be certain we are within our budget."

To elicit the positive formulations of intentions and values, an effective mentor will ask questions such as: "If (stress/expense/failure/waste) is what you do not want, then what is it that you *do* want?" or "What would it get for you (how would you benefit) if you were able to avoid or get rid of what you do not want?"

The following are some examples of positive reformulations of negative statements.

Negative Statement	Positive Reformulation
too expensive	affordable
waste of time	use available resources wisely
fear of failure	desire to succeed
unrealistic	concrete and achievable
too much effort	easy and comfortable
stupid	wise and intelligent

Turning Criticisms Into Questions

Once the positive intention of a criticism has been discovered and stated in positive terms, the criticism can be turned into a question. It could be said that "behind every negative criticism is a really good question." When a criticism is transformed into a question, the options for responding to it are completely different than if it is stated as a generalization or judgment. Say, for instance, that instead of saying, "It is too expensive," the Critic asked, "How are we going to afford it?" When asked this question, the other person is given the possibility of outlining the details of the plan, rather than having to disagree with, or fight with the Critic. This is true for practically every criticism. The criticism, "That idea will never work," can be transformed into the question: "How are you going to actually implement that idea?" "That's not a realistic plan," can be restated as: "How can you make the steps of your plan more tangible and concrete?" The complaint, "It requires too much effort," can be reformulated to, "How can you make it easier and simpler to put into action?" Typically such questions serve the same purpose as the criticism, but are actually more productive.

Notice that the questions above are all *how* questions. These types of questions tend to be the most useful. Why questions, for instance, often presuppose other judgments, which can lead back into conflict or disagreement. To ask, "Why is this proposal so expensive?" or "Why can't you be more realistic?" still presuppose a problem frame. The same is true with questions like, "What makes your proposal so expensive?" or "Who is going to pay for it?" In general, *how* questions are most effective for refocusing on an outcome frame or feedback frame.

Mentoring Toolbox: Helping Critics to Be Advisors

In summary, in order to help someone to be a "constructive" Critic, or an advisor, it helps to: (1) find the positive purpose behind the criticism, (2) make sure the positive intention is stated (framed) positively, and (3) turn the criticism into a question—and in particular, into a *how* question.

This can be accomplished by using the following sequence of questions:

1. What is your criticism or objection?

   e.g., "This plan will never work."

2. What is the value or positive intention behind that criticism? What is it that you are attempting to achieve or preserve through your criticism?

   e.g., "Put my efforts into reaching goals that are achievable and timely."

3. Given that that's the intention, what is the HOW question that needs to be asked?

   e.g., "How can you be sure that the plan addresses the key issues that are necessary to achieve the goal in a timely fashion?"

To apply this process, have your client think of his or her performance in some important project or key area of his or her life or job. Ask the client to go into a Critic position with respect to himself or herself in relation to this context. What criticisms does the client have with respect to what he or she is doing?

When you have identified some criticisms or objections, lead the client through the steps defined above, in order to help the client turn his or her criticisms into questions. Find the positive intention and the *how* question related to the criticism.

(Once the criticisms have become questions, the client can pose these questions to his or her own internal Dreamer or Realist in order to formulate appropriate answers.)

Ultimately, the objectives of the Critic phase of a project are to make sure an idea or plan is ecologically sound and preserves any positive benefits or by-products of the current way(s) of achieving the goal. When a Critic asks *how* questions, then he or she shifts from being a "spoiler" or "killer" to being an "advisor." In this regard, Critics can even be viewed as advisors or mentors in disguise.

Summary

Mentors advise and support others at the level of values and beliefs. People's values and beliefs determine the degree of motivation and permission that they feel with respect to applying their capabilities and taking action—either opening doors to change or setting limits and boundaries. Thus, values and beliefs can either strengthen or inhibit the client's ability to perform effectively.

Effective mentors help clients to establish, reinforce, express and align empowering values and beliefs through their encouragement and also through their own example. One task of a mentor is to provide a good role model for key values and beliefs that clients can use as a reference point in their own lives. This type of mentoring often becomes internalized as part of the client's inner model of the world, so that the external presence of the mentor is no longer necessary. Thus, helping clients to recognize and call upon inner mentors can be as valuable to them as having mentors who are physically present.

A main task of mentoring is helping clients to become more clear about their core values and hierarchies of values. Mentoring tools such as the Values Audit and Aligning Values with Vision and Action support clients to clarify values and organize their thoughts, actions and environments in order to better achieve and express those values. Values Planning, Putting Values into Action and Establishing Practices are ways of helping clients to define the behavioral and environmental support necessary to ensure that they consistently achieve what is most important to them.

Helping clients to believe in themselves and in their ability to perform effectively is one of the most important tasks of a good mentor. Supporting clients to believe that success is possible, that they are capable to achieve their goals, and that they deserve to succeed is vital to helping them perform optimally. The Belief Assessment process allows both clients and coaches to define the areas in which the client's beliefs are strong with respect to key beliefs, as well as identify areas of doubt. Inner mentors can be used to help build confidence and strengthen belief in areas where clients experience doubt or incongruence.

The "as if" frame is a simple but important mentoring tool to help clients get past perceived boundaries and limitations. Acting "as if" allows clients to drop their current perception of the constraints of reality and use their imagination more fully as means to bypass doubts and limiting beliefs.

Reframing is another essential tool for mentors. Reframing involves the use of language in order to influence the way that experiences and events are interpreted and responded to by redirecting the client's focus of attention to a broader perspective. One-word reframes involve rephrasing the key words used to express a particular idea or concept to other words that put a different slant on the concept by presenting a different or wider perspective, leading to a more positive connotation. Values Bridging is a mentoring process that applies several one-word reframes in order to "chain" seemingly incompatible values together in a way that makes them more harmonious or complementary.

Helping clients to address potential interference from criticism is another key goal of mentoring. Finding the positive intention behind criticisms and transforming criticisms into questions (particularly *how* questions) is a powerful way to diffuse the negative aspects of criticism and yet still retain whatever valuable feedback the criticism carries.

Chapter 5

Sponsorship

Overview of Chapter 5

- **Sponsorship**
  - Identity
  - The Style and Beliefs of a Sponsor
  - Sponsorship Messages
  - Non-Sponsorship and Negative Sponsorship
- **An Example of Sponsorship**
- **Skills of Sponsorship**
- **Sponsorship Toolbox: Finding the Source of your Resources**
- **Sponsorship Toolbox: Active Centering**
- **Sponsorship Toolbox: Listening Partnerships**
- **Sponsorship Toolbox: "I See" and "I Sense" Exercise**
- **The Hero's Journey**
- **Sponsorship Toolbox: Mapping the Hero's Journey**
- **Sponsorship Toolbox: Beginning the Hero's Journey**

Overview of Chapter 5 (continued)

- Archetypic Energies
- Sponsorship Toolbox: Co-Sponsoring Archetypic Energies
- Sponsorship Toolbox: Proper Naming
- Sponsorship Toolbox: Sponsoring a Potential
- Sponsorship Toolbox: Group Sponsorship Format
- Sponsorship Toolbox: Recovering Lost Sponsors
- Summary

Sponsorship

Our deepest fear is not that we are inadequate. Our fear is that we are powerful beyond measure. It is our light, not our darkness, that frightens us. We ask ourselves, "Who am I to be brilliant, gorgeous, talented, fabulous?"

Actually, who are you not to be? You are a child of god. Your playing small does not serve the world. There is nothing enlightened about shrinking, so that other people won't feel insecure around you.

We are all meant to shine, as children do. We are born to make manifest the glory of god that is within us. It is not in some of us; it is in everyone. As we make our own light shine, we unconsciously give others permission to do the same. As we are liberated from our fear, our presence automatically liberates others.

—Marianne Williamson (as quoted by Nelson Mandela)

Let everything you do be done as if it makes a difference.
—William James

One of the most important functions of a large "C" Coach is to support the personal growth of clients at the identity level. A person's sense of identity goes even deeper than his or her values and beliefs, focusing on the individual's perception of self, role and mission. Identity issues are a function of *who* a person or group perceives themselves to be. Growth and change at the level of identity is fostered through a special type of coaching relationship known as *sponsorship*.

In general, "sponsorship" has to do with *promotion*. An organization that "sponsors" a particular program or research project, "promotes" that program or project by providing needed resources. A group that "sponsors" a seminar or workshop, provides the space and promotional effort necessary to create the context for the workshop leader to present his or her ideas and activities, and for others to receive the benefits of these ideas and activities. When top management "sponsors" a project or initiative, it is giving its recognition and "blessing" to that project or initiative as something that is important for the identity and mission of the company. From this perspective, sponsorship involves creating a context in which others can optimally perform, grow and excel.

While the notion of "sponsorship" today has a commercial implication to many people, the term "sponsor" originally derives from the Latin *spondere* ("to promise") and was used to denote a person who had undertaken responsibility for the spiritual welfare of another (the word "spouse" shares the same root).

We can refer to the commercial form of sponsorship as small "s" sponsorship. "Sponsorship" at the identity level (what we might call "Sponsorship with a capital 'S'") is the process of recognizing and acknowledging ("seeing and blessing") the core characteristics of another person. This form of sponsorship involves seeking and safeguarding fundamental qualities and potentials within others and providing the conditions, support and resources that allow the group or individual being sponsored to express and develop their unique aptitudes and capabilities to the fullest degree. In short, sponsorship involves promoting the unique identity of the client.

It is also possible to engage in one's own "self-sponsorship," in which one is able to learn to promote and safeguard core qualities within oneself.

Identity

As was stated above, "identity" relates to our sense of *who* we are. According to the NeuroLogical Levels model, identity is a level of change and experience that is distinct from our values, beliefs, capabilities, behaviors and environmental input. If you have ever looked at infants when they are first born it is obvious that they are not simply "blank slates." They are born with their own unique personalities. Even before they have perceived much of their environment, coordinated their behavior, formed mental maps or established particular beliefs and values, they have an identity; their own special way of being in the world.

It is our perception of our identity that organizes our beliefs, capabilities and behaviors into a single system. Our sense of identity also relates to our perception of ourselves in relation to the larger systems of which we are a part, determining our sense of "role," "purpose" and "mission." Thus, perceptions of identity have to do with questions such as "Who am I?" "What are my limits?" and "What is my role and mission?"

Clarifying the "deep structure" of our identity allows us to express ourselves even more fully at the level of our behavioral "surface structure." It involves:

- Finding and clarifying our life's direction

- Managing boundaries between "self" and "others"

- Becoming clear about beliefs that support our identity and those which limit us

- Expanding our sense of self

- Incorporating new dimensions of being

The Style and Beliefs of a Sponsor

Sponsorship at the identity level is different from mentoring, teaching and coaching. Unlike a teacher, coach or mentor, the skills and resources of the sponsor may be quite different from the person or group that is being sponsored. The sponsor is not necessarily a role model for the individual or group being sponsored. Rather, the sponsor provides the context, encouragement and resources that allow the group or individual being sponsored to fully focus on, develop and use their own unique abilities and skills.

Sponsorship, then, involves awakening and safeguarding potential within others. It is founded upon the commitment to promote something that is already within a person or group, but which is not being manifested to its fullest capacity.

The beliefs of the sponsor include:

At the level of identity, everyone is inherently good. People are fundamentally positively intended.

It is important to recognize and acknowledge people's fundamental goodness and potential.

Each person is on his or her own "Hero's Journey."

The more light that this person shines, the more light there will be in the world.

My presence and undivided attention, and my ability to "see" others will help to naturally release their deepest potentials.

The person I am with is precious. He or she is an important and valuable being. He or she is worth my attention and acknowledgment.

The leadership style of a sponsor is that of *individualized consideration*. This involves giving attention to the needs and potential of the individual moreso than to the task. It includes giving personalized attention to the client and treating him or her as a unique individual.

Sponsorship Messages

A good sponsor believes in his or her client, makes that client feel important and shows the person that he or she can make a difference. Thus, the process of sponsorship is primarily expressed through the communication (verbally and non-verbally) of several key messages. These messages have to do with the acknowledgment of the client in a very fundamental way.

The basic sponsorship messages include:

You exist. I see you.
You are valuable.
You are important / special / unique.
You have something important to contribute.
You are welcome here. You belong.

These fundamental identity messages are frequently accompanied by the following empowering beliefs (which we explored in the previous chapter on Mentoring):

It is possible for you to succeed.
You are capable to succeed.
You deserve to succeed.

Clearly, the intention of these messages is to promote the client's sense of being unconditionally valued, feeling of belonging and desire to contribute and succeed. The impact of these messages is generally quite profound and lead to a number of positive and resourceful emotional responses.

When people feel that they are seen, for instance, there is a sense of safety and acknowledgment that comes with it; they no longer feel it is necessary to have to do something to get attention. The result is that they feel relieved and relaxed.

When people feel that they exist, are present in mind and body, and that their existence is not threatened, they experience a sense of being centered and at peace.

When people know that they have value and are valued, they feel a sense of satisfaction.

The knowledge that a person is unique leads to a natural desire and tendency to express that uniqueness which unleashes the person's natural creativity. It is important to keep in mind that being unique, important or special, does not mean that one is "better than" or superior to others. Uniqueness is the quality that gives a person his or her own special identity as distinct from all others.

People's recognition that they have something to contribute brings with it tremendous motivation and energy.

The belief that they are welcome makes people feel at home and engenders a sense of loyalty. Similarly, the feeling of belonging creates a sense of commitment and responsibility.

The impact of positive sponsorship messages is summarized in the following table.

Positive Sponsorship Message	Emotional Response
"You are seen." ⟶	*relief, relaxed*
"You exist." ⟶	*centered, at peace*
"You have value." ⟶	*satisfied*
"You are unique." ⟶	*creative*
"You have something to contribute." ⟶	*motivated and energetic*
"You are welcome here." ⟶	*at home, loyal*
"You belong." ⟶	*committed*

Emotional Impact of Positive Sponsorship

Non-Sponsorship and Negative Sponsorship

The importance of sponsorship and the sponsorship messages can be illustrated by making a comparison to contexts in which there is no sponsorship and those in which there is what could be called "negative sponsorship."

In situations of *non-sponsorship*, there is essentially an absence of positive sponsorship messages. But this in and of itself is a type of message, leading to the conclusions and responses summarized below:

Received Non-Sponsorship Message	Emotional Response
"I am not seen." ⟶	*anxious, invisible*
"I do not exist." ⟶	*desperate for attention*
"I am not valued." ⟶	*empty*
"I am not unique/nothing special. I am no different than anyone else." ⟶	*passive*
"I have nothing to contribute." ⟶	*worthless and unwanted*
"My contributions are not valued." ⟶	*taken advantage of*
"I am not part of the group." ⟶	*displaced*
"I can be easily replaced." ⟶	*uneasy*

Emotional Impact of Non-Sponsorship

In contexts of *negative sponsorship*, the opposite of the sponsorship messages is actually communicated. This leads to emotional reactions along the lines of non-sponsorship, but more exaggerated. Some examples of negative sponsorship messages and the resulting responses are:

Negative Sponsorship Message   Emotional Response

"You should not be here.
  You should hide/disappear."———▶   *afraid*

"Who do you think you are?
  You are nothing.
  You should not exist."   ———▶   *undeserving*

"You will never be good enough.
  You are a problem."   ———▶   *blamed and ashamed*

"You are worse than everyone else."———▶ *inadequate*

"You are detracting and
  holding us back."   ———▶   *guilty and a burden*

"You are unwelcome."———▶ *desire to leave or escape* (sneaky)

"You do not deserve to be here.
  You don't belong with us." ———▶   *rejected and abandoned*

Emotional Impact of Negative Sponsorship

The following table provides a comparative summary of the emotional impact of positive sponsorship, non-sponsorship and negative sponsorship.

Positive Sponsorship	Non-Sponsorship	Negative Sponsorship
You are seen. *relief, relaxed*	You are not seen. *anxious, invisible*	You should not be here. *afraid*
You exist. *centered, at peace*	You are not noticed. *desperate for attention*	You are nothing. *undeserving*
You have value. *satisfied*	You are not valued. *empty*	You are a problem. *blamed and ashamed*
You are unique. *creative*	You are nothing special. *passive*	You are worse than others. *inadequate*
Your contribution is important. *motivated and energetic*	You contribute nothing. *worthless and unwanted*	You detract. *guilty and a burden*
You are welcome. *at home, loyal*	You are not part of the group. *displaced*	You are unwelcome. *desire to leave or escape*
You belong. *committed*	You can be easily replaced. *uneasy*	You do not deserve to be here. *rejected and abandoned*

Comparative Impact of Sponsorship, Non-Sponsorship and Negative Sponsorship

Many of us have probably experienced non-sponsorship and even negative sponsorship from significant others. Strangely enough, negative sponsorship messages frequently come from some positive (though misguided) intention, or from simple ignorance.

In fact, there is sometimes an interesting paradox in which coaches and other professionals ignore sponsorship because they are so focused on some other level of support (caretaking, guiding, teaching, etc.). Someone can be a very effective caretaker, for example, but do so at the expense of sponsorship. Examples of this occur in many hospital environments where patients are watched over constantly for their physical needs, but get very little coaching, hardly any teaching, no mentoring and, instead of being sponsored, are not "seen" as individuals at all . Instead a patient might be referred to as "the asthmatic in bed three."

Sponsorship is also frequently ignored in organizational settings. It is obvious when you walk into a company where sponsorship is not practiced. It is as if no one there really exists. When people feel that they are not seen, not valued, don't really contribute (or their contributions are not recognized), can be easily replaced and don't really belong, their performance will reflect this sentiment. When people do feel sponsored, however, they feel present, motivated, loyal, creative and will perform beyond expectation.

Incidentally, employees are not the only ones who do not receive sponsorship in companies. CEOs and top managers also rarely receive real sponsorship. Frequently this is because everyone else expects them to be the sponsors. It also often happens that, instead of seeing the CEOs or top managers, people only see their roles and are only interested in them because of their power and the possible political advantages associated with being "close" to them.

Even NLP practitioners can get so caught up in "guiding" their clients through the latest techniques that they become more concerned about the client's "submodalities" and "accessing cues" than the client him/herself.

The key, of course, is that effective sponsorship is something that can be added to any of the other levels of support. A person can be a caretaker, guide, coach, teacher, mentor and sponsor at the same time.

An Example of Sponsorship

The power of combining sponsorship with other levels of support is beautifully illustrated in the following story by Elizabeth Silance Ballard. The original story was written in 1976 and was published as "Three Letters From Teddy" in *A Second Helping of Chicken Soup for the Soul* (Health Communications, Deerfield Beach, FL, 1995).

Her name was Mrs. Thompson. And as she stood in front of her 5th grade class on the first day of school, she told the children a lie. Like most teachers, she looked at her students and said that she loved them all the same. However, that was impossible, because there in the front row, slumped in his seat, was a little boy named Teddy Stoddard. Mrs. Thompson had watched Teddy the year before and noticed that he didn't play well with the other children, that his clothes were messy and that he constantly needed a bath. In addition, Teddy could be unpleasant. It got to the point where Mrs. Thompson would actually take delight in marking his papers with a broad red pen, making bold X's and then putting a big "F" at the top of his papers.

At the school where Mrs. Thompson taught, she was required to review each child's past records and she put Teddy's off until last. However, when she reviewed his file, she was in for a surprise. Teddy's first grade teacher wrote, "Teddy is a bright child with a ready laugh. He does his work neatly and has good manners...he is a joy to be around." His second grade teacher wrote, "Teddy is an excellent student, well liked by his classmates, but he is troubled because his mother has a terminal illness and life at home must be a struggle." His third grade teacher wrote, "His mother's death has been hard on him. He tries to do his best but his father doesn't show much interest and his home life will soon affect him if some steps aren't taken." Teddy's fourth grade teacher wrote, "Teddy is withdrawn and doesn't show much interest in school. He doesn't have many friends and sometimes sleeps in class."

By now, Mrs. Thompson realized the problem and she was ashamed of herself. She felt even worse when her students brought her Christmas presents, wrapped in beautiful ribbons and bright paper, except for Teddy's. His present was clumsily wrapped in the heavy, brown paper that he got from a grocery bag. Mrs. Thompson took pains to open it in the middle of the other presents. Some of the children started to laugh when she found a rhinestone bracelet with some of the stones missing, and a bottle that was one quarter full of perfume. But she stifled the children's laughter when she exclaimed how pretty the bracelet was, putting it on and dabbing some of the perfume on her wrist. Teddy Stoddard stayed after school that day just long enough to say, "Mrs. Thompson, today you smelled just like my Mom used to."

After the children left she cried for at least an hour. On that very day, she quit teaching reading, and writing, and arithmetic. Instead, she began to teach children. Mrs. Thompson paid particular attention to Teddy. As she worked with him, his mind seemed to come alive. The more she encouraged him, the faster he responded. By the end of the year, Teddy had become one of the smartest children in the class and, despite her lie that she would love all the children the same, Teddy became one of her "teacher's pets."

A year later, she found a note under her door, from Teddy, telling her that she was still the best teacher he ever had in his whole life.

Six years went by before she got another note from Teddy. He then wrote that he had finished high school, third in his class, and she was still the best teacher he ever had in his whole life.

Four years after that, she got another letter, saying that while things had been tough at times, he'd stayed in school, had stuck with it, and would soon graduate from college with the highest of honors. He assured Mrs. Thompson that she was still the best and favorite teacher he ever had in his whole life. Then four more years passed and yet another letter came. This time he explained that after he got his bachelor's degree, he decided to go a little further. The letter explained that she was still the best and favorite teacher he ever had. But now his name was a little longer, the letter was signed, Theodore F. Stoddard, MD.

The story does not end there. You see, there was yet another letter that spring. Teddy said he had met this girl and was going to be married. He explained that his father had died a couple of years ago and he was wondering if Mrs. Thompson might agree to sit in the place at the wedding that was usually reserved for the mother of the groom.

Of course, Mrs. Thompson did. In addition, guess what? She wore that bracelet, the one with several rhinestones missing. In addition, she made sure she was wearing the perfume that Teddy remembered his mother wearing on their last Christmas together.

They hugged each other, and Dr. Stoddard whispered in Mrs. Thompson's ear, "Thank you Mrs. Thompson for believing in me. Thank you so much for making me feel important and showing me that I could make a difference."

Mrs. Thompson, with tears in her eyes, whispered back. She said, "Teddy, you have it all wrong. You were the one who taught me that I could make a difference. I didn't know how to teach until I met you."

Skills of Sponsorship

As the story of Mrs. Thompson and Teddy Stoddard demonstrates, sponsorship is something that results from a personal decision, and can be added to whatever else one is doing. Mrs. Tompson's determination to "quit teaching reading, and writing, and arithmetic" and instead "teach children" clearly displays a shift in her focus from being only a "teacher" to also becoming a "sponsor." The fact that Teddy's "mind seemed to come alive," and that "by the end of the year Teddy had become one of the smartest children in the class" also illustrates the deeper level benefits of sponsorship.

In addition to the shift in focus, the switch from teacher to sponsor requires the application of a different set of tools and skills. Stephen Gilligan, Ph.D., (1997) identifies a number of principles and skills of positive or "therapeutic sponsorship." From Gilligan's perspective, a sponsor helps others not so much by *doing* anything in particular. Rather, sponsors transform others by first recognizing or seeing something latent in them, and then by *being there* for them as a kind of reference point. According to Gilligan, the outcomes of positive sponsorship are to "awaken awareness of self and of the world, and to introduce skills and traditions to develop 'self-in-world' and 'world-in-self'."

Gilligan defines a number of specific skills associated with "therapeutic sponsorship." Many of these skills can be adapted to a more general application of sponsorship than therapy. The following is a subset of Gilligan's skills of therapeutic sponsorship that encompass the primary skills of sponsorship for the large "C" Coach:

1. **Internal congruence**

According to Gilligan , the most important commitment a sponsor has is to him/herself. Gilligan contends that, without a connection to him/herself, "a person will tend to be reactive rather than responsive," and end up being more concerned with "dominance" and "submission" than being truly engaged with supporting the other. Personal congruence, alignment and integrity are the source of positive sponsorship. It is not possible to truly make the commitment to support another person, for instance, unless one is in contact with oneself. It is in this way that the sponsor *is* a type of role model for others. If the sponsor is insincere or disconnected from him/herself, he or she cannot authentically "commit" to anything.

2. **Connecting with the other**

In some West African cultures the traditional greeting is not "How are you doing?" "What's happening?" or "How is it going?" as it is in many Western cultures. Rather, the typical greeting is "I see you." In response, the other person replies, "I am here." This exchange symbolizes a type of contact that is deeper than that which is only on the surface (environmental or behavioral). Sponsorship involves *seeing* and fostering the potential within another person. This requires connecting with something in the other person.

The existentialists contend that until a person is seen and acknowledged or blessed by another person, he or she does not yet fully exist. Thus, an effective sponsor not only acknowledges, "I see you," but adds, "It is good to see you (again)." Without this type of connection with and acknowledgment of the other, the notion of "I see you," becomes just another hollow and empty phrase. It is important to remember that sponsorship cannot be imposed on people. It is the felt sense of connection that is the basis for true sponsorship.

3. Curiosity

Acknowledgment of others is characterized by curiosity about how they are doing. The purpose of sponsorship is to help clients get beyond perceived internal boundaries and support the release and development of the client's deepest potential. Curiosity is characterized by questions rather than demands, rules or advice. According to Gilligan, the questions of the sponsor would include things like: What's going on? What's the problem? How is it a problem? What do you think you need to resolve the problem or make progress?

4. Receptivity

Sponsors can provide the questions, but they cannot really provide the answers to those whom they are sponsoring. In the same way that curiosity involves "asking," receptivity involves "listening." Receptivity involves being comfortable, to a certain degree, with uncertainty. It involves creating and safeguarding the space for the other person to be able to think and find his or her own answers. While suggestions can be offered as a stimulus, they should not be perceived as "the answer" for the other.

5. Proper naming

The names we give things determine their meaning to us. In the same way that a parent helps a child learn to understand and effectively interact in the world by teaching the child the proper names of objects, events and emotions, sponsorship involves giving voice to the type of language that supports the client's core values, personal qualities and health.

Studies made on the relationship between language and health (Rodin, 1986), for instance, indicate a connection between physical health, sense of control and "symptom labeling." That is, a patient's sense of control effected the way he or she experienced and labeled bodily sensations as symptoms relevant to health or illness. In other words, people who have less of a sense of control are more apt to label a physical sensation as a "symptom" of illness. Likewise the label given a particular physical sensation will effect the degree of control a person feels about it.

A "proper" name can be defined as one which brings out the best in oneself, acknowledges the positive intention of any others involved in the situation and, at the same time, tells the truth of the experience. Phrases like, "I failed," "I am not good enough" and "I did my best, but did not yet achieve my goal" for instance, could all be used to describe the same situation. Each, however, will have a different impact on the internal state of the speaker.

A name that brings out the best in oneself while demeaning others would not yet be a "proper name." Clearly, labeling something in a way that puts oneself down or negates one's own resources, would also not yet be a proper name. A name that highlights positive aspects of oneself or others, but which hides or denies the hurt or pain of an experience, in also not a "proper name."

6. Identifying and transforming self-negating influences

The attempt to personally grow and evolve can sometimes bring up confusion and conflict associated with change. Limiting beliefs, or "thought viruses," such as, "It isn't possible for me to change," "I am not capable of reaching my goals," or "I do not deserve to succeed," can thwart peoples' attempts to successfully grow or change.

One of the tasks of sponsorship is to help identify and transform such limiting beliefs. Effective sponsorship involves supplying other perspectives that allow people to see the positive side of their actions and behavior. This involves helping the other person recognize the needs, intention, consequences and assumptions related to a particular situation or interaction. To do this a sponsor needs to stay creative and to periodically "stand in the shoes" of the client.

The purpose of the rest of this chapter is to provide a toolbox that supports these fundamental skills of sponsorship.

Sponsorship Toolbox: Finding the "Source" of Your Resources

All of the skills of sponsorship defined in the previous section stem from the ability of the sponsor to be centered and internally congruent. Being internally congruent comes from having a felt sense of contact with yourself and your "center." Having a felt sense of your center is a powerful resource. Think of times when you were in very challenging situations and managed to stay resourceful. It is likely that, in those times, you were able to feel internally centered and clear, even though the situation may have been tough and confusing on the outside.

Now think of times when you have not been centered, or lost the sense of your center. It was probably much more difficult to find or maintain your resources, even in situations that were not externally very challenging.

Being centered is like being in touch with the "source" of your resources. In fact, it is interesting to note that the term "re-source" implies that, when we are capable and resourceful, we are somehow back in contact with our "source." Consider, for instance, the many diverse processes and internal states that we call "resources"—"focus," "flexibility," "commitment," "creativity," "openness," "boundaries," etc. In terms of their contents, many of these are exact opposites of one another. Why, then, do we use the same name to categorize all of them. Perhaps the common factor is that, when they do function as a resource, it is because they are indeed putting us back in touch with our inner center or source.

The following process applies the different levels of learning and change in order to get in touch with the "source" of your resources. This is a very useful strategy for sponsors to use to prepare themselves to be ready to sponsor others. It is also a process that coaches and sponsors may guide their clients through in order to help the client become more centered and in contact with his or her own resources.

1. Sit in a "neutral" or "resting" position with your feet on the floor and your hands folded comfortably in your lap. "Center" yourself so that you feel internally relaxed, calm and aware of the physical center of your body.

2. Begin to become aware of your *external environment*. Think of other environments (home, work, social) which help you to feel resourceful. In many ways, these environments may seem to be a source of your resources. Notice, however, that there are also environments which are challenging, in which you must access resources from some other source within yourself. Be aware that there is a "source" of your resources that is something deeper than your environment. When you have the awareness of a source of your resources coming from something deeper than your external environment, place your hands palm down on your *upper legs* or thighs. Then, return your hands to the "neutral/resting" position in your lap.

3. Allow your attention to shift to your *physical body and behavior*. Notice your eyes, your ears, your hands, your feet, your breathing, and the subtle movements you make to maintain your balance. Think of some of the resources that you associate with your physical body, strength and energy. In many ways, your physical being is a source of your resources. Also notice, however, that there have been many times when you have had to be resourceful even though you may have been physically weak, exhausted or ill. Become aware that there is a

"source" of your resources in these instances that is deeper than your physical body and actions. Allow your hands to move up and touch your *lower belly*, just below your naval to communicate your recognition that there is a source of your resources that comes from something much deeper than your physical being. Then, return your hands to the "neutral/resting" position in your lap.

4. Now become aware of your *mind and thoughts*. Become aware of your inner voice, your memories, your fantasies and your feelings. Think of some of the resources that you most associate with your mind and mental capacities. In many ways, your mind can be a powerful source of resources for you. Also notice, however, that there have been many times when you have had to be resourceful even though you may have been mentally confused, uncertain or blank. You may even be aware of thoughts and mental processes which challenge your ability to be resourceful at times. Become aware that the "source" of your resources in these instances is something beyond your mind and mental capabilities. Allow your hands to move up and touch your *diaphragm*, just below your chest bone where your ribs join together, to communicate your recognition that there is a source of your resources that comes from something even deeper than your mind and mental processes. Then, return your hands to the "neutral/resting" position in your lap.

5. Turn your attention to your *beliefs, values and belief system*. Identify some of the core values and beliefs that empower you. Your beliefs and values can be a very important source of your resources. Notice, however, that you probably also have some beliefs and values which challenge your ability to be resourceful at times, and that you have had to be resourceful at times that you were doubtful and in conflict. Become aware that

the "source" of your resources in these instances is something deeper than your beliefs and value systems. Allow your hands to move up and touch your *heart* area, at the center of your chest, to communicate your recognition that there is a source of your resources which comes from something deeper than your beliefs and values. Then, return your hands to the "neutral/resting" position in your lap.

6. Shift your awareness to your *perceptions of your identity* and your *sense of self*. Become aware of the many different parts of yourself. Notice what kind of positive self-image and self-concept you have. These different parts and aspects of yourself are a source of many your resources. Notice, however, that you have probably also struggled with negative self-image and self-concept at times, which challenged your ability to be resourceful. There have probably been times when you had to find resources even when you were unsure of yourself, or did not know who you were anymore. Become aware that the "source" of your resources in these instances is something even deeper than your perceptions of identity and sense of self. Allow your hands to move up and gently touch the *base of your throat*. Allow your touch to communicate your recognition that there is a source of your resources that is something beyond your self-image and personality. Then, return your hands to the "neutral/resting" position in your lap.

7. Once you have the awareness of the difference between yourself and all of these other levels of experience, notice what is left that is "you" at your deepest level. Many people experience this as a "space," a "soul," an "essence," or an "energy." Notice what that experience is for you. When you have a sense of your deepest self, "essence" or "source," allow your hands to move up and

touch the *center of your forehead*. Allow your touch to create an "anchor" for this experience of your deepest self, "essence" or "source." Then, return your hands to the "neutral/resting" position in your lap.

8. Now, lift your eyes, take a deep breath and raise your hands above your head and open your arms, opening yourself to a *system that is larger than yourself* (i.e., "universal mind," "spirit," "collective consciousness," etc.). Notice that your "essence" or "energy" is not alone. It is part of a larger "field" of consciousness, energy or spirit. Imagine feeling a sense of connection with the "energy" from that field. When you have a felt sense of connection with the "field," place your hands on the *crown of your head*. Allow your touch to communicate your connection to something beyond yourself.

9. Allow your hands to gently retrace each level of your being, bringing this sense of the "field" into all aspects of your identity.

   • Moving your hands down, touch the *center of your forehead*. As you do, connect your felt sense of the field to your experience of your "soul," "essence" or "center." Watch, listen and feel for any insights or inspiration.

   • Now touch the *base of your throat*. Connect your felt sense of the field and your center to your self-image and self-concept. Again, watch, listen and feel for any insights or inspiration.

   • Next, touch your *heart*, and imagine the field connecting your throat with your heart, values and beliefs, feeling a deep sense of congruence. Watch, listen and feel for any insights or inspiration.

- Touch your *diaphragm* imagining the field moving through your spirit, heart and mind into the center of your body. Watch, listen and feel for any insights or inspiration.

- Now touch your *lower belly* and imagine the field filling every cell of your body and physical being. Watch, listen and feel for any insights or inspiration.

- Finally, place your hands palm down on your *upper thighs*. Feel the field or collective energy you experienced filling each location, flowing through your whole body and out into the environment through your feet. Watch, listen and feel for any insights or inspiration.

10. When you are done, return your hands to the "neutral/resting" position in your lap and spend some time feeling and acknowledging your sense of centeredness, wholeness and alignment. Imagine that this state could be a type of "holographic" resource for you—a resource in which all other resources are contained. When you can get to this state, it becomes the gateway to all of your other resources. Create a symbol representing this state that you can use as an anchor to get back to it quickly and easily.

Sponsorship Toolbox: Active Centering

Being centered and internally congruent is a fundamental skill of sponsorship. It is also a very useful resource state. People who practice martial arts (Karate, Judo, Kung Fu, etc.), for instance, often talk about the importance of being "centered" and calm, even when they are in the middle of intense competition. In fact, they say that "if you give away your center to your opponent, you have already lost the competition." When you lose your center and get upset, you begin to lose other resources and often start working against yourself.

The following tool offers a way to apply the experience of being centered in order to respond more resourcefully to challenging situations.

1. Have the client identify and associate into a challenging context in which it is difficult for him or her to stay centered and resourceful.

2. Ask the client to step out of the experience and enter an inner state in which he or she feels aligned, relaxed and centered. (This can be done by using the symbol from the Source of Your Resources process, if the client has already been through that procedure.)

3. When the client is ready, gently begin to physically push and pull the client in different directions, from different angles (from the shoulders, waist, front, back, side to side, etc.), while he or she practices staying centered, balanced and aligned both physically and mentally. As the client becomes more comfortable and confident with his or her ability to remain in the state, you can make it more challenging by pushing or pulling a little harder.

4. When the client feels ready, have him or her hold the centered state, step back into the challenging situation and notice how his or her experience is different. He or she will usually feel much more able to deal with the situation in a resourceful manner.

Sponsorship Toolbox: Listening Partnerships

Stephen Gilligan maintains that sponsors transform others by first recognizing or "seeing" something latent in them, and then by *being there* for them as a kind of reference point. Listening is one of the ways in which sponsors can "be there" for their clients.

The key to effective listening, from the sponsorship perspective, is staying fully in your center while simultaneously fully connecting with the client. This allows you to create and hold a "space" for your client to genuinely reflect and speak from his or her own center. Listening from your center allows you to be "touched" by what your client is saying and helps you to be both curious and receptive.

Listening partnerships are a way to apply this type of listening as a simple but effective tool for sponsorship and "co-sponsorship." The notion of a "Listening Partnership" was developed by Patty Wipfler of the Parents Leadership Institute in Palo Alto, CA. According to Wipfler (1989), "Listening is a tool which can powerfully address the needs of parents [and others] for learning assistance and stress release." She contends that we all have "the natural ability to assist each other by listening, and, when this ability is developed over time, we become more resourceful, more able to care effectively, and . . . surer of ourselves. . .".

Wipfler encourages people to create a simple, but powerful, structure through which to anchor and direct this ability to listen by forming "listening partnerships":

The agreement [in a listening partnership] is to exchange regular listening time . . . During this listening time, equal turns are taken. One person talks, and the other listens and cares. The listener offers no advice, no helpful hints, and asks no questions to satisfy his own curiosity. He communicates full respect and appreciation. The listener makes the basic assumption that talking things through will help the other person to sort and learn from his own experience. When time is up, the two change roles, and the person who listened then has time to examine his experience, feelings, and thoughts, with the full attention of his listening partner.

This kind of time to think, uninterrupted, about oneself and one's own life. . . helps us untangle the web of experience, feelings, and expectations that can snarl our [thoughts and] relationships. . . When we can examine our own experience in detail, we become freer to think of new approaches, to problem-solve, and to act intentionally when difficult situations arise. We are assisted to think and learn.

(From *Listening: A Tool For Caring Parents*, Wipfler, P., Parents Leadership Institute, Palo Alto, CA, 1989.)

Again, the key to creating an effective listening partnership is to create and "hold the space" for the speaker to reflect spontaneously and authentically. This is facilitated by the first four skills of sponsorship:

- Being centered and internally congruent
- Being connected with the other
- Having curiosity about the other
- Being receptive to whatever the other has to say

From the NLP perspective, it is also useful to take on the following beliefs while listening to another person as a "sponsor" in a listening partnership.

Beliefs of the Sponsor (Listening Partner)

The person to whom I am listening is intelligent.

He or she is on a "Hero's Journey."

This person can solve his or her own problems if he or she could think it all the way through.

The most important thing this person needs is my presence and undivided attention.

This is the most important thing for me to be doing right now.

I have the time. This time is a gift. My time spent listening is valuable and will not be wasted.

I will be enriched by what this person has to say.

Nothing is random. Every detail is significant.

Everything is a metaphor for everything else.

I feel generous and grateful towards this person.

Establishing listening partnerships among team members can be a powerful way to encourage mutual sponsorship and establish a sponsorship culture.

Sponsorship Toolbox: "I See" and "I Sense" Exercise

Sponsorship involves seeing and affirming positive qualities in others. One way to encourage mutual sponsorship among a group of people is to have them practice looking for and acknowledging what they observe and like about their fellow group members.

Since sponsorship is about seeing and supporting people at an identity level, it useful to have people notice positive characteristics both at a literally observable level and also at a deeper level.

The following process, initially developed by NLP trainer Robert McDonald, encourages people to sponsor one another by having them focus on what they perceive and authentically like about one another.

The process is best done in a small group of 5 or 6 people.

Group members take turns being Person A, the person to be focused on by the rest of the group.

Starting to Person A's left and going clockwise around the group, each member of the group is to comment on one thing that he or she sees and likes about Person A, and something he or she senses and likes about person A. "Seeing" is sensory based. "Sensing" is an intuition about identity.

Each person is to use the following format:

"I see_____. And I like it."

"I sense that you _____. And I like it."

Repeat this process until everyone in the group has the opportunity to be Person A and receive these comments from all of the other group members.

The Hero's Journey

Managing the process of personal growth and life change can be likened to what Joseph Campbell called the "Hero's Journey" (*The Power of Myth*, 1988). Campbell searched for the connections in the myths and stories of change that cross cultural boundaries. He examined stories of heroes, historical and mythical, spanning all ages, cultures, religions and genders.

Campbell discovered that certain themes are repeated in many cultures and appear to be deeper threads connecting all of humanity, reflecting the overall path that we take from birth to death regardless of our individual circumstances. Just as we are born the same and die the same, there are other deep patterns held in the collective memory of our species.

Campbell described the commonalities of our overall life path in terms of the steps of the "Hero's Journey"—the sequence of events that seem to be shared in the epic myths and stories of every culture. Campbell's notion of the hero's journey provides a powerful road map for effective coaches and sponsors to use to help their clients deal with the challenges of change, especially change at the identity level.

According to Campbell, the fundamental steps of the hero's journey include:

1. *Hearing a calling* that relates to our identity, life purpose or mission. We can choose to either accept or try to ignore the calling.

2. *Accepting the calling* leads us to confront a boundary or threshold in our existing abilities or map of the world. (Attempting to ignore the calling frequently leads to the formation or intensification of problems or symptoms in our lives.)

3. *Crossing the threshold* propels us into some new life "territory" outside of our current comfort zone; a territory that forces us to grow and evolve, and requires us to find support and guidance.

4. *Finding a guardian*, mentor or sponsor is something that often comes naturally from having the courage to cross a threshold. (As it has been said, "When the student is ready, the teacher appears.") Because the territory beyond the threshold is new for us, we cannot necessarily know what type of guardianship we will need ahead of time or who those guardians will be.

5. *Facing a challenge (or "demon")* is also a natural result of crossing a threshold. "Demons" are not necessarily evil or bad; they are simply a type of "energy" or "power" that we need to learn to contend with or accept. Often, they are simply a reflection of one of our own inner fears and shadows. Frequently, the demon is an expression of some type of negative sponsorship message, either from oneself in response to an external challenge, or from a significant other.

6. *Transforming the "demon"* into a resource or advisor is typically accomplished by either:
   a) *Developing a special skill*;
   b) *Discovering a special resource or tool*.

7. Completing the *task* for which we have been called, and *finding the way* to fulfill the calling is ultimately achieved by creating a *new map of the world* that incorporates the growth and discoveries brought about by the journey.

8. *Finding the way home* as a transformed person, and sharing with others the knowledge and experience gained as a result of the journey.

While the hero's journey is clearly a metaphor, it captures a good deal of the reality facing clients as they seek to build a path to a successful future and contend with the uncertainties of change. The notion of a "calling," for instance, clearly symbolizes the vision and mission that the client, team or organization is pursuing.

The "threshold" represents the new territory, and unknown and uncertain elements that the client must confront in order to put the vision and mission into action.

The symbol of the "demon" reflects the challenges of upheaval, competition, internal politics and other obstacles and crises which emerge from circumstances beyond our control. It is here that we confront "negative sponsorship"—messages, coming from either inside of us or from significant others, that imply, "You should not be here," "You do not deserve to exist," "You are incapable," "You will never be good enough," "You are unwelcome," etc. The demon is ultimately something that appears to oppose or negate us as heroes with something to contribute.

The resources that help us to cross the threshold into new territory and transforms the demon are the values, behavioral skills and business practices we are able to put into action in order to deal with complexity, uncertainty and resistance. This is the area where we ourselves must grow in order to develop the flexibility and increased requisite variety necessary to successfully navigate the new territory and overcome the obstacles which arise along the way.

"Guardians" are the sponsors and relationships we develop that support us to build skills, believe in ourselves and stay focused on our objectives.

It is sometimes tempting for coaches to think that the client is the victim and the coach is the "hero" who will slay the client's demon with his or her wonderful coaching techniques. It is important to keep in mind, however, that the client is the hero and the coach is the guardian. Our job as coaches and sponsors is to help the client recognize his or her own hero's journey and support him or her on that journey.

Sponsorship Toolbox: Mapping the Hero's Journey

While Campbell's description of the journey begins with hearing and accepting a "calling," our real life experiences often call us to the hero's journey by presenting us with the challenge first. The many heroes who emerged as a result of the September 11 terrorist attacks, for instance, were thrown into their journey by a direct confrontation with the "demon." They had to face their threshold and recognize their calling within the crisis they were facing.

This is also frequently the case with our clients. It is a crisis which presents the calling. Certainly, dealing with any sort of crisis is a type of hero's journey in and of itself.

To help clients explore and prepare themselves for some of the key aspects of their own heroes' journeys, pick a project, transition or initiative that they are currently involved in or planning and ask the following questions:

1. What is the "demon" (challenge) you must face? What is a situation in which you feel more of a "victim" than a "hero?"
   [Again, this will typically be a situation in which the client is confronting some type of negative sponsorship messages, either from himself or herself in response to an external challenge, or from a significant other.]

2. What is your "threshold"? What is the unknown territory, outside of your comfort zone, that either a) the crisis is forcing you into or b) you must enter in order to deal with the crisis?

3. Given the demon you are facing and the threshold you must cross, what is the "call to action"—what are you being "called" to do or become? (It is often useful to answer this question in the form of a symbol or meta-

phor; e.g., "I am being called to become an eagle/warrior/ magician, etc.")

4. What resources do you have and which do you need to develop more fully in order to face the challenge, cross your threshold and accomplish your calling?

5. Who are (will be) your "guardians" for those resources?

When the client has identified his or her guardians, ask the client to imagine where they would be located physically around him or her in order to best support the client. One by one, have the client put him/herself into the shoes of each of the guardians, and look at him/herself through their eyes (second position). What message or advice does each guardian have for the client?

Have the client return to his or her own perspective (first position) and receive the messages.

Sponsorship Toolbox: Beginning the Hero's Journey

When you have completed helping your client to map his or her hero's journey, you can then help the client to begin this journey by guiding him or her through the following format. This process uses a physical time line and the "as if" frame to help clients identify and transform any resistances they have to crossing their "threshold" and beginning their hero's journey.

1. Create an imaginary time line on the floor. Place the "calling" and the "demon" where they belong with respect to the future dimension of the time line.

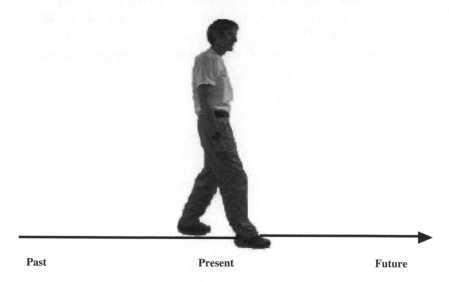

Past   Present   Future

A Physical Time Line Can Be Used to Recall the Past and Anticipate the Future.

2. Have the client stand in the present and get a felt sense of the threshold he or she must cross in order to successfully deal with his or her "demon" and achieve

his or her "calling." Ask, "What holds you back?" "Where is the resistance?"

3. Assist your client/hero by helping him or her to "physicalize" this resistance; i.e., interact with the client to create a physical metaphor for the feeling of resistance (i.e., holding the client back, pushing the client back, dragging the client down, pulling the client off track, etc.). Role play various possibilities until you find one that the client intuitively feels is "right."

The Sponsor Helps the Client Physicalize His or Her Resistance to Crossing the Threshold By Role Playing a Physical Metaphor for the Resistance.

4. The sponsor and client then switch places, so that the client is in the role of his or her own resistance. From this perspective, the client considers the questions, "What is the positive intention of the resistance?" "What are the resources I need to fulfill the positive intention in a new and more appropriate way?" "How can I change the physical expression of the resistance so that it becomes a 'guardian' for me with respect to the positive intention rather than a limitation?"

The Sponsor and Client Switch Places, So that the Client Is in the Role of the Resistance and Can Reflect on Its Positive Intention.

5. The client leaves the present on his/her time line and walks to the future, acting "as if" he or she were able to cross the threshold and go to a place in the future that represents the "calling." The client stands in the location representing the calling and gets a felt sense of being successful and centered.

6. From the location of the calling, the client/hero turns and looks back to the present, where he or she has struggling with the threshold. From this location, the client becomes his or her own guardian and self-sponsor, and offers a resource and a message to his or her present self.

7. The client returns to the present, bringing the message and necessary resources from the future position, and transferring them to the present. The client reflects upon how these resources help to further transform the former resistance into a guardian.

8. Taking these resources, the client again walks to the future location on his or her time line that represents the calling.

Archetypic Energies

According to Stephen Gilligan, there are three fundamental "archetypic energies" required to successfully complete one's "hero's journey": *strength* (power, determination, ferocity), *compassion* (softness, openness, gentleness) and *humor* (playfulness, flexibility, creativity, deviousness).

Strength is needed to stay committed and set boundaries. Strength without the balancing forces of compassion and humor can become violence and aggression.

Compassion is needed to connect with others, have emotional wholeness and to effectively give and receive the support necessary to grow. Compassion and softness without strength and humor, though, can become weakness and dependence.

Humor is necessary to find new perspectives, be creative and have fluidity. Humor without strength and compassion, however, can become cynicism and superficial trickery.

According to Gilligan, it is necessary to maintain a balance of these three forces, and to "humanize" them by bringing them into your "center." Gilligan points out that when we give up or lose our center to any one of these energies they become unintegrated and develop a "shadow side." Strength, for example, is clearly the energy of the "warrior." When this warrior energy is not centered, humanized and balanced with the others, then warrior becomes merely a killer or destroyer. Similarly, compassion and humor can have their shadow side as well.

The key is to be able to ground, harness and integrate these energies by selectively bringing them "through" our internal center.

A good capital "C" Coach will want to sponsor all three of these archetypic energies within his or her clients in order to be sure that they have the fundamental resources necessary for their heroes' journeys. Clients will also want to see that their coaches and "guardians" have these energies in a balanced way in order to be confident and comfortable that their coach is whole, integrated and resourceful.

The following format is a variation of a process designed by Stephen Gilligan in which a coach and client can co-sponsor these fundamental resources in each other.

Sponsorship Toolbox: Co-Sponsorsing Archetypic Energies

1. Sit together in a pair (A and B) facing each other. Both A and B take the time to "center" themselves coming fully in contact with their internal physical, emotional and spiritual centers.

2. Person A begins by accessing the energy of strength and bringing it into his or her center. When he or she feels the presence of the energy of strength in his or her body, A makes eye contact with B and makes the invitation: *See my strength.*

   B maintains eye contact with A, and when he or she is able to authentically see or sense A's strength, B says: *I see your strength.*

3. A then internally contacts the energy of compassion or softness and bringing it into his or her center. When he or she feels the presence of the energy of softness in his or her body, A makes eye contact with B and makes the invitation: *See my softness.*

   Again, maintaining eye contact with A, when B is able to authentically see or sense A's softness, B says: *I see your softness.*

4. Person A now accesses the energy of humor and brings it into his or her center. When he or she feels the presence of the energy of humor throughout his or her body, A makes eye contact with B and makes the invitation: *See my playfulness.*

When B is able to authentically see or sense A's humor, B says: *I see your playfulness.*

5. Finally, Person A focuses his or her attention on the felt sense of his or her center. When he or she feel fully present throughout his or her body, A makes eye contact with B and makes the invitation: *See me.*

When B is able to authentically see or sense the full presence of A, B says: *I see you.*

A and B repeat the exercise, switching roles, so that B makes the invitation to A to see B's strength, softness, humor and presence.

Sponsorship Toolbox: Proper Naming

In many ways, proper naming is a type of verbal reframing. Proper naming helps people to view their experiences in a way that awakens a wider perspective and puts them in touch with potential resources and solutions. Proper naming is particularly important for experiences at the identity level.

As described earlier, a proper name is one which brings out the best of yourself or the person you are sponsoring, acknowledges the positive intention of any others involved in the situation and, at the same time, tells the truth of the experience.

A name that brings out the best in oneself while demeaning others would not yet be a "proper name." Clearly, labeling something in a way that puts oneself down or negates one's own resources, would also not yet be a proper name. A name that highlights positive aspects of oneself or others, but which hides or denies the hurt or pain of an experience, is also not a "proper name."

Let's say that someone becomes upset with another person for hurting his or her feelings and says, "You are a jerk." That is certainly one way to name the experience, and it may tell a certain truth about what happened. On the other hand, such a statement is not likely to bring out the best in the person saying it, nor does it acknowledge the positive intent of the other. In fact, it is a form of negative sponsorship.

The same experience could be labeled with the words, "Your behavior reminds me that I need to stay strong and resourceful so that I won't get hurt." This labeling is more likely to brings out the best in yourself, so that you can actually learn from something from the experience, and acknowledge the truth and positive intention of your emotional response, but without negating the identity of the other person (which would just be treating that person the way he or she treated you).

Some other examples of proper naming might be:

"I let people take advantage of me." ⟶ "I need to show my strength and set clearer boundaries."

"I hate my boss." ⟶ "I feel that my boss does not see or value me."

"I want to hurt you." ⟶ "See my strength."

One of the most common ways coaches and sponsors can apply proper naming involves recategorizing self-negating identity statements to statements about capabilities or behavior. Negative identity judgments are often the result of interpreting particular behaviors, or the lack of ability to produce certain behavioral results, as statements about one's identity. Shifting a negative identity judgment back to a statement about a person's behavior or capabilities greatly reduces the impact it has on the person mentally and emotionally.

As an example, a client might make a statement like "I am a failure." The sponsor could point out, "It is not that you are a 'failure', it is just that you have not yet mastered all of the elements necessary for success." Again, this puts the limiting identity level judgment back into a more proactive and solvable framework.

These types of reframes can be accomplished using the following steps:

a) Identify the negative identity judgment:

I am _____ (e.g., "I am <u>a burden to others</u>.")

b) Identify the positive intention behind the negative identity judgment.

(e.g., "To take care of myself and solve problems on my own.")

c) Identify a missing or needed capability or resource that is implied by the positive intention behind the identity judgment. In particular, think in terms of the three archetypic energies (strength, compassion, playfulness) and the capacity to be centered.

(e.g., *"compassion* to care for myself and *strength* to solve problems on my own.")

d) Verbally substitute the capability or behavior for the negative identity judgment:

Perhaps it is not that you are a _____ (negative identity: e.g., "burden to others"), *it is just that you need more* _____ (e.g., "compassion to care for yourself and strength to resolve problems on your own").

In summary, this type of "proper naming" frames or reframes the client's experience in a way that:

1. Acknowledges that the client is a hero on a hero's journey.

2. Describes key issues in terms of the presence or lack of one of the three archetypic energies.

3. Acknowledges and addresses the positive intentions of the initial statement or belief.

Sponsorship Toolbox: Sponsoring a Potential

Effective sponsorship involves recognizing and safeguarding potential qualities and characteristics in others, helping them to surmount boundaries and transform self-negating influences. This is largely done by "being there" for others and communicating the basic sponsorship messages: "I see you." "You exist." "You are valuable." "You are unique." "You have something to contribute." "You belong and are welcome here."

Positive sponsorship is a profound and powerful way to help people establish and strengthen key resources and personal characteristics. The following format provides a way for coaches to be a sponsor and "guardian" and help clients identify and strengthen key resources that will support them on their "hero's journey."

1. Have the client create a physical time line and move back to a location that represents the very beginning of his or her life—a point before his or her conception. Instruct the client to get in touch with his or her center and the "source" of his or her resources.

2. Ask the client to choose a characteristic or potential (such as "strength," "compassion" or "playfulness") that, if it had been nurtured or protected during the client's life, would allow him or her to more fully: (a) establish healthy boundaries, (b) overcome barriers, or (c) evolve him/herself more completely.

3. Invite the client to create a symbol for this resource or characteristic and share it with you. Listen carefully from your center, and let the client's description "touch" you. If necessary, ask a few questions, until you are able to authentically and congruently "see" or sense the reality of this potential within your client.

4. Turn so that you are standing perpendicular to your client, facing his or her side. Ask your client to get in touch with his or her center or "source" and do the same yourself. When you are in touch with your center and source, and are able to congruently connect with your client and sense his or her resources and potential, signal the client by offering him or her one of your hands. When the client is ready to accept your sponsorship, he or she is to signal you by taking your hand and placing your hand over his or her heart. Place your other hand on the upper center of your client's back.

The Coach Extends His or Her Hand as a Signal that He or She Is Centered and Ready to be a Sponsor. When the Client Is Ready to Accept Sponsorship, He or She takes the Coach's Hand and Places It Over His or Her Heart. The Coach Places His or Her Other Hand on the Upper Center of the Client's Back.

5. Ask the client to focus on the resource or characteristic that he or she would like to have nurtured and protected and walk along the time line to the present, re-experiencing the events of his or her life. Accompany the client along the time line, maintaining your hands over his or her heart and upper back, keeping your attention on the client and the resource or characteristic he or she would like to have nurtured and continually repeating the sponsorship messages: "I see you." "You exist." "You are valuable." "You are unique." "You have something to contribute." "You belong and are welcome here."

[If you wish, you can also add some empowering belief statements with respect to the characteristic or resource that the client desires to strengthen: i.e., "It is possible for you to have more of this resource." "Your are capable of having even more of this resource." "You deserve to have more of this resource."]

6. When the client reaches the present, and no longer requires your ongoing sponsorship, he or she is to release your hand from his or her heart. You will then gently remove your other hand from the client's back. The client may then continue walking into his or her future, allowing the resource/characteristic to continue to blossom and develop.

7. The client will eventually reach a place on the future of his or her time line at which he or she feels that the resource/characteristic has become so fully developed that it is now part of his or her identity. Have the client stop at this place and turn around to look back across his or her time line. The client can now become his or her own self-sponsor for this potential. Invite the client to find the message, from this location in his or her future, that he or she most needs to send back through his or her life.

8. Invite the client to take this message, return to the beginning of his or her time line and repeat the process, being his or her own self-sponsor by getting in touch with his or her potential, placing his or her own hands over his/her heart, and walking up the time line again spreading the message from his or her future self. You may accompany the client at a distance (walking with him or her but not touching the client). Have the client move all the way back to his or her future, then return to the present and share his or her experiences with you.

During the walk through the client's personal history, it is important to remember that the sponsor is not trying to be a therapist, teacher or "rescuer" for the client. The purpose of this process is not to try to change the client's personal history or intervene to "fix" things. The sole purpose of the sponsor is to ensure that, no matter what happens, his or her attention remains on the client and the desired characteristic or resource. The process is not about changing the external details of the client's personal history. It is about making sure that the client is in touch with his or her center and inner resources no matter what happens in his or her life, and that the client always knows that he or she exists, is seen, is valuable, is unique, has something to contribute and is welcomed.

Sponsorship Toolbox: Group Sponsorship Format

Sponsorship does not only have to come from a single individual. In fact, the experience of being sponsored is often intensified and amplified when it comes from a whole group or team.

The following format provides a way for a number of people to act as sponsors for different key beliefs for another member of the group.

Note: This process is best done in a group of five (although it can be relatively easily adapted for groups of other sizes).

1. One group member is to volunteer to be the "receiver" and the others will be "sponsors." The sponsors are to stand around the receiver; one in front, one behind, one to the left, and one to the right.

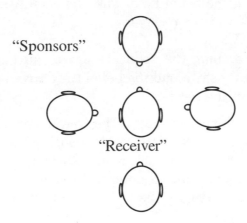

The Sponsors Form a Group Around the "Receiver"

2. The receiver is to select some positive life change that he or she would like support in making, or to choose some project, dream or personal potential or quality that he or she would like achieve or evolve. The receiver is also to reflect upon the inner resources that would help him or her to achieve the desired state (i.e., strength, compassion, playfulness).

3. The receiver is then to select each of the group members to be a sponsor for a belief that is necessary or important in order to be able to establish the practice, achieve the dream or develop the potential. Some common beliefs include:

   It is possible for you.
   It is desirable and important for you.
   You are capable.
   You deserve it.

   Each sponsor is to be sure that he or she can truly "see" and sense the belief he or she has been asked to be the sponsor for in the receiver.

4. One at a time, the sponsors are to authentically and congruently say aloud the belief they have been asked to sponsor in the receiver.

   [When each sponsor has verbalized his or her belief, the sponsors may want to rotate (clock-wise) around the receiver and repeat each belief statement from another location. This can be done until each sponsor reaches his or her starting place.]

5. Each sponsor is then to begin to repeat his or her belief statement at the same time the others are saying theirs, in any order and at any time they feel like it.

6. Finally, after a few minutes of repeating the messages, each sponsor is to "anchor" the receiver by touching him or her as they verbalize their beliefs. After touching the receiver, the sponsor stops speaking and stands in silence for a few minutes holding the anchor.

Another group member then volunteers to be the receiver and the process is repeated, until all group members have been in the receiver position.

A version of this process can also be done in which each sponsor selects, or is selected, to communicate one of the basic sponsorship messages:

You are valuable.
You are important / special / unique.
You have something important to contribute.
You are welcome here. You belong.

Both of these processes can have a very profound positive impact on the "receiver."

Sponsorship Toolbox: Recovering Lost Sponsors

Sometimes we lose people who have been important sponsors to us. This loss can come from death, physical separation or changes in life conditions which force a detachment of some type. This can create a painful void in our lives, leading to feelings of grief, abandonment, betrayal, guilt, etc. The loss of an important sponsor can even create a type of life crisis for some people.

Similar to having inner mentors, however, people can internalize sponsors, and learn to become their own self-sponsors. The following format is a way to help clients recover their relationship with past sponsors who have gone out of their lives for some reason. While this process is very symbolic and metaphoric, people find it to be quite emotionally meaningful.

1. Identify and associate into an experience or situation in which you most feel the loss of a past sponsor.

2. Step away from that experience and go to a centered and resourceful state in which you feel aligned and in contact with the "source of your resources."

3. Choose two existing inner sponsors to be your "guardian angels." Select individuals who have been sponsors in your life previously and are no longer physically present, but whom you know and feel will always be a part of you.

4. Turn slightly to your right and, physically using your hands, sculpt a life size "hologram" of the lost sponsor. Create a representation of the person as he or she was at the time that he or she was your sponsor. You may choose to create a symbolic representation if you wish. (Sometimes this is more meaningful than an anatomically accurate one.)

Note: If any negative or painful memories come up, put them on imaginary balloons and let them go. (Images can go on the outside of the balloon, voices and sounds can go inside the balloon.)

5. When you have finished the sculpture, symbolically "breathe life" into the hologram and give your sponsor the voice that is most appropriate for him or her to have.

6. Face the representation of the sponsor you have created and ask, "What is your gift for me?" Go to "second position" with your sponsor, by putting yourself into his or her shoes, and answer the question from his or her perspective. Create a symbol for the gift (e.g., a golden heart).

7. Return to "first position," by associating back into yourself, and answer the question, "What is my gift for you?" Create a symbol of your gift to that sponsor (e.g., a fountain pen that writes in many colors).

8. Exchange gifts with the past sponsor and imagine that you could connect your hearts with an eternal silver thread of light.

9. Honor the gift you have received from this sponsor by finding others who are currently in your life that you can share it with. Imagine how you will share this gift and keep it alive through your behavior. Use your inner sponsor as a guardian and mentor to help you share this gift.

10. Imagine your past sponsor now joining and being welcomed by your two "guardian angels" and other inner sponsors.

11. Bring your gift, your new inner sponsor and your other "guardian angels" into the situation in which you had previously experienced the loss of sponsorship, and notice how your experience is transformed.

Summary

Sponsorship involves supporting people to grow and change at the level of identity. A person's sense of identity relates to his or her perception of his or her self, role and "calling." Being an effective sponsor involves "being there" for others, recognizing and acknowledging them at a deep level, and communicating key messages such as "I see you." "You exist." "You are valuable." "You are unique." "You have something to contribute." "You belong and are welcome here."

Non-sponsorship and negative sponsorship occur when either no sponsorship messages are given or when people receive the opposite of sponsorship, being put down instead of supported. When people feel that they are not seen, not valued, don't really contribute (or their contributions are not recognized), can be easily replaced and don't really belong, their ability and motivation to perform diminishes dramatically.

Being an effective sponsor requires both a strong internal intention to support others and a unique set of personal skills. The skills of sponsorship include being centered and internally congruent, connecting emotionally with others, being curious and receptive, the ability to properly name the experiences of the client in a way that helps to bring out his or her best, and the capacity to identify and transform self-negating influences which could interfere with the client's personal growth.

Finding the Source of your Resources and Active Centering are sponsorship tools that help both sponsors and clients to achieve a state of centeredness, alignment and congruence, and maintain a felt sense of their centers even in challenging situations.

Listening Partnerships involve learning to listen to others from one's center, creating and holding a "space" for them to authentically reflect upon and think through important life situations and decisions. Listening Partnerships are also an effective way to encourage mutual sponsorship within a group or team.

Another way to encourage mutual sponsorship among a group of people is to have them practice looking for and acknowledging what they observe and like about their fellow group members. The "I See and I Sense" process creates an environment in which members of a group or team can co-sponsor one another by looking for and acknowledging what they appreciate about their fellow group members on the inside as well as the outside.

Meeting life's challenges can be likened to a "hero's journey." A main task of sponsorship is to support others to recognize and succeed in this journey. Frequently when clients seek coaching, however, they do not feel at all like heroes. Instead they feel like victims, and are looking for someone to rescue them. It is important for coaches to keep in mind that the client is the hero, not the coach. Large "C" Coaches do not best serve their clients by slaying their demons for them or allowing them to stay locked within their own comfort zone. A good coach and sponsor acts as a guardian for clients' resources and helps clients to recognize that they are indeed on a hero's journey by putting them in touch with their calling. The process of Mapping the Hero's Journey is a way of supporting clients to sort and recognize significant patterns in their lives, identifying the "calling" within challenging situations and crises and shifting from a "victim" mentality.

Coaches can help clients to take the steps necessary to begin their hero's journey by placing the key elements on a time line and addressing resistances to moving forward. By helping clients to recognize the positive intention of their own internal resistances, seeming interferences may be transformed into "guardians" with respect to that positive intention rather than operating as limitations to progress.

Several core resources, or "archetypic energies," are needed for people to perform effectively at the identity level and successfully complete their hero's journeys. These include strength, compassion and humor. Co-Sponsoring Archetypic Energies involves the coach and client seeing and acknowledging these resources in one another, bringing balance and mutual confidence into their interaction.

Proper naming is a type of verbal reframing that allows clients to get a more positive perspective on situations and events and to bring out their best by shifting the way it has been "named." One of the most common ways coaches and sponsors can apply proper naming involves recategorizing self-negating identity statements to statements about capabilities or behavior. This puts the limiting identity level judgment back into a more proactive and solvable framework.

A key goal of sponsorship is also to recognize and safeguard positive qualities and characteristics in clients, helping them to surmount boundaries and transform self-negating influences. This is largely done by "being there" for others and communicating the basic sponsorship messages: "I see you." "You exist." "You are valuable." "You are unique." "You have something to contribute." "You belong and are welcome here." When clients are able to review challenging situations from their personal history with the appropriate sponsorship—as in the Sponsoring a Potential format—key qualities and resources become nurtured and safeguarded, allowing clients to more fully: (a) establish healthy boundaries, (b) overcome barriers, or (c) evolve themselves more completely.

Sponsorship does not only have to come from a single individual. In fact, the experience of being sponsored is often intensified and amplified when it comes from a whole group or team. This can be accomplished by having several group members act as sponsors for different key beliefs for another member of the group.

Sometimes we lose people who have been important sponsors to us, creating a painful void in our lives, and leading to feelings of grief, abandonment, betrayal and guilt. Similar to having inner mentors, people can internalize sponsors, and learn to become their own self-sponsors. The Recovering Lost Sponsors format is a way to help clients recover their relationship with past sponsors who have gone out of their lives.

The toolbox of sponsorship contains process that are simple in many ways but also which require significant commitment and presence on the part of the sponsor and a certain degree of intimacy between coach and client. While there are many tools described in this chapter that need to be done in a one-on-one setting which may seem challenging for people who are not experienced coaches, the fact remains that sponsorship is as simple as sending those key messages: "I see you." "You exist." "You are valuable." "You are unique." "You have something to contribute." "You belong and are welcome here."

Chapter 6

Awakening

Overview of Chapter 6

- **Awakening**
  - **"Spirit" and "Field"**
  - **Coach as an Awakener**
- **Not Knowing**
  - **Nerk-Nerk**
- **Uptime**
- **Awakener's Toolbox: Creating an "Uptime" Anchor**
- **Getting Access to the Unconscious**
- **Awakener's Toolbox: Active Dreaming**
  - **Active Dreaming Exercise**
- **Awakener's Toolbox: Awakening to Freedom**
  - **Awakening to Freedom Format**
- **Double Binds**
- **Awakener's Toolbox: Transcending Double Binds**

Overview of Chapter 6 (continued)

Awakening

A human being is a part of the whole called by us "universe". . . a part limited in time and space. He experiences his thoughts and feelings as separated from the rest—a kind of optical delusion of his consciousness. This delusion is a kind of prison for us, restricting us to our personal desires and to affection for a few persons nearest us. Our task must be to free ourselves from this prison by widening our circle of compassion to embrace all living creatures and the whole of nature in its beauty. —Albert Einstein

Webster's Dictionary defines *awakening* as "rousing from sleep," "emerging from a state of indifference, lethargy or dormancy" or "becoming fully conscious, aware and appreciative."

Times of growth and transformation in our lives are usually accompanied by such "awakenings." It is as if we were roused from a type of sleep—coming out of a self-imposed stupor—or had been blind and suddenly regained sight. Our mental maps of who we are and what is possible in the world become broader, and we perceive old limitations in a completely new way. In these experiences, we succeed in breaking through our old mind set and "get outside of the box."

The results of awakening are frequently a renewed sense of purpose and meaning, expanded awareness, clear perception and emotional and physical revitalization.

Awakening is often associated with cognitive or mental expansion, but can also be related to one's heart and emotions. Awakening frequently has to do with reconnecting with our motivations at the deepest level. Consequently, awakenings usually accompany significant transitions in our personal and professional lives.

"Spirit" and "Field"

Awakening goes beyond coaching, teaching, mentoring and sponsorship to include the level of vision, purpose and spirit. This relates to our sense of something that goes beyond our own image of ourselves, and involves our vision of the larger system surrounding specific roles, values, beliefs, thoughts, actions or sensations. It relates to who and what else we perceive to be in the world around us, and addresses the question of *for whom* or *for what* a particular path has been selected (the purpose).

The term *spiritual* is used in the NeuroLogical Levels model to refer to the subjective experience of being part of a larger system or "field"; one that reaches beyond ourselves as individuals to our family, community and global systems. It is the awareness of, what anthropologist and systems theorist Gregory Bateson called, "the pattern which connects" all things together into a larger whole. We, as individuals, are a subsystem of this larger system.

"Spiritual" level experience relates to what could be called *the larger "S" self*—a sense of being that goes beyond our own image of ourselves, our values, beliefs, thoughts, actions or sensations. It involves our connection with who *else* and what *else* are in the larger system surrounding us. It is this level of experience that typically provides the greater context that gives our lives meaning and purpose.

Spiritual pursuits, in the form of accomplishing one's "vision," life "mission" and "purpose" are the motivation behind some of the greatest human achievements. Many of the world's most important leaders and geniuses acknowledge the significance of some type of spiritual guidance of this sort in their lives and work. Of his work in the area of physics, for example, Albert Einstein claimed, *"I want to know how God created this world. I am not interested in this or that phenomenon, in the spectrum of this or that element; I want to know his thoughts; the rest are details."*

According to the NeuroLogical Levels model, the notion of the *spiritual* may be likened to what Einstein was referring to as "God's thoughts."

Neurologically, spiritual level processes have to do with a type of *relational field* between our own nervous systems and those of other people, forming a type of larger, collective nervous system. The result of this field of interaction is sometimes referred to as a group "mind," a group "spirit," or a "collective consciousness." This field also includes the "nervous systems," or information processing networks, of other creatures and beings, and even our environment. As Gregory Bateson described it:

> *The individual mind is immanent but not only in the body. It is immanent in pathways and messages outside the body; and there is a larger Mind of which the individual mind is only a sub-system. This larger Mind is comparable to God and is perhaps what people mean by "God," but it is still immanent in the total interconnected social system and planetary ecology.*
> (Steps to an Ecology of Mind, 1972)

Coach as Awakener

In many ways, coaches, consultants, therapists, teachers and leaders are awakeners; opening up new vistas and possibilities for their students, clients and collaborators by helping them get in touch with this larger Mind or field. Awakening others involves supporting them to grow at the level of vision, mission and spirit. An awakener supports another person by providing contexts and experiences which bring out the best of that person's understanding and awareness of purpose, self, and the larger systems to which he or she belongs.

Being an awakener requires the abilities of a coach, teacher, mentor and sponsor to some degree, but has other dimensions. It is obvious that it is not possible to awaken others if you yourself are still asleep. So the first task of the awakener is to wake up and stay awake. An awakener "awakens" others through his or her own integrity and congruence. An awakener puts other people in touch with their own missions and visions by being in full contact with his or her own vision and mission.

Another key goal of an awakener is to help people "get outside the box" in which they are currently confined; breaking out of old habits and transcending conflicts and double binds.

The great Danish physicist Nils Bohr pointed out that there are two types of truth: superficial truth and deep truth. According to Bohr, "In a superficial truth, the opposite is false. In a deep truth, the opposite is also true." Bohr was no doubt referring to notion that fundamental physical elements, such as electrons, are both waves and particles. The fact that electrons are waves of energy does not mean that they are not also particles of matter, even though the two are opposite.

The same is true of deep psychological truths. Beauty and ugliness, for instance, are both deep truths. The fact that there is great beauty and hope in the world does not mean that it cannot also be ugly. And the fact that people are capable of acting horribly and violently, does not mean that they are not also capable of heroism and creating miracles. Awakeners often awaken others to this type of deeper truth. And, once we know that both are true, then we have a choice. Where do we choose to put our energy? Do we devote ourselves to beauty or get lost in the ugliness?

In fact, it is important to point out that sometimes "the brighter the light, the darker the shadows." When people have even a minor spiritual awakening, they suddenly see shadows that they did not see before, because the light has gotten brighter.

Waking up in this way is usually exhilarating, but not always pleasant. Thus, helping others to awaken requires skill and sensitivity. Awakening others involves the unconditional acceptance of who they are and how they are; yet, at

the same time, includes the suggestion that there are possibilities and choices for expansion and evolution. Awakening
can be either gradual or sudden (such as a moment of
"epiphany" or sudden insight). Awakening often leads to
learning at the level of what Gregory Bateson called "Learning IV"—the creation of something "completely new."

When interacting with others, the beliefs of the awakener
include:

Life is a vast mystery with incredible possibilities.

*We are all on a journey together through life; and, in
this respect, we are all the same.*

*All people are inherently valuable and acceptable as
they are.*

*Everybody makes the best choices that they perceive
available to them.*

*Nobody could have responded any differently than
they did to any past situation.*

*People are, however, completely free to choose how to
respond at each moment.*

*People limit the possible choices they perceive because
they, or some part of them, is "asleep."*

*If people know that they are valuable and acceptable
as they are, they will perceive more choices, and make
the right choices, and, thus, become free to evolve in
any direction.*

The leadership style most associated with awakening is
that of "charismatic" or "visionary" leadership. Visionary
leaders have a sense of vision and mission that gives collaborators a sense of purpose. Charismatic or visionary leaders
are models that others want to follow. Their congruence and
integrity gain the respect and trust of others.

Not Knowing

The state of "not knowing" is a special state used for modeling and information gathering in NLP. When a person enters a state of "not knowing," he or she attempts to drop any pre-existing assumptions, and get a fresh and unbiased view of a particular situation or experience. That is, he or she attempts to "not know" anything about the particular person or situation being explored or examined in order to avoid any preconceptions that may color his or her experience.

The state of "not knowing" can be characterized by the following anecdote:

> *An NLP Practitioner, Master Practitioner and a Modeler went for the first time on a walk in the redwood forest in Santa Cruz. On the path in front of them they saw a yellow banana slug. "Oh look," said the Practitioner, "The slugs in Santa Cruz are yellow."*
>
> *The Master Practitioner replied, "Not necessarily. All we really know is that some slugs in Santa Cruz are yellow."*
>
> *The Modeler retorted, "Well, to be precise, there is at least one path in Santa Cruz, with at least one slug on it which is yellow — at least on one side."*

The state of "not knowing" is a strategy that has been used by many exceptional people to produce innovations and new perspectives. Albert Einstein, for instance claimed that many of the ideas forming the theory of relativity emerged because he asked himself questions about space and time without any preconceptions, as a child would wonder about it.

The famous hypnotherapist Milton Erickson claimed that he always put aside all of his presuppositions when he worked with a client, and checked his assumptions. Did the client have two eyes (he or she could have a glass eye)? Did the client have two hands (if he or she is wearing gloves, the client may have a prosthetic hand)? Did the client have all of his or her hair (the person could be wearing a wig)? And so on.

World renowned healer and teacher Moshe Feldenkrais maintained, *"I start each case as if it were my first, and ask myself more questions than any of my assistants or critics ever do."* By entering a state of "not knowing," and starting each case as if it were his first, Feldenkrais, like Erickson, was able to be more aware, more creative, have more contact with his patients, and did not fall prey to limiting presuppositions that may in the end not have been valid. As a result, people like Einstein, Erickson and Feldenkrais were able to make breakthroughs in areas where others were held back by the presuppositions and assumptions of the time. As Feldenkrais pointed out, *"This mode of thinking is often successful in situations were specialists with greater knowledge than mine have failed."*

Not knowing is thus a powerful gateway to "awakening," and is an important skill for both large "C" Coaches and their clients in order to "get outside the box."

Nerk-Nerk

One way to help oneself and others achieve a state of not knowing is through the character of "Nerk-Nerk." "Nerk-Nerk" is the name of a fictitious character invented by NLP trainer Todd Epstein used to facilitate the process of information gathering and modeling. "Nerk-Nerk" is the name of a make-believe space alien who has the exact same nervous system and physical characteristics of human beings, but none of the perceptual, linguistic or cultural assumptions. Nerk-Nerk has studied and is familiar with all forms of human language, but is incapable of making the deletions, generalizations and distortions that most human beings do habitually while communicating verbally with one another. Nerk-Nerk is only able to understand and respond to fully specified sensory based descriptions and instructions.

Epstein used the character of Nerk-Nerk to facilitate the processes of entering a state in which all previous mental maps and assumptions are put aside with reference to one's ongoing experience. When a coach enters a "Nerk-Nerk" state, he or she attempts to drop pre-existing assumptions, and get a fresh and unbiased view of a particular situation or experience.

Such as state is a basic skill for awakeners. Try it out for yourself. Imagine for a few moments that you are Nerk-Nerk and examine familiar objects around you as if you had never seen them before. Watch television or observe people interacting if you were an alien or extra-terrestrial. What type of things would you pay attention to, and what type of patterns would you notice that are different from your everyday understanding?

If you were to observe or listen to your clients from this perspective, what kinds of questions would you ask them? What would you notice or perceive about their problems and life situations?

Uptime

The state of "not knowing" is also similar to the "uptime" state, in which all of a person's sensory channels are tuned externally. In a state of "uptime" there is no internal dialog, imagery, or emotional tension. All one's sensory awareness is focused on the external environment in the "here and now." The notion of "uptime" as used in NLP was formulated by NLP founders Richard Bandler and John Grinder. The term is borrowed from early computer terminology. "Uptime" meant the computer was inputting data. "Downtime" indicated that the computer was internally processing the data it had received.

Uptime is another powerful resource for awakening. It is essentially an awakening of the senses that opens the door to a deeper awakening to the world around us. You can use the following procedure to help promote and anchor the state of uptime in yourself and your clients.

Awakener's Toolbox: Creating an "Uptime" Anchor

1. Find a place, either indoors or outdoors, where you can sit or walk around for a while and enjoy the world around you.

2. As you observe your surroundings, practice focusing and tuning your awareness of your external environment to each of your sensory representational systems:

   a) *seeing* things—using both panoramic and detailed viewing of the various objects, colors and movements in your environment.

b) *feeling* the temperature of the air, the textures, shapes and hardness of the objects around you, and the feelings of your skin and muscles as you sit or move through the environment.

c) *listening* for the differences in the tones and location origins of the various sounds around you—and for the changes in your breathing and the pitch and tempo of any voices near you.

d) *smelling* the air and the objects around you—noticing which smells are sharper, which are more subtle— and, if you wish, take note of any changes in the taste in your mouth.

As you access each of these systems, you may screen out your other channels by closing your eyes and plugging your ears and nose in various combinations. Be sure to access each system as completely as possible without any internal dialogue, internal pictures or feelings.

3. With your right hand grab hold of your left wrist. As you judge that you are able to access each system in succession, squeeze your wrist only as tightly as you are able to completely access the sensory channel you are using. The more you can see, hear, feel and smell clearly the experiences around you, the tighter you squeeze your wrist..

4. Begin to tune into all representational systems simultaneously so that you attention is completely focused outside of you through all of your channels. Squeeze your wrist only as tightly as you are able to do this successfully.

5. Keep repeating the process until all you have to do is reach over and squeeze your wrist and your attention automatically begins to turn outside of you to your external environment, without any conscious effort.

Getting Access to the Unconscious

"Not knowing" and "uptime" are special states that help people to gain access to unconscious processes. Almost all creative and successful performers acknowledge the importance of unconscious processes in their work and accomplishments. It seems that once one has set up all the appropriate circuitry (as a result of caretaking, guiding, coaching, teaching, mentoring and sponsorship), it is important to maximize unconscious competence—to get out of the way of the process and let it run on its own.

Many creative people, for instance, claim they get their most brilliant ideas at times when they are not directly focusing on the problem or issue they are trying to resolve, such as when they are in the shower in the morning. A number of people have said something to the effect of, "I stuff my mind full of the information that I can find until I am completely exhausted and I can't fit anything more in there. Then I go to sleep. When I wake up, I have the answer!" Mozart described his creative process for writing music as being like a "pleasing, lively dream." Leonardo da Vinci even went so far as to suggest some processes for stimulating unconscious associations by staring at walls and describing methods for producing mental states similar to day dreaming.

Clearly, the link between conscious and unconscious is a key element of "awakening." In fact, a large part of the experience of awakening involves bringing into consciousness what is already known at an unconscious level.

Sigmund Freud pointed out that *mental processes are essentially unconscious* and that *those which are conscious are merely isolated acts and parts of the whole psychic entity.* Freud maintained that most of the processes that take place within our nervous system occur outside of our conscious awareness. Claiming that *the acceptance of unconscious mental processes represents a decisive step toward a new orientation in the world and in science,* Freud asserted:

[W]e resolve to think of the consciousness or unconsciousness of a mental process as merely one of its qualities and not necessarily definitive. . . . Each single process belongs in the first place to the unconscious psychical system; from this system it can under certain conditions proceed further into the conscious system.

People demonstrating mastery or excellence in the world have a high quality relationship between conscious and unconscious. They continually find ways to enhance and develop the quality of the relationship between that small piece that we call "consciousness," and the vastness of the unconscious. Consciousness feeds back into the larger unit, the unconscious, and affects the quality of the relationship. People who experience mastery also understand that this relationship is an ongoing process, an evolution which is continually enhanced as time goes by.

Developing the quality of the conscious/unconscious relationship involves a balance between practice and spontaneity. Sometimes it is important for your goal to be to "not have a goal." There comes a point in our learning when all we have to do is to act completely spontaneously. At this moment there is no self-reflection. There is only the systemic loop between the conscious and unconscious mind and between ourselves and the outside world.

In martial arts like Aikido, for example, you go onto the mat and you practice and practice. When you meet an opponent, you don't stop to talk to yourself or think about what you are doing. You don't even decide beforehand what maneuver to use. You really can't know what you are going to do until you interface with the opponent, because you are in a dance with the outside world.

Gregory Bateson pointed out, a master knows when to use the "tight thinking" of the cognitive conscious mind, and when to use the "loose thinking" of the more creative unconscious mind. Hypnotherapy icon Milton Erickson used the metaphor of the horse and the rider to describe the interplay between the conscious and unconscious mind; the horse being our unconscious mind and the rider being our conscious mind. Of course, anyone who has ridden a horse knows what happens when the rider wants to go in one direction and the horse in another. Neither one easily reaches their destination, and it requires a lot of time and uses up a lot of energy.

It is thus important to have strategies and methods to continually develop the relationship between your conscious and unconscious processes. Some typical mechanisms are meditation, prayer and self-hypnosis. These are processes that require that the whole unit of mind participate completely and honestly, as Gregory Bateson would say.

States of meditation, prayer and self-hypnosis are similar to "not knowing" and "uptime" in that they are all characterized by:

a. The use of peripheral (as opposed to foveal) vision.

b. Focus on external sounds (absence of internal dialog).

c. A relaxed physiology (no excess emotional or physical tension).

These appear to be key qualities in creating the bridge between our conscious and unconscious.

Dreaming is an altered or "other than conscious" state. It too can be used to enhance your thinking and learning processes and to review and integrate new information. You can use your dreams to review your day, with the intention of exploring what aspects of your day went well and/or how you might want to do things differently in the future. Dreaming can be used to seek answers to questions, challenges, or choice points you may be working on. The unconscious does not think in literal or material terms, but processes in terms of relationship, patterns, and patterns of relationships. What is offered by the unconscious mind to the conscious mind during dreaming is metaphoric. It is best to accept dreams as metaphors, and trust that you understand the teaching involved.

Awakener's Toolbox: Active Dreaming

Active dreaming is a tool for awakening, formulated by long-time NLP trainer and developer Judith DeLozier, that was inspired by certain Native American groups. Active dreaming is a process which involves setting an intention to be achieved during either sleep or day dreams. The intention may be to get an answer, solve a problem, make a decision, get more information, understand something better, etc. Intentions are typically stated in more general terms than a goal or outcome. For example, a person might say, "My intention is to dream about something that I can safely and ecologically let go of." The intention serves as a filter or guide which directs unconscious processes.

Answers may be either literal or symbolic. One person might awaken the following morning, and realize, "It is time for me to let go of the anger that I have been holding onto about a relationship that ended five years ago." Another person may go for a walk, and find herself fantasizing about leaves falling from a tree. The person may have no conscious understanding of what the leaves symbolize, but feel lighter and more at ease.

One way to explore the symbols is to take "second position" with them—imagining being the leaves or the tree, for instance. One can then explore the relationship between the symbols and one's original intention.

The following exercise is a way to help clients apply the practice of active dreaming to enhance the loop between their conscious and unconscious processes and gain deeper insight into some project, problem or transition in which they are involved.

Active Dreaming Exercise

1. Place an "intention" in the back of your mind; for example, a decision you are making, a problem you are solving, something you want to be more creative about, an issue you want more information about, etc.

2. Create a state of "not knowing" or an "uptime" state by:

   a. Using only peripheral (as opposed to foveal) vision.

   b. Focusing your hearing on external sounds (turn off any internal dialog).

   c. Establishing a relaxed physiology (no excess emotional or physical tension).

3. Commit to this state for a ten minute walk. While walking, notice what appears to "jump out at you," or where you attention is pulled; i.e., a tree, grass, the wind, the sound of a bird, etc.

4. As these phenomena present themselves (there may be more than one), take second position with each symbol or object. What are the characteristics of that object or symbol? What would be your attributes if you were a tree, for example? Time would probably change, the speed with which objects or people move would be different, you would be stationary on the bottom with movement on the top, etc.

5. Take all of the knowledge and characteristics that you have discovered by taking second position with the object or symbol and create a third position or meta position with respect to your original intention. Explore what new news, data, or understandings you have learned with respect to your original intention.

Awakener's Toolbox: Awakening to Freedom

Awakening is the goal of many spiritual disciplines and practices. Students of Zen Buddhism, for instance, interact with a Zen master, who assigns koans and assists the student in breaking free from conventional thought and awareness. A *koan* (which literally means "a public case") is a theme for meditation used by Zen masters to help their disciples break through the barriers of the rational, "conscious mind" in order to achieve enlightenment. Koans usually consist of a saying from a great Zen master of the past or an answer given by him to a question. For example, a monk asked Dongshan "Who is Buddha?" and received the reply "Three jin of flax." By meditating on such a koan, which is nonrational, Zen students open their minds to other types of thought, intuition and inspiration.

The "resolution" of a koan is a classic example of Albert Einstein's dictum that "you cannot solve a problem with the same type (or level) of thinking that is creating the problem." The "solution" to a koan involves "jumping" logical levels, or "thinking outside of the box." When this happens, rather than being a source of struggle, a koan becomes a stimulus for creativity and "enlightenment."

Anthropologist Gregory Bateson asserted that tackling a koan had much in common with dealing with psychological double binds. A "double bind" is a situation in which it appears that there is no right answer—whatever answer one gives or action one takes is "wrong." Bateson believed that such binds were a key factor in the development of mental illness, but could also be the source of great creativity and awareness, if a person were able to shift to the appropriate level of thinking and perception.

As an example, Bateson frequently cited a common feature of Zen training. A Zen master picks up a stick and raises it over one of his students, saying, "If you say that this stick is real, I will hit you with it. If you say that this stick is not real, I will hit you with it. Is this stick real or not?" As long as the student stays at the same level of thinking that the master has used to create the double bind, he or she is stuck. If the student simply reaches up and grabs the stick, begins to sing, picks up his or her own stick and pretends to "sword fight," etc., he or she has transcended the double bind, and shifted the context of the relationship. This was a level of learning that Bateson called "Learning III." (Such processes could also possibly lead to Learning IV.)

The practices of Zen Buddhism, and their emphasis on increasing awareness, expanding consciousness, and challenging the presuppositions and limitation of our thinking processes, provide useful insight into the process of "awakening." The following is an awakening exercise, inspired by NLP trainer and developer Richard Clarke, who has combined his more than 30 years of Zen training with NLP as a key element in his coaching practice.

Awakening to Freedom Format

Before beginning the process, the awakener needs to put himself or herself into a state of complete and unconditional acceptance of the identity and "spirit" of the client.

1. Ask the client to reflect on some unwanted or unproductive life pattern. Note the basic structure of the pattern. (For example, a person might think, "This is just going to be like all the other times I've tried to make a change in my life. I just know it. It won't work and I'll just feel hopeless again. With the family background I've had what can I expect!") Instruct the client to recall the many examples of the pattern in his or her life, the consequences that resulted, and the ways in which it has affected the client's life.

   a. Ask the client to consider what it would be like in the future to be free of that pattern and to reflect upon

how his or her life would be different if this pattern
were no longer in his or her life.

b. Then ask the client reflect on what this pattern does
   for him or her—i.e., how the continuation of the
   pattern may be functioning in his or her life. Check
   whether it is "helping" the client in any way. For
   example, it may help the client to avoid responsibility,
   escape criticism or domination by another person,
   manipulate or attempt to control others, give him or
   her a sense of familiar identity, etc. If those "advantages" are still valuable to the client, explore how he
   or she can get them in ways other than through the
   continuation of the undesired behavior.

As you discuss these issues with the client, remain in a
state of complete and unconditional acceptance of the
identity of the client and the "spirit" of his or her
answers.

2. Now, say to the client, with a respectful voice and
   manner, "You are free . . . so you <u>could</u> continue to do,
   think, or believe that, even for the rest of your life. You
   will continue to be an acceptable human being no matter
   what you do. You are completely OK as you are, and will
   continue to be so whether or not you ever change
   anything at all in your life. And you are free . . . so you
   really <u>could</u> continue this pattern and be perfectly alright
   . . . but why?"

3. Ask the client to sincerely and carefully consider this
   question, notice his or her internal response to this
   question and share it with you. Frequently, this response will be to bring up other beliefs about the pattern
   or the client. (For instance, the client might respond,
   "It's been this way for so long, I can't expect to be able to
   change things just like that. Besides, I am going to get

resistance every step of the way from my family/coworkers/boss.")

4. Shifting your focus to this response, repeat your comments of step 2; again reminding the client, "You are free . . . so you really could continue <u>this</u> response as well, and be perfectly alright . . . but why?"

5. Again ask the client to sincerely and carefully consider this question, notice his or her internal response to this question and share it with you.

6. Repeat this process a number of times; each time reminding the client, "You are free . . . so you really <u>could</u> continue this response as well, and be perfectly alright . . . but why?"

After several repetitions, the client will quickly get beyond his or her typical justifications with respect to the issue and get deeper and deeper insights into the pattern. Eventually, the client will find him or herself "out of the box" of his or her habitual thinking patterns, free of old beliefs and assumptions and with new awareness of areas in which he or she genuinely has a choice.

Because there is no "push back" from the coach, the client is lead to confront his or her own inner map more and more deeply, making self-discoveries that have not before been possible. Thus, it is very important that when the coach asks "but why?" he or she be genuinely curious and receptive and accept the client and whatever he or she says unconditionally.

Double Binds

In the previous section, we touched upon the notion of a double bind. A *double bind* is essentially a "no-win" situation; i.e., a situation in which you are "wrong if you do, and wrong if you don't." According to anthropologist Gregory Bateson, who originally defined the notion of the double bind, such dilemmas are at the root of both creativity and emotional confusion. The difference is whether or not one is able to recognize and transcend the bind in an appropriate way.

The essential structure of a double bind is:

> If you *do not* do A, you will not (survive, be safe, have fun, be OK as a person, etc.). But if you *do* do A, you will *not* (survive, be safe, have fun, be OK as a person, etc.).

The Salem witch trials are a classic illustration of such a bind. Apparently, one of the tests to see if a person was a witch was to bind the person and cast her into the water. If the person floated and survived, then she was determined to be a witch, and was put to death. If the person sank and drowned, she was exonerated with respect to being a witch, but was, of course, also dead.

It is not uncommon for clients to feel that they are "on trial" in such a way. Less dramatic double binds occur quite frequently in everyday life. One example is the dilemma of the husband who, when he asked his wife what she was thinking about certain topics, was told angrily that it was "none of his business." If he did not ask, however, he was criticized for "not caring" about her opinions. His inability to sort out the meaning of the two messages and respond appropriately made him feel that he was an inadequate husband.

Double binds also arise in business situations. Consider the situation of the person whose workload has become so large that he or she is not able to handle it. Doing one part of his or her job will mean that some other part does not get done. On the other hand, not doing that part of the job means that it will not get done. Either way, the person is not doing his or her job.

Another frequent double bind in business relates to the process of "downsizing." A manager, faced with reducing the people in his or her organization, is often caught in the bind of wanting the people to be "successful" and the business to be "successful." If the manager cuts the people, then they will not have incomes, may lose their homes, etc. Thus, the manager has failed in his or her outcome to make the people he or she works with "successful." On the other hand, if the manager doesn't reduce the people, then the business may be unprofitable, or even fail—in either case, unsuccessful. The manager is in the double bind of either failing with respect to his or her co-workers, or failing with respect to the business.

The most intense double binds occur in the context of significant interpersonal relationships. They often involve what appears to be a power struggle in which one person is "negatively sponsoring" the other or trying to "make the other person wrong."

As an illustration, Bateson cites an example of a boy who had been hospitalized with the diagnosis of "schizophrenia." After some time in the hospital, the boy had become stable enough that he was able to receive visitors. One day, the boy's mother came to visit. Upon greeting her son, the mother said, "How about giving your mother a hug?" The boy dutifully put his arms around her. As he embraced her, however, the boy's mother visibly stiffened, clearly uncomfortable with the physical contact. Responding to the nonverbal message, the boy withdrew his arms, somewhat confused. At this point, the mother asked, "What's wrong, don't you love your mother?" Becoming even more confused and uncomfortable, the boy started to tense up and look away. At this, his mother admonished, "You really must learn to control your emotions." The interaction continued in this way until the boy's anxiety escalated, ending in a violent episode for which he had to be physically restrained.

Even though the situation is not as dramatic as that of the Salem witch trials, all of the ingredients for a double bind are present. The first message is, "If you do not hug me, you do not love me (and thus will not have my approval)." The second message, however, is, "If you do hug me, you will make me uncomfortable and I will withdraw (and thus you will not have my approval)."

There is also a third message, in this example, about the boy's reaction to his dilemma. Her comment that, "You really must learn to control your emotions," implies that the source of the problem is with the boy's inability to control his emotions rather than in her own incongruity. The implication is, "The fact that you feel confused means that something is wrong with *you*. You are the cause of the problem, confusion, etc."

This third message seems to be an important part of the double bind pattern. The other person interprets the individual's discomfort or confusion as a sign of (1) incompetence, or (2) negative intent coming from a position of power on the part of the individual who is in the double bind (reversing the reality). The third message is also typically on an identity level and is essentially a "negative sponsorship" message. The implication being that the individual's sense of confusion is an evidence that he or she is defective at the level of his or her identity; i.e., your distress about being in a double bind is a sign of a defect in your character. It is this third aspect of the double bind that makes them most emotionally intolerable.

Awakener's Toolbox: Transcending Double Binds

Being in a double bind is a lot like having a nightmare. It has been pointed out that when you are having a nightmare, there are many things that you can do to attempt to escape the danger that you perceive to be pursuing you. You can run, hide, call for help, and, because it is a dream, you can even do things that defy typical reality like fly, change shape, etc. There is, however, only one real solution to the nightmare, and that is to wake up from it.

NLP trainers and developers Tim Hallbom and Suzi Smith suggest the practice of taking *multiple "meta positions"* as a way to help clients "awaken" from double binds. Taking a "meta position" typically involves shifting to what we have referred to earlier as "third position"—disassociating from yourself and taking the perspective of an observer of your current situation. This change in perspective is also facilitated by using "third person" language (he, she, they, them, etc.) when describing yourself and any others involved in the interaction. Usually, the emotional intensity associated with the situation is immediately reduced if one can accomplish this shift in perceptual position.

Because of the multi-level nature of double binds, however, simple disassociation is often not enough. Frequently, addressing double binds involves the ability to take a three-place (watching yourself watch yourself) or four-place (watching yourself, watch yourself, watching yourself) disassociation. If necessary, the process could be extended even further (there is an unlimited number of potential meta positions). Each new level of disassociation not only distances a person further from the emotional intensity of the situation, but also allows him or her to take a broader and potentially wiser perspective.

To help clients use this method to break free of double bind situations and find new options, you can offer them the following instructions:

1) Recall a situation in which you feel that you have been in a double bind.

2) Imagine that you can float out of your body, to a point above and behind yourself, so that you are watching yourself and the other person(s) in the interaction. See "them" interacting "over there" as if you were an uninvolved observer. Notice what new awareness, understandings or learnings you gain from this perspective.

3) Imagine that you are able to move to a point above and behind this "observer" perspective, such that you are watching yourself watch yourself and the other(s) in the situation "over there." Again notice any new awareness, understandings or learnings you gain from this perspective.

4) Continue to repeat step 3 several times for each new observer position you are able to reach. You may find yourself achieving a kind of "spiritual" perspective and awareness that can help to bring a sense of inner peace and wisdom. What would be "God's thoughts" with respect to this situation?

5) Retrace your steps back to the original situation, reentering each observer perspective and taking with you the awareness, understandings and learnings you have gained from each of the observer positions. Your experience should be very different when you reassociate back into your memory of the double bind situation.

Awakener's Toolbox: Creating a Positive Double Bind

As was mentioned earlier, the most challenging double binds have the characteristic of including a number of negative sponsorship messages: i.e., "You are wrong if you do." "You are wrong if you don't." and "You are wrong if you cannot decide." This tends to produce the opposite of awakening. Instead of "becoming fully conscious, aware and appreciative" and having greater wisdom, clarity and creativity, the person feels confused, stuck and shut down.

One way of creating antidotes to double binds is to set up a situation in which the person receives multiple positive sponsorship messages instead. That is, that he or she is assured "You are OK if you do." "You are OK if you don't." and "You are OK if you cannot decide." This creates what could be called a "positive double bind," a no-lose situation in which the person is validated and supported at the identity level, no matter what.

Similar to the Awakening to Freedom format, this type of support allows the person to separate identity from behavior, get "out of the box" of the type of thinking associated with the problem and genuinely reflect on his or her beliefs, assumptions and choices with respect to the situation.

One of the keys to Awakening to Freedom, Positive Double Bind and dealing with double binds in general is helping clients to experience Nils Bohr's principle of the deep truth; the notion that in a deep truth the opposite is also true. The awareness of the deeper truth brings a greater sense of wisdom and choice. The goal of creating a positive double bind is to help clients become aware of this type of deeper truth with respect to themselves and their patterns of behavior.

A positive double bind is a useful awakening tool for many types of situations. The following is a format for creating a positive double bind that involves sending a combination of particular positive sponsorship messages to a client. While it is possible for one person to deliver all these messages to a client, the process is most easily done in a group of four.

1. Ask the client to identify a behavior pattern with respect to which he or she is stuck or undecided. It may be either desired or undesired (e.g., procrastinating, writing a book, changing jobs, breaking off a relationship, etc.).

2. Persons A and B stand on either side of the client and make the following comments over and over:

   Person A: "You are OK if you do."
   Person B: "You are OK if you do not.
   Persons A and B together: "You are OK if you cannot decide."

3. At the same time, person C continually repeats:

   "There is a larger purpose to your life and actions."
   "You have the capacity to make good decisions."
   "You can trust in your larger self and your unconscious."
   "You will be guided to make the right choice."
   "You have the capability to deal effectively with life challenges."
   "You can be strong, compassionate and playful."
   "You can learn. There is something important to learn."

Note that the emphasis of the messages of A and B is that "*You* are OK," not "*It* is OK." To say "*You* will be OK if you procrastinate or do not procrastinate," is different than saying "*It* is OK if you procrastinate or do not procrastinate." The term "it" implies a general judgment about the behavior rather than a message about the identity of the individual. The critical point of this exercise is to emphasize that the client will be OK at an identity level, no matter what. This helps the client to separate his or her identity from the behavior in question and gives the client the genuine freedom to choose.

The third set of messages helps to remind the client of key resources and beliefs that can help him or her to make effective decisions and find his or her path.

Clients who have gone through this process frequently find that the first set of messages basically neutralizes any internal conflicts or struggles. The second set of messages helps them to bring the resources necessary to wisely and ecologically make the appropriate decision or resolve the issue.

Bateson's Levels of Learning and Change

The process of awakening is clearly one of shifting levels of experience and awareness. People often talk about responding to things on different *levels*. For instance, someone might say that some experience was negative on one level but positive on another level. In our brain structure, language, and perceptual systems there are natural hierarchies or levels of experience. The effect of each level is to organize and direct the information on the level below it. Changing something on an upper level would necessarily change things on the lower levels; changing something on a lower level could but would not necessarily affect the upper levels.

Anthropologist Gregory Bateson (1973) identified four basic levels of learning and change—each level more abstract than the level below it but each having a greater degree of impact on the individual. Bateson proposed his categorization of different "logical levels" of learning based on Bertrand Russell's mathematical theory of logical types. (See Appendix A.) Each level functioned by making corrective changes and refinements in the next lowest level upon which it operated.

According to Bateson:

> *Zero learning is characterized by specificity of response [i.e., having a specific behavior in a specific environment - RD] which—right or wrong—is not subject to correction.*
>
> *Learning I is change in specificity of response by correction of errors of choice within a set of alternatives.*
>
> *Learning II is a change in the process of Learning I, e.g., a corrective change in the set of alternatives from which choice is made, or it is a change in how the sequence is punctuated.*

Learning III is change in the process of Learning II, e.g., a corrective change in the system of sets of alternatives from which choice is made.

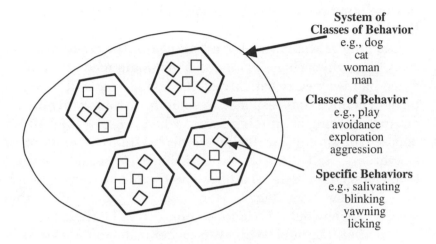

System of
Classes of Behavior
e.g., dog
cat
woman
man

Classes of Behavior
e.g., play
avoidance
exploration
aggression

Specific Behaviors
e.g., salivating
blinking
yawning
licking

Different Levels of Learning Relate to Changes in Different Levels of Behavior

As an example, consider the situation of Pavlov and his dogs. Pavlov discovered that he could condition his dogs to salivate to the sound of a bell by repeatedly ringing the bell when he fed them. The dogs learned to associate the sound of the bell with receiving food. Pretty soon all Pavlov needed to do was ring the bell and, even if he had no food, the dogs would begin to salivate, triggered by the sound alone.

According to Bateson's levels of learning model, the dogs' initial act of salivating when given food is a case of *Learning Zero*. It is a preprogrammed, instinctual response that is inherited and which would be difficult, if not impossible, to extinguish.

Learning to extend the reaction of salivation from the sight and smell of the food to the sound of the bell is an example of *Learning I*. Through repetition and reinforcement, the dog is learning to associate the specific response of salivating (as opposed to other responses, such as yawning, licking, blinking, etc.) with the specific stimulus of a particular bell.

Learning II would involve a "change in the *set* of alternatives from which choice is made." This would mean that, once a dog had learned to salivate at the sound of a bell, it would have to change that response to something completely different (say barking or running away) when it heard the bell (as opposed to simply increasing or decreasing the amount of salivation). Salivating is a member of a set of "eating" behaviors. Other "sets" of alternatives would be "play," "avoidance," "exploration," "aggression," etc. Making a shift at this level would obviously be more complex than Learning I.

Learning III would be an even bigger change. Bateson says it would be a "change in the system of sets of alternatives from which choice is made." A dog, for instance, is one "system" of sets of alternatives. Other animals (cats, birds, humans, wolves, etc.) would constitute different systems. To accomplish Learning III, Pavlov's dogs would have to suddenly shift from "dog-like" behaviors to "cat-like" behaviors (meowing, climbing trees, etc.) when the bell rang. This would clearly be quite challenging and, as Bateson pointed out, is practically impossible for adults of most species (although imitating other animals like dogs, cats and birds is a natural and normal pastime for human children).

Thus, in Bateson's framework, a simple, mechanical reflex would be a case of "zero learning." *Learning Zero* processes could also include habits, addictions and other patterns that seem fixed and unchangeable. Learning Zero is a common state of affairs for many people and organizations. Many of our behaviors become unconscious and embedded habits that make it difficult to adapt and adjust effectively to changes in the world around us. This frequently leads to stuckness, resistance, complacence and inefficiency.

Behavioral conditioning, psychomotor learning, process reengineering or incremental quality improvement would be operations relating to "corrective changes" with respect to particular behaviors and actions in people and organizations—*Learning I*. Learning I is essentially about behavioral flexibility; updating and improving the procedures and patterns of behavior that are already in place. Learning I is best facilitated by helping people to develop better "metacognition," the awareness of one's actions, internal experience and thinking processes. This is done by providing basic coaching and teaching techniques such as contrastive analysis and providing feedback.

Changing higher level processes like policies, values and priorities would relate to operations which address entire sets of alternatives—*Learning II*. If a company, for instance, decides to shift to being more "service oriented" than "product oriented," it will require large scale changes across whole areas of procedures and behaviors, and likely the establishment of new sets of behaviors and procedures modeled from others.

Another example of change at the level of Learning II in an individual would be an abrupt switch from exploratory behavior to avoidance, or from aggression to exploration or play. To accomplish such an immediate and dramatic turnaround requires shifts in beliefs and values. If one believes that a certain context is "dangerous," for instance, he or she will more than likely select "avoidance" behaviors rather than those in the class of "play." On the other hand, if a person believes that a context is "safe," he or she is not likely to choose behaviors from the classes of "fight" or "flight."

A good illustration of this is the rapid drop off in the number of people choosing to travel in airplanes after the September 11, 2001, hijackings. It was not a gradual change brought about by higher airfares or poorer service (which would have been an instance of Learning I). Rather, it was an immediate and intense shift brought on by the belief that it was not longer "safe" to fly. Clearly, the effects of Learning II are more immediate and far reaching than Learning I.

With respect to humans, Learning II shifts are supported by the ability to take "meta position"—that is, to disassociate from oneself and consider one's actions in context, and in comparison to other "sets of alternatives." This is one of the main goals of mentoring.

"Imprinting" and personality development would relate more to the establishment of change in whole "systems" of alternative behaviors—*Learning III*. Shifting such "systems" essentially involves a change at the level of identity. It involves expanding our range of behavior to include possibilities outside of our current role or collection of "sets" of alternatives. The Internet and the "new economy," for instance, forced many companies to stretch into completely new management and marketing approaches, sometimes far beyond what they were used to or comfortable with.

Modeling, benchmarking and taking "second position" with others are ways to support the process of Learning III. They facilitate us to reach beyond the threshold and limits of our current sense of self and identity. As Bateson maintained, "To the degree that man achieves Learning III . . . his 'self' will take on a sort of irrelevance." Bateson asserted that change at the level of Learning III was quite difficult, and that "to demand this level of performance in some men and some mammals is sometimes pathogenic." This is why sponsorship is so essential for supporting people to expand their identity.

Learning IV

Beyond these three levels, Bateson also hinted at the possibility of a *Learning IV*—a level of learning that he believed was not possible to achieve by any individual member of a species, but only collectively as a group or species as a whole. Learning IV would involve the establishment of completely new behaviors that do not fit any current system of classes of behavior. Learning IV would be a truly revolutionary type of learning, that would involve the creation of whole new archetypes or systems of behavior.

When our ancestors stood up on two feet and spoke the first words, they were not selecting from some existing set of alternatives, nor were they modeling some other species or creature that already existed. They began something completely new that revolutionized our role on the planet.

Acts of genius frequently have the characteristics of Learning IV—unprecedented and transformative—leading to revolutions in the way we understand and interact with the world around us. In the Silicon Valley world of technology ontroprcncurs, people often distinguish between "evolutionary" and "revolutionary" technologies. Evolutionary technologies are those which make a significant improvement on what already exists, extending its functionality or characteristics in some important way or integrating it with other technologies. Revolutionary technologies are those which change or create a new industry and transform the way that people work or communicate. Things like the printing press, automobile, airplane, radio, television, personal computer, Internet, for example, could be considered revolutionary technologies.

While some type of "awakening" accompanies each level of learning in Bateson's model, the awakenings at Learning IV are the most profound and transformative. The revolutionary aspects of Learning IV are clearly examples of a type of awakening in which we are not only able to get "outside the box," but begin to create a whole new set of boxes.

As Bateson suggests, the insights and awakenings that constitute Learning IV most likely come in the form of some type of inspiration or revelation that has its source beyond the individual and in the larger system or "field" surrounding us—what Bateson referred to as the "larger Mind" or "pattern which connects," and what Einstein implied when talked about "God's thoughts" or "universe."

Access to Learning IV requires a strong connection with our unconscious mind and derives from states of "not knowing," "uptime," "active dreaming," which involve being centered and open to all possibilities, without making any judgments or interpretations. These special states give us the experience of being able to unconsciously tap into the possibilities present in the larger "field" or "Mind" around us—what we have been calling the "spiritual" level of learning and experience.

Overview of the Four Levels of Learning

To summarize Bateson's levels of learning:

- **Learning 0** is *no change*. It involves repetitive behaviors in which the individual, group or organization is stuck in a rut or trapped "inside the box"—e.g., habits, resistance, inertia.

- **Learning I** is gradual, *incremental change*. It involves making corrections and adaptations through behavioral flexibility and stretching. While these modifications may help to extend the capabilities of the individual group or organization, they are still "within the box"—e.g., establishing and refining new procedures and capabilities. Learning I is the focus of coaching and teaching.

- **Learning II** is rapid, *discontinuous change*. It involves the instantaneous shift of a response to an entirely different category or class of behavior. It is essentially the switch from one type of "box" to another—e.g., change in policies, values or priorities. Learning II is best facilitated through the process of mentoring.

- **Learning III** is *evolutionary change*. It is characterized by significant alterations which stretch beyond the boundaries of the current identity of the individual, group or organization. We could say that not only are they outside the "box," they are outside of the "building"—e.g., transition of role, brand or identity. Shifts at this level require effective sponsorship.

- **Learning IV** is *revolutionary change*. It involves awakening to something completely new, unique and transformative. At the level of Leaning IV, the individual, group or organization is out of the box, out of the building and in a new world—e.g., completely new responses, technologies or capabilities that open the door to previously unknown and uncharted possibilities.

Bateson's levels provide another very useful road map for coaches when seeking to help their clients. New outcomes and the need for change created by shifts in the environment force clients to confront behaviors and patterns that have become stuck at the level of Learning 0. The question then becomes, at which levels (I, II, II or IV) does learning need to take place in order for the client to reach his or her goals and move from his or her current state to the desired state?

Clearly, different types of life situations and transitions bring about and require different levels of learning. It is important to be able to identify the level(s) of learning required in order for the client to reach his or her desired state and apply the appropriate approach and support that will facilitate those levels of learning. Frequently, individuals and organizations unknowingly try to apply a Learning I solution to a Learning II or III problem. This is ineffective at best, and sometimes makes things even worse.

Some issues and goals will require learning at several or all of the levels. Accomplishing major life transitions and breaking free of double binds clearly require adjustments at several levels of learning, including Learning IV at times. Another common issue that arises for clients, requiring multiple levels of learning and change, is that of updating "survival strategies."

Survival Strategies

Survival strategies are deep and often unconscious internal patterns that are usually established at a very early age. Typical survival strategies are responses like *fight* (attack), *flight* (escape) or *freeze* (paralysis). Survival strategies form a part of our core programming and function as a kind of fundamental meta program which shapes our approach to life and relationships. They are a part of our deepest programming which we share with and have evolved from other animals. All creatures must develop some form of survival strategy.

These fundamental strategies can take many forms in our daily life, such as feeling the need to shrink, trying to become small and invisible, going blank, dissociating from feelings, submitting, becoming passive, trying to seduce the aggressor, believing in the necessity to hold one's ground at all costs, etc. "Survival" in many cases, extends beyond physical survival to include the preservation or protection of our sense of identity and personal integrity, key beliefs and values, significant roles and relationships to which we have devoted ourselves, and so on.

As with all strategies, it is most effective to have a range of possibilities with respect to our survival strategies and apply them flexibly according to the context. Frequently, however, we become stuck in one strategy or overgeneralize its effectiveness. This leads us to act inappropriately, and frequently produces a paradoxical result in which we are actually escalating the situation, and end up putting ourselves even more at risk in some way.

As an analogy, it is known that different survival strategies are more effective with different types of predatory mammals. If a person is attacked by a bear, for instance, it is best to lie down, become passive, and pretend to be dead. If approached by a mountain lion, on the other hand, it is best for a person to stand one's ground, make oneself appear as big as possible, and slowly back away. Trying the wrong strategy with the wrong animal can result in disastrous consequences (and attempting to outrun the predator is not likely to be effective in either situation).

Thus, it is important to periodically review, enrich and update our survival strategies, expanding our options to include new possibilities such as centering, acceptance, forgiveness, commitment and fluidity. Because they are so deep and vital to our existence, changing survival strategies is not simply a matter of making superficial adjustments. Updating survival strategies involves reviewing key life situations and bringing new resources into these experiences at several levels.

Awakener's Toolbox: Updating Survival Strategies through Bateson's Levels of Learning

The following format applies Gregory Bateson's Logical Levels of Learning to help clients identify and update survival strategies that may have become outdated and ineffective. It involves systematically moving from Learning 0 all the way to Learning IV.

Learning I, II and II are like the rungs of a ladder that help us to achieve the possibility of Learning IV. This process demonstrates the various types of approaches and support that help people to make the types of adjustments and changes in perspective necessary to successfully accomplish each level of learning, building upon the insights and knowledge generated by each level to support the capacity of Learning IV.

The process involves leading the client through the following steps:

1. Think of a problem situation or relationship in which you continue to fall back into an old survival strategy, even though it is ineffective (Learning 0). Associate into an example of the experience and internally "relive" what it is like. Demonstrate or role play the behavioral response that you have in that situation, and identify the structure of the survival strategy (i.e., fighting back, trying to escape, freezing up, shrinking, making yourself invisible, etc.). Keep in mind that the pattern may involve a combination or sequence of survival strategies.

2. Take a step back from the situation and reflect upon this pattern of behavior. Notice how you are responding both mentally and physically in that situation. Explore how you could adjust or adapt your behavior (Learning I) if

you were able to have more inner strength (power), softness (compassion) and playfulness (humor). Role play some possibilities exploring how you could vary the current behavior you are engaging in; i.e., exaggerate it, dampen it, shift it, etc. Think of a key coach or teacher in your life who can help you to be more flexible.

3. Take a further step back from the situation and go to an "observer" position, such that you are "watching yourself" in the problem situation.

    a. Notice how you have been categorizing or classifying this situation up until now. What do you perceive as the survival issue? What beliefs have you been holding about yourself, others or the context that have triggered you to perceive it as a "survival" situation?

    b. Think of some other time and situation in which you were able to act or respond in a completely different and more resourceful way (Learning II)—e.g., a state of "uptime." Associate into a situation in which you were able to enact this other class of behavior.

    c. Create a "belief bridge" to the problem situation: What is the belief that you have that allows you to act resourceful in this other situation? What belief would you need to have in order to support the new class of behavior in the problem situation? Think of an important mentor in your life who can help you hold that belief.

    d. Revisit the problem situation and act "as if" you had this belief and the different class of behavior associated with it in the problem situation. What would be different?

4. Step back again so that you are outside of yourself, reflecting on yourself and the range of behaviors that you have had available to you in your life. Consider the possibility of a completely different system with a completely different range of behavior (identity) that is not your own (Learning III).

   a. Find a person, animal or being that would have a completely different strategy than you in that situation. Identify a role model for that system of behavior and put yourself fully "into his or her shoes" (second position). [If you need to, create a "belief bridge" to get into the perceptual position of the model (i.e., What belief would you need in order to be able to put yourself fully into the other?)]

   b. From the perspective of the role model, what is your metaphor for yourself as that model? What is your "calling" as that model? Think of a sponsor in your life who helped you to expand your perception of who you are and imagine putting yourself back into the problem situation and responding "as if" you were this other person, applying the calling and the metaphor you have created.

5. Step back beyond the Learning III location. Enter a state of "not knowing," in which you feel centered and open to all possibilities, without making any judgments or interpretations. Open yourself up to what Gregory Bateson called the "pattern which connects" and the "larger Mind," and what Einstein referred to as "God's thoughts" and "universe." Think of an awakener in your life who helped you widen your view of what was possible. Create an anchor or symbol for this state. Using the anchor or symbol to hold the state, step back through each of the other levels of learning and back

into the problem situation and act spontaneously. What is a behavior you could do that would not fit <u>any</u> current system of classes of behavior? (Learning IV)

This same process can be used to help clients resolve many types of issues. In addition to survival strategies and double binds, the same steps can be applied to any situation in which a client feels stuck or trapped in any pattern of behavior.

Summary

Awakening involves assisting people to grow and evolve at the level of vision, purpose and spirit. Awakeners support others by helping them to develop greater awareness of their calling, their unconscious resources, and the larger systems to which they belong. This is accomplished by helping clients to "get outside the box" in which they are currently confined; breaking out of old habits, transcending conflicts and double binds, and updating ineffective survival strategies.

A key condition for achieving deep insights and awakenings is the ability to achieve a state of "not knowing." When a person enters a state of *not knowing*, he or she attempts to drop any pre-existing assumptions, and get a fresh and unbiased view of a particular situation or experience.

Uptime is another gateway to awakening. Being in a state of uptime involves placing our attention on the here and now, opening our senses completely to the world around us. In doing so we bypass conscious assumptions and interferences and create a clear channel to our unconscious competencies.

The link between conscious and *unconscious* is a key element of "awakening." In many ways, awakening is the result of bringing into consciousness what is already known at an unconscious level.

Active dreaming is a way of utilizing the channel between the conscious and unconscious by setting an intention and entering a state in which you are:

- Using only peripheral (as opposed to foveal) vision.

- Focusing your hearing on external sounds (turn off any internal dialog).

- Maintaining a relaxed physiology (no excess emotional or physical tension).

Knowledge and information arising from the active dreaming process is frequently symbolic or metaphoric, stimulating clients to become aware of other levels of meaning with respect to particular situations and their lives in general.

Awakening to Freedom is a large "C" Coaching format which helps clients to "get outside of the box" of current limiting life patterns and finding "a type of thinking different from the one that has been creating the problem." By offering complete and unconditional acceptance of the client, the awakener creates a context in which the client can confront his or her own mental maps, beliefs and assumptions more and more deeply, making self-discoveries that have not before been possible.

Double binds are no-win situations that require significant insight and awakening to resolve. The conditions surrounding double binds generally create a result directly opposite from "awakening," a state in which the person feels confused, stuck and shut down. *Transcending double binds* involves taking multiple "meta positions" in which the client can disassociate from and reflect upon the double binding situation with an absence of the emotional trauma and negative sponsorship messages associated with the situation. This allows the client to achieve a broader and wiser perspective from which to find new insights, options and solutions.

Positive double binds serve as an antidote to the negative sponsorship messages embedded in typical double binds and also form a gateway to transcending the limitations of unproductive life patterns. Positive double binds are created by simultaneously sending multiple positive sponsorship messages which serve to neutralize any internal conflicts or struggles and stimulate the resources necessary to think innovatively and make wise and ecological decisions.

Gregory Bateson's *levels of learning* provide an important and useful road map for coaches and awakeners to help clients to travel the path from incremental improvement to revolutionary change by getting successively farther out of the box of current thinking patterns and behaviors.

Bateson's hierarchy culminates in *Learning IV*—the ability to come up with ideas and actions that are completely new and transformational. True Learning IV has its source beyond the individual, within the larger system or "field" surrounding us. Access to Learning IV requires a strong connection with our unconscious and involves being centered and open to all possibilities, without making any judgments or interpretations. This makes it possible to tap into the insight present in the larger "field" or "Mind" around us.

A key application of Bateson's levels of learning, and in particular Learning IV, is that of updating ineffective survival strategies that have become rigidified at the level of Learning 0. *Survival strategies* are deep and often unconscious internal patterns (e.g., fight, flight, freeze) that are usually established at a very early age. Updating survival strategies involves systematically leading clients from Learning 0 to Learning IV, building upon the insights and knowledge generated by each level to reach life-transforming insights and awakenings.

Conclusion

The purpose of this book has been to explore the skills and tools necessary to be an effective large "C" Coach. This involves the integration of a number of support roles ranging from caretaker to awakener. Each chapter has focused on a particular level of change and the types of issues that typically need to be addressed by coaches at that level. For each level of change we have also defined the skills, characteristics and the leadership style most associated with supporting people to effectively perform, learn and improve with respect to that level.

These key interrelationships can be summarized in the following table:

Level of Change	Types of Issues To Be Addressed	Type of Support Needed	Leadership Style
Environment	*Where and When*	**Guide Caretaker**	Management by Exception
Behavior	*What*	**Coach**	Contingent Reward
Capabilities	*How*	**Teacher**	Intellectual Stimulation
Values and Beliefs	*Why*	**Mentor**	Inspirational
Identity	*Who*	**Sponsor**	Individualized Consideration
Spiritual	*For Whom For What*	**Awakener**	Charismatic Visionary

Levels of Support Provided by a Large "C" Coach

A major portion of each chapter of this book has also been devoted to providing a toolbox of techniques, formats and exercises to be used in the context of each support role (caretaker, guide, coach, teacher, mentor, sponsor and awakener) in order to facilitate the process of effective performance, learning and change for each level. Most of these tools and techniques have been drawn from or inspired by the principles and technology of Neuro-Linguistic Programming (NLP) and founded upon what we have termed the coaching-modeling loop.

The significance of modeling in particular has been emphasized through tools and processes such as:

- Intervision
- Contrastive Analysis and Mapping Across
- T.O.T.E. Elicitation
- Second Position
- Meta Position

The coaching-modeling loop combines knowledge about *what* a person needs to do in order to perform effectively with information about *how* to achieve those results. Modeling augments coaching by defining how key tasks and activities may best be done, and coaching augments modeling by helping people to internalize and put into practice what has been modeled.

Creating an Aligned Path from Caretaker to Awakener

It is important to point out that the various levels of tools and support covered in the chapters of this book are not mutually exclusive, but rather complement one another in fundamental ways. The lower levels support the upper levels, and the upper levels provide a framework and direction for the lower levels. In fact, all of the levels of tools and support are needed to some degree in order to help clients bring their dreams and visions into reality.

Thus, even though they have been presented separately, the tools and roles are best used in combination with one another.

Perhaps the best way to summarize and align the roles and styles that make up the path from caretaker to awakener is in the form of an experiential review which serves as a final tool in our coaching toolbox.

Capital "C" Coach Alignment Process

The purpose of the following process is to help you to establish an effective and aligned capital "C" Coaching state.

Begin by laying out six spaces for the various levels of support we have been exploring in this book—*caretaker* and *guide*, performance *coach, teacher, mentor, sponsor* and *awakener*. For each role, you will be directed to identify the level of focus and type of resources you will need to be effective in that role. To help you build those resources at each location you will be guided to:

a. think of the individuals in your life who have been effective role models for that level of support.

b. put yourself into the perceptual position of those role models in order to get a felt sense of what it is like to support people at that level, including the appropriate leadership style.

c. identify personal reference experiences for times when you were able to effectively be in that role and express the supporting leadership style.

You will also be directed to identify the types of posture, movements, voice tone and internal state related to each role and style.

As a final step, you will align all of the roles and styles within the context of your vision and environment, as an integrated large "C" Coaching state.

Awakener	Sponsor	Mentor	Teacher	Coach	Caretaker Guide
Visionary	Individual Consideration	Inspirational	Intellectual Stimulation	Contingent Reward	Management by Exception
Spiritual	*Identity*	*Values & Beliefs*	*Capabilities*	*Behavior*	*Environment*
6	5	4	3	2	1

1. Identify an *environment* in which you would like to be a more effective large "C" Coach. Where and when are you called upon to be a large "C" Coach? Associate into that environment, as if you were there, seeing, hearing and feeling the key features of that environment. Think about the physical resources you need that would most support you and any guidance that would help you to understand or manage that environment better.

   a. Think about the people in your life who have been your caretakers and guides. Notice how they were ready and available if you needed care or knowledge about your surroundings. Recall some situations in which you received effective caretaking or guidance and how important it was for you to know that you could get the physical support or information you needed. Think of the characteristics of the people who have been good caretakers and guides for you.

   b. Now, put yourself into the shoes of some of those caretakers and guides. Feel what it is like to be a caretaker or guide for others. What is it like to be ready and available to help others with physical care or knowledge?

   c. Also, think of times when you yourself have been in the role of caretaker or guide. Get a strong sense of the "energy" of the caretaker and guide. Feel that energy in your body and find a physical expression, in terms of your posture, gestures and voice tone, that expresses the energy of the caretaker and guide and creates within you the state of readiness that goes with management by exception. When you have a good sense of that physical expression, anchor it strongly to this location and then let it go.

2. Step back to the *performance coach* location. Reflect upon the *behaviors* you will need to be an effective large "C" Coach in the environment you have selected. *What* will you be doing as an effective coach? Feel your physical body and identify some of the actions for which it would be important for you to receive feedback and encouragement. What areas of your own performance will be most critical?

a. Recall the people in your life who have been performance coaches for you. Notice how they were able to help you set clear goals, encourage you to stretch, give you high quality feedback, and let you know what would happen if you performed well and what would happen if you did not. Recall how their feedback and encouragement helped to draw the best out of you and what it was like to stretch and improve through time with their support.

b. Now, put yourself into the shoes of some of those coaches. Feel what it is like to be an effective coach. What is it like to help set clear goals, encourage people to stretch and give good feedback?

c. Also, think of times when you yourself have been in the role of a coach for others. Get a strong sense of the "energy" of the coach. Feel that energy in your body and find a physical expression, in terms of your posture, gestures and voice tone, that expresses the energy of the coach and creates within you the state of determination, attentiveness and focus that goes with defining clear goals, and providing feedback and the encouragement to stretch. When you have a good sense of that physical expression, anchor it strongly to this location and then let it go.

3. Step back to the *teacher* location. Reflect upon the *capabilities* you will need to use and/or strengthen in order be an effective large "C" Coach in the environment you have selected. *How* will you accomplish your objectives as a coach? Which cognitive strategies and mental abilities will help you most with your "inner game" in that environment? In which areas will it be most critical for you to be intellectually stimulated?

   a. Recall the people in your life who have been your most effective teachers. Notice how they were able to help you find new perspectives and think of situations and issues in new ways. Recall what it is like to be highly intellectually stimulated, with your mind alive and ready to learn.

   b. Put yourself into the shoes of some of your teachers. Feel what it is like to be a good teacher. What is it like to stimulate others intellectually, helping them to develop clarity, new understanding and a wider map of the world?

   c. Think of times when you have been in the role of a teacher for others, helping them to find new ideas and think more clearly. Get a strong sense of the "energy" of the teacher. Feel that energy in your body and find a physical expression, in terms of your posture, gestures and voice tone, that expresses the energy of the teacher and creates within you the state of intellectual curiosity and lucidity. When you have a good sense of that physical expression, anchor it strongly to this location and then let it go.

4. Take a step back to the *mentor* location. Reflect on the *values and beliefs* that will motivate and guide you as an effective large "C" Coach in the environment you have chosen. *Why* is it important for you to be a large "C" Coach in this environment? What are the core values and key beliefs that inspire you and your clients to be your best?

    a. Recall the people in your life who have been your mentors. Notice how they shaped or influenced your life in a positive way by "resonating" with, releasing, or unveiling something deeply within you. Recall what it is like to feel a strong sense of belief in the future and to give the very best of yourself.

    b. Put yourself into the shoes of some of the key mentors in your life. Feel what it is like to be a mentor. What is it like to inspire others with your words and actions and be an example looked up to by others?

    c. Think of times when you yourself have been in the role of a mentor for others, touching their hearts and helping them to establish empowering beliefs. Get a strong sense of the "energy" of the mentor. Feel that energy in your body and find a physical expression, in terms of your posture, gestures and voice tone, that expresses the energy of the mentor and creates within you the state of inspiration and motivation. When you have a good sense of that physical expression, anchor it strongly to this location and then let it go.

5. Take a step back to the location of the *sponsor*. Reflect upon your *identity* and *who* you are or will be as an effective large "C" Coach within the environment you have chosen. What is your role and calling as a coach?

a. Recall the people in your life who have been your sponsors and have truly "seen" and "blessed" you. Notice how their attentiveness and acknowledgment made you feel that you were seen, were valuable, were unique, had something to contribute and were welcomed. Recall what it is like to feel a strong sense of self-esteem and acknowledgment for who you are as a person.

b. Put yourself into the shoes of some of the significant sponsors in your life. Look through the eyes of these sponsors. What is it like to be fascinated by others, recognizing, promoting and safeguarding the potential that you know is there?

c. Think of times when you yourself have been a sponsor to others, recognizing and acknowledging them at a fundamental level, giving them personalized attention, making them feel important and showing them that they can make a difference. Get a strong sense of the "energy" of the sponsor. Feel that energy in your body and find a physical expression, in terms of your posture, gestures and voice tone, that expresses the energy of the sponsor and creates within you the state of strong internal centeredness and contact with your "source," and at the same time the sense of fascination and deep connection with others. When you have a good sense of that physical expression, anchor it strongly to this location and then let it go.

6. Take a final step back to the location of the *awakener*. Reflect upon the larger vision and sense of spiritual purpose that calls you to be a large "C" Coach within the environment you have chosen. *For whom* and *for what* are you committing yourself and your resources? What is your sense of the larger system, "Mind" or universe to which you belong and the role you have in it?

a. Recall the people in your life who have been your awakeners and have helped you become more fully conscious, aware and appreciative of this larger "Mind" or universe. Notice how they broadened your mental maps of who you were and what was possible in the world, and how they opened the possibility for you to perceive old boundaries and limits in a completely new way. Recall what it is like to feel a renewed sense of purpose and meaning, expanded awareness, clear perception and emotional and physical revitalization.

b. Put yourself into the shoes of some of the important awakeners in your life. Feel what it is like to be the role of an awakener for others. What is it like to help others succeed in breaking through their old mind sets, "get outside of the box" and become aware of possibilities that are completely new?

c. Think of times when you have been an awakener for others, helping them to recognize and be more fully in touch with their own visions and missions by being congruently aligned and in touch with your own. Get a strong sense of the "energy" of the awakener. Feel that energy in your body and find a physical expression, in terms of your posture, gestures and voice tone, that expresses the energy of the sponsor and creates within you the state of congruence, integrity and complete alignment with your vision and purpose.

7. Instead of letting go of your physiology and internal state this time, keep it and hold it in your body.

a. Step forward to the *sponsor* location, bringing with you the skills and resources of the awakener. Awaken your sponsor to the larger vision and purpose you are aware of in your life. Awaken more fully in your sponsor the contact with your "source" and the connection with others. Explore ways to blend and mix the physiological expressions of both sponsor and awakener.

b. Step forward again, into the location of the *mentor*. Bring with you the skills and internal resources of both the awakener and the sponsor. Sponsor and awaken your mentor to the core values and key beliefs that will inspire you and your clients to be your best. Explore ways to blend and mix the physiological expressions of the mentor with those of both sponsor and awakener.

c. Move forward now into the location of the *teacher*. Bring with you the skills and internal resources of the awakener, sponsor and mentor. Mentor, sponsor and awaken your teacher to be intellectually stimulated and stimulating, having full access to the cognitive strategies and mental abilities that will help you most with your "inner game" as a large "C" Coach. Explore ways to blend and mix the physiological expressions of the teacher with those of mentor, sponsor and awakener.

d. Step forward another time, into the location of the *small "c" coach*. Bring with you the skills and internal resources of the awakener, sponsor, mentor and teacher. Teach, mentor, sponsor and awaken your small "c" coach to embody the vision, calling, values, beliefs and strategies that drive you as a large "C" Coach, and support you to maintain the state of determination, attentiveness and focus that help you to bring out the best in others. Explore ways to blend and mix the physiological expressions of the coach with those of teacher, mentor, sponsor and awakener.

e. Step forward again, into the location of the *caretaker* and *guide*. Bring with you the skills and internal resources of the awakener, sponsor, mentor, teacher and performance coach. Coach, teach, mentor, sponsor and awaken your caretaker and guide to be ready and available at all levels and whenever needed. Recall the environment that you identified at the beginning of this process. Notice how you can feel fully present and resourceful in that environment, ready to respond and perform in whatever ways are appropriate.

8. Blend all of the physiologies, resources and internal states associated with each role together into a single, aligned large "C" Coaching state. Find a symbol for this state and anchor it with the belief that you are a proficient caretaker, you are a good guide, you are a competent performance coach, you are a stimulating teacher, you are an effective mentor, you are a committed sponsor, you are an awakener, you are a large "C" Coach.

I hope you have enjoyed this journey from coach to awakener. It is my sincere wish that this book has been and will continue to be an effective road map and toolbox for you to support your mission and calling as caretaker, guide, coach, teacher, mentor, sponsor and awakener.

Afterword

I hope you have enjoyed this exploration into the path leading *From Coach to Awakener.* If you are interested in exploring the principles and technology of Neuro-Linguistic Programming in more depth, other resources and tools exist to further develop and apply the distinctions, strategies and skills described within these pages.

NLP University is an organization committed to providing the highest quality trainings in basic and advanced NLP skills, and to promoting the development of new models and applications of NLP in the areas of health, business and organization, creativity and learning. Each Summer, NLP University holds residential programs at the University of California at Santa Cruz, offering extended residential courses on the skills of NLP, including those related to business consulting and coaching.

For more information please contact:

NLP University
P.O. Box 1112
Ben Lomond, California 95005
Phone: (831) 336-3457
Fax: (831) 336-5854
E-Mail: Teresanlp@aol.com
Homepage: http://www.nlpu.com

In addition to the programs I do at NLP University, I also travel internationally, presenting seminars and specialty programs on a variety of topics related to NLP and large "C" Coaching. I have also written a number of other books and developed computer software and audio tapes based on the principles and distinctions of NLP.

For example, I have produced several software tools based on my modeling of Strategies of Genius: *Vision to Action*, *Imagineering Strategy* and *Journey to Genius Adventure*. I also have audio tapes and CDs describing the creative processes such as Mozart and Walt Disney.

For more information on these programs, my schedule of seminars or other NLP related products and resources, please contact:

Journey to Genius
P.O. Box 67448
Scotts Valley, CA 95067-7448
Phone (831) 438-8314
Fax (831) 438-8571
E-Mail: info@journeytogenius.com
Homepage: http://www.journeytogenius.com

ISVOR DILTS Leadership Systems is another resource for coaches and consultants. ISVOR DILTS provides innovative leadership development paths, programs and tools to companies of all sizes. These programs leverage leading edge e-learning solutions and other new technologies to serve corporate clients around the world.

ISVOR DILTS Leadership Systems, Inc.
One Bay Plaza
1350 Old Bayshore Highway, Suite 700
Burlingame, CA 94010
Phone: (650) 558-4140
Fax: (650) 558-4147
E-Mail: info@isvordilts.com
Homepage: http://www.isvordilts.com

Appendix A: A Brief History of Logical Levels

The notion of *logical levels* refers to the fact that some processes and phenomena are created by the *relationships* between other processes and phenomena. Any system of activity is a subsystem embedded inside of another system, which is embedded inside of another system, and so on. This kind of relationship between systems produces different levels of processes, relative to the system in which one is operating. Our brain structure, language, and social systems form natural hierarchies or levels of processes.

As a simple example, consider the *rate of change*, or "speed" of an automobile. Speed is a function of how much ground the vehicle covers in a certain amount of time (e.g., 10 miles per hour). Thus, speed is the relationship *between* distance and time. The car's velocity in moving from the garage to the highway can be said to be at a different level than a car, garage, highway, or clock, because it is a property of the relationship between them (and does not exist without them).

Similarly, the "profitability" of a company is at a different level than the machinery used by that company; and an idea is at a different level than the neurons in the brain which produces that idea.

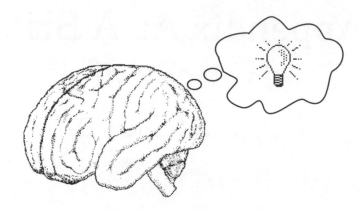

**An Idea Is at a Different Level than the Particular Neurons
in the Brain which Produce that Idea**

Logical Levels of Learning and Change

The concept of logical levels of learning and change was
initially formulated as a mechanism in the behavioral sciences by anthropologist Gregory Bateson, based on the work
of Bertrand Russell in logic and mathematics. Bateson identified four basic levels of learning and change—each level
encompassing and organizing elements from the level below
it, and each having a greater degree of impact on the
individual, organism or system.

The term *logical levels*, as I have used it in NLP, was
adapted from Bateson's work, and refers to a hierarchy of
levels of processes within an individual or group. The function of each level is to synthesize, organize and direct the
interactions on the level below it. Changing something on an
upper level would necessarily "radiate" downward, precipi-
tating change on the lower levels. Changing something on a
lower level could, but would not necessarily, affect the upper
levels. These levels include (in order from highest to lowest):
(1) identity, (2) beliefs and values, (3) capabilities, (4) behavior and (5) environment. A sixth level, referred to as "spiri-

tual," can be defined as a type of "relational field" which encompasses multiple identities, forming a sense of being a member of a larger system beyond one's individual identity.

Historical Background

Gregory Bateson

I first became acquainted with the notion of different logical types and levels of learning, change and communication while attending Gregory Bateson's *Ecology of Mind* class at the University of California at Santa Cruz in 1976. Bateson (1904-1980), an anthropologist by training, had the greatest depth and scope of thought of anyone I have ever known. His lectures would cover topics ranging from communication theory, to Balinese art, to Maxwell's equations for electromagnetic fields, to schizophrenia, to genetic deformities in beetles' legs. His talks, however, were never a disjointed collection of thoughts or jumbled group of ideas as the diversity of topics might suggest. Bateson's version of cybernetics and systems theory was able to tap into the deeper structure, or "pattern which connects," all of these topics into a single fascinating weave of life and existence.

Reflecting back, attending Bateson's class was one of the most transformative experiences of my life. I would sit in his class, listening to his deep voice and distinctive Cambridge accent, which sounded to me like the voice of wisdom. To me, he was, and remains, a type of "spiritual guide." Thoughts, ideas and revelations would flow into my mind, some relating to his lecture and some from completely other areas of my life, education, and experience. Usually they came so quickly I couldn't write them down fast enough. (It was also in Bateson's class that I first met wife to be, Anita. Sharing Bateson's wisdom has always been one of the strongest bonds between us.)

These were "heady" times, when NLP was first taking shape. A year earlier Richard Bandler and John Grinder had published their first book, *The Structure of Magic Volume I*. Grinder, also a professor (of linguistics) at UC Santa Cruz, had shown Bateson the manuscript of the book, which outlined the language patterns known in NLP as the "Meta Model." Bateson was impressed with the work, and wrote in a preface, "John Grinder and Richard Bandler have done something similar to what my colleagues and I attempted fifteen years ago. . . . They have tools which we did not have—or did not see how to use. They have succeeded in making linguistics into a base for theory and simultaneously into a tool for therapy. . . making explicit the syntax of how people avoid change, and, therefore, how to assist them in changing."

It was after reading *The Structure of Magic* that Bateson made arrangements for Bandler and Grinder to meet Milton Erickson, a long time colleague and friend, to see if they could create a similar model of the complex communication patterns used by Erickson in his hypnotic and therapeutic work. This led to more books, and some of the most seminal work in NLP.

Bateson's earlier work, to which he referred in his preface to *The Structure of Magic*, was his attempt to apply principles of cybernetics and communication theory to psychotherapy and the understanding of psychological pathology. Stimulated by Norbert Wiener (the founder of cybernetics), Bateson had adapted cybernetic thinking to human communication and interaction in order to develop generalizations about the behavior and mental characteristics of individuals, groups and families, and the influences behind functional and dysfunctional systems. Bateson's ideas fueled a whole generation of behavioral scientists, and psychotherapists. People such as Virginia Satir, Mara Selvini Palazzoli, Jay Haley, John Weakland, and others, for example, applied Bateson's formulations to the treatment of individual and family problems.

One of the central ideas introduced by Bateson into the behavioral sciences was that of "logical types" of communication and learning—which he called the "most important" criterion of "mind" in his book *Mind and Nature* (1979). Bateson derived the notion of different logical types of communication and learning from Bertrand Russell's mathematical theory of logical types—which states that a class of things cannot be a member of itself. According to Bateson (*Steps to an Ecology of Mind*, p.202):

> *Our approach is based on that part of communications theory which [Bertrand] Russell has called the Theory of Logical Types. The central thesis of this theory is that there is a discontinuity between a class and its members. The class cannot be a member of itself nor can one of the members be the class, since the term used for the class is of a different level of abstraction— a different Logical Type—from terms used for members.*

As an example, the *class* of even numbers cannot itself also be an *even number*. Similarly, the *class* of cats is not a particular cat. Likewise the physical object "cat" cannot be treated the same as the class of cats. (The class of cats does not require milk and kitty litter, but the members of the class frequently do.) In other words, the notion of logical types distinguishes between a particular "map" and the "territory" to which the map relates; i.e., between a mental "form" and its "content."

The Origins of Bateson's Model

Bateson first formally introduced the concept of "logical types" in his article *A Theory of Play and Fantasy* (1954). In it Bateson argued that "play" involved distinguishing between different *logical types* of behavior and messages.

Bateson noted that when animals and humans engage in "play" they often display the same behaviors that are also associated with aggression, sexuality, and other more "serious" aspects of life (such as when animals "play fight," or children play "doctor"). Yet, somehow, animals and humans were able to recognize, for the most part, that the play behavior was a different type or class of behavior and "not the real thing." According to Bateson, distinguishing between classes of behavior also required different types of messages. Bateson referred to these messages as "meta messages"—messages *about* other messages—claiming that they too were of a different "logical type" than the content of a particular communication. He believed that these "higher level" messages (which were usually communicated non-verbally) were crucial for people, and animals, to be able communicate and interact effectively.

Animals at play, for instance, may signal the message "This is play" by wagging their tails, jumping up and down, or doing some other thing to indicate that what they are about to do is not to be taken for real. Their bite is a playful bite, not a real bite. Studies of humans also reveal the use of special messages that let others know they are playing, in much the same way animals do. They may actually verbally "meta-communicate" by announcing that "This is only a game," or they laugh, nudge, or do something odd to show their intent.

Bateson claimed that many problems and conflicts were a result of the confusion or misinterpretation of these messages. A good example is the difficulties that people from different cultures experience in interpreting the non-verbal subtleties of each other's communications.

In fact, Bateson next applied the concept of logical types as an explanation for some of the symptoms of serious psychological problems and mental illness. In *Epidemiology of Schizophrenia* (1955), Bateson maintained that the inability to correctly recognize and interpret meta messages, and to distinguish between different classes, or logical types, of behavior, was at the root of many seemingly psychotic or "crazy" behaviors. Bateson cited the example of a young mental patient who went into the pharmacy of the hospital. The nurse behind the counter asked, "Can I help you?" The patient was unable to distinguish whether the communication was a threat, a sexual advance, an admonishment for being in the wrong place, a genuine inquiry, etc.

When one is unable to make such distinctions, Bateson contented, that individual will end up, more often than not, acting in a way that is inappropriate for the situation. He likened it to a telephone switching system that was unable to distinguish the "country code" from the "city code" and the local telephone number. As a result, the switching system would inappropriately assign numbers belonging to the country code as part of the phone number, or parts of the phone number as the city code, etc. The consequence of this would be that, again more often than not, the dialer would get the "wrong number." Even though all of the numbers (the content) are correct, the classification of the numbers (the form) is confused, creating problems. [It should be noted that this is a fundamentally different communication problem than simply having "noise" on the telephone line which obscures the numbers. The causes of logical typing confusions are quite different than the causes of noisy signals.]

In *Toward a Theory of Schizophrenia* (co-authored with Don Jackson, Jay Haley and John Weakland, 1956), Bateson applied the notion of different logical types as a key element of the "double bind." According to Bateson, double binds (special situations in which a person finds himself or herself "damned if I do, and damned if I don't") resulted from confusions and paradoxes created by conflicting messages of different logical types, which consequently led to conflicts of behavior.

Bateson believed that the ability to sort out the different logical types of messages and classifications which were at the root of such double binds was essential for effective therapy. Bateson's ideas about the applications of the theory of logical types to communication and psychotherapy were further explored by his colleagues Watzlawick, Bavelas and Jackson in *Pragmatics of Human Communication* (1967).

Applications to the Process of Learning

Bateson's next application of the theory of logical types was to the process of learning. In *The Logical Categories of Learning and Communication* (1964) he extended the notion of logical typing to explain different types and phenomena of learning as well as communication. He defined two fundamental types, or levels, of learning which must be considered in all processes of change: "Learning I" (stimulus-response type conditioning) and "Learning II", or *deutero learning*, (learning to recognize the larger context in which the stimulus is occurring so that its meaning may be correctly interpreted). The most basic example of Learning II phenomena is set learning, or when an animal becomes "test-wise"—that is, laboratory animals will get faster and faster at learning new tasks that fall into the same class of activity. This has to do with learning *classes* of behavior rather than single isolated behaviors.

An animal trained in avoidance conditioning, for instance, will be able to learn different types of avoidance behavior more and more rapidly. It will, however, be slower at learning some "respondently" conditioned behavior (e.g., salivating at the sound of a bell) than some animal that has been conditioned in that class of behavior earlier. That is, it will learn quickly how to identify and stay away from objects that might have an electric shock associated with them but will be slower at learning to salivate when a bell rings. On the other hand, an animal trained in Pavlovian type conditioning will rapidly learn to salivate to new sounds and colors, etc., but will be slower to learn to avoid electrified objects.

Bateson pointed out that this ability to learn patterns or rules of a class of conditioning procedures was a different "logical type" of learning and did not function according to the same simple stimulus-response-reinforcement sequences used to learn specific isolated behaviors. Bateson noted, for instance, that the reinforcement for "exploration" (a means of learning-to-learn) in rats is of a different nature than that for the "testing" of a particular object (the learning content of exploration). He reports (*Steps to an Ecology of Mind* p. 282):

> . . . *you can reinforce a rat (positively or negatively) when he investigates a particular strange object, and he will appropriately learn to approach it or avoid it. But the very purpose of exploration is to get information about which objects should be approached or avoided. The discovery that a given object is dangerous is therefore a success in the business of getting information. The success will not discourage the rat from future exploration of other strange objects.*

The ability to explore, learn a discrimination task, or be creative is a higher level of learning than the specific behaviors that make up these abilities—and the dynamics and rules of change are different on this higher level.

Bateson also identified several other levels of learning— each responsible for making corrective changes and refinements in the other class of learning upon which it operated.

> *Zero learning is characterized by specificity of response [i.e., having a specific behavior in a specific environment RD] which—right or wrong—is not subject to correction.*
>
> *Learning I is change in specificity of response by correction of errors of choice within a set of alternatives.*

Learning II is a change in the process of Learning I, e.g., a corrective change in the set of alternatives from which choice is made, or it is a change in how the sequence is punctuated.

Learning III is change in the process of Learning II, e.g., a corrective change in the system of sets of alternatives from which choice is made.

(Steps to an Ecology of Mind p. 293)

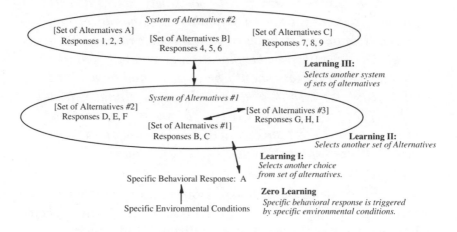

Bateson's "Logical Levels" of Learning

Bateson also defined a level of *Learning IV*, which would involve change in Learning III. That is, Learning IV would involve changes in the larger "system of systems."

I have addressed this model extensively in this book, in chapter 6, providing examples and an exercise which specifically applies each of Bateson's levels of learning to help someone update his or her "survival strategy." (See pages 266-280.)

Chapter 6 summarizes Bateson's levels of learning in the following manner:

- **Learning 0** is *no change*. It involves repetitive behaviors in which the individual, group or organization is stuck in a rut or trapped "inside the box"—e.g., habits, resistance, inertia.

- **Learning I** is gradual, *incremental change*. It involves making corrections and adaptations through behavioral flexibility and stretching. While these modifications may help to extend the capabilities of the individual group or organization, they are still "within the box"—e.g., establishing and refining new procedures and capabilities.

- **Learning II** is rapid, *discontinuous change*. It involves the instantaneous shift of a response to an entirely different category or class of behavior. It is essentially the switch from one type of "box" to another—e.g., change in policies, values or priorities.

- **Learning III** is *evolutionary change*. It is characterized by significant alterations which stretch beyond the boundaries of the current identity of the individual, group or organization. We could say that not only are they outside the "box," they are outside of the "building"—e.g., transition of role, brand or identity.

- **Learning IV** is *revolutionary change*. It involves awakening to something completely new, unique and transformative. At the level of Leaning IV, the individual, group or organization is out of the box, out of the building and in a new world—e.g., completely new responses, technologies or capabilities that open the door to previously unknown and uncharted possibilities.

To use a computer analogy, data stored in a computer is like Learning 0. It just sits there, unchanging, to be used over and over again whatever programs are running on the computer. Running a spell checking program on that data would be like Learning I. A spell check program makes corrective changes in a particular set of data.

If the data being checked, however, is not text but numbers and financial figures that need to be updated, no amount of running the spell checker will be able to make the proper corrections. Instead, the user would have to switch to a spread sheet or some type of accounting software. Getting "out of the box" of one program and switching to another is like Learning II.

Sometimes the computer one is using is incapable of running the needed program and it is necessary to switch computers altogether, or change operating systems. This would be like Learning III.

To develop a completely new device, such as a programmable molecular computing machine composed of enzymes and DNA molecules instead of silicon microchips, would be like Learning IV.

The Development of "NeuroLogical Levels"

Bateson went on to apply the theory of logical types more generally to many aspects of behavior and to biology. To him, logical typing was a "law of nature," not simply a mathematical theory. He contended that a tissue that is made up of a group of cells, for instance, is a different logical type than the individual cells—the characteristics of a brain are not the same as a brain cell. The two can affect each other through indirect feedback—i.e., the functioning and connections of the overall brain can influence the behavior of a single brain cell and the activity of a single brain cell contributes to the overall functioning of the brain. Indeed, a cell may be said to affect itself through the rest of the brain structure.

As a student in his Ecology of Mind class, Bateson instilled in me the importance of considering logical types and levels in all aspects of life and experience. And, because I was exposed to these ideas at the same time I was becoming involved in NLP, Bateson's approach has always been an integral part of my understanding of NLP. His distinctions about different logical types and levels of learning seemed of particularly profound significance.

In a paper I wrote in November 1976 (published in *Roots of NLP*, 1983), for instance, I attempted to distinguish between logical types and logical levels.

I vividly remember discussing the power of Bateson's notions of logical levels and logical types with a participant in an NLP course that I was teaching in Oslo, Norway in 1986. The person was also familiar with Bateson's work and we were reflecting on the deep importance of logical types and levels of learning. We both agreed, however, that these ideas had not been applied as fully and pragmatically as they could be. I recall saying, "Yes, someone really should apply the notion of logical levels in a more practical everyday sense." As soon as the words left my mouth, it was as if I had given myself the command.

I was already empirically aware that there was an important distinction between people's physical actions and behaviors and the deeper cognitive representations and strategies which took place in their minds. It was also obvious that processes on a behavior level were different than those on a mental level. Tying someone up, for instance, could stop that person from physically taking revenge, but could not keep him or her from continuing to plan revenge; in fact, it will often encourage it. It was also clear that developing a cognitive capability involved different dynamics than simply influencing someone physically. My work with learning strategies, for instance, had convinced me that it was much more expedient to teach a person to spell by providing an effective strategy for spelling rather than to simply punish them whenever they misspelled a word.

I had also begun to work with people's beliefs and belief systems. As I did, it became evident that they were not simply another type of strategy. Instead, they often tended to operate upon particular strategies. That is a certain belief could either function as motivation or interference to the development of a strategy.

This seemed to be to fit with Bateson's notion of a "hierarchy" of logical levels. The term "hierarchy" comes from the Greek *hieros*, meaning "powerful, supernatural, or sacred," and *arche*, which means "beginning." The implication is that the levels of a hierarchy get closer and closer to the source or beginning of that which is sacred or powerful. This implication has also led to the use of the term hierarchy to refer to any graded or ranked series, such as a person's "hierarchy of values," or a machine's "hierarchy of responses." The connotation of this being that those elements at the top of the hierarchy "come first," or are "more important" than those at the lower levels.

It was this aspect of hierarchy that first led me to choose the particular labels I have used to describe the various levels in my NeuroLogical Levels model. As with all key NLP distinctions, these labels did not arise as a result of some rationalization. Rather, as part of my NLP training work, I was frequently teaching seminar participants the usage of a set of verbal reframing patterns I had developed, known as "Sleight of Mouth." This often involved people responding to negative statements made about them by others. I began to notice that certain types of statements were typically more difficult for people to handle than others, even though the type of judgment being asserted was essentially the same. For example, compare the following statements:

That object in your environment is dangerous.

Your actions in that particular context were dangerous.

Your inability to make effective judgments is dangerous.

Your beliefs and values are dangerous.

You are a dangerous person.

The judgment being made in each case is about something being "dangerous." Intuitively, however, most people sense that the "space" or "territory" implied by each statement becomes progressively larger, and feel an increasing sense of emotional affect with each statement.

For someone to tell you that some specific behavioral response made was dangerous is quite different than telling you that you are a "dangerous person." I noticed that if I held a judgment constant and simply substituted a term for environment, behavior, capabilities, beliefs and values, and identity, people would feel progressively more offended or complimented, depending on the positive or negative nature of the judgment.

Try it for yourself. Imagine someone was saying each of the following statements to you:

- Your *surroundings* are (stupid/ugly/exceptional/beautiful).

- The way you *behaved* in that particular situation was (stupid/ugly/exceptional/beautiful).

- You really have the *capability* to be (stupid/ugly/exceptional/beautiful).

- What you *believe and value* is (stupid/ugly/exceptional/beautiful).

- *You* are (stupid/ugly/exceptional/beautiful).

Again, notice that the evaluations asserted by each statement are the same. What changes is the aspect of the person to which the statement is referring.

Environment
Behavior
Capability
Beliefs and Values
Identity

This intuitive sensibility seemed to reflect something fundamentally "neurolinguistic" in relation to these statements.

These distinctions fell into place even more solidly when it occurred to me that they corresponded to the six fundamental "W" questions that we use to organize our lives: where, when, what, how (the backward "w" question), why and who.

Environment: Where? When?
Behavior: What?
Capability: How?
Beliefs and Values: Why?
Identity: Who?

It was in the Fall of 1987 that I first applied the labels in common usage today as the "ABC's of NLP":

a. what I **A**m (A)—identity
b.what I **B**elieve (B)—beliefs and values
c. what I am **C**apable of (C)—capabilities
d. what I **D**o (D)—Behavior
e. my **E**nvironment (E)

My understanding of how each level functioned was directly parallel to Bateson's notion of the various level of learning:

• A particular behavioral response in a particular environment is Learning 0.

• Change in behaviors involves the development of a new capability—Learning I.

- Shifts in capabilities arise from changes in beliefs and values (a recategorization of the context and/or cause-effect assumptions concerning the context)—Learning II.

- Changes in an entire *system* of beliefs and values, capabilities and behaviors would essentially amount to a change in identity —Learning III.

- Getting outside the system (into the larger "system of systems"—i.e., the "field" or "spirit") would be necessary to achieve a change within a particular system itself— Learning IV.

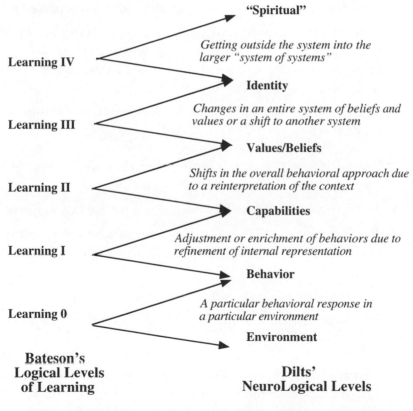

"Spiritual"

Learning IV

Getting outside the system into the larger "system of systems"

Identity

Learning III

Changes in an entire system of beliefs and values or a shift to another system

Values/Beliefs

Learning II

Shifts in the overall behavioral approach due to a reinterpretation of the context

Capabilities

Learning I

Adjustment or enrichment of behaviors due to refinement of internal representation

Behavior

Learning 0

A particular behavioral response in a particular environment

Environment

Bateson's
Logical Levels
of Learning

Dilts'
NeuroLogical Levels

Relationship of Bateson's Levels of Learning to NeuroLogical Levels

Each level functions by integrating and operating upon the level beneath it. Clusters of change or activity at any particular level will also influence the level above it. Consider the following examples:

- The speed of a car is a function of the change in distance it makes in relationship to time (*environment*).

- Pushing the gas peddle or brake of a car with one's foot is a *behavior* which alters its speed.

- The *capability* of maintaining the speed limit is a function of integrating a mental map with one's perceptions in order to regulate the way in which one uses one's foot.

- Respecting the speed limit is a result of *valuing* laws and *believing* that there are consequences if they are not kept. If one does not value the speed limit, one will not maintain it, even if one is capable.

- Being a "good driver" (*identity*) is a function of aligning all of them.

- The keys of a piano, the sound it makes and notes on a page of sheet music are in the *environment*.

- Pushing down a piano key with one's finger is a *behavior*

- Playing music (sight reading the notes and coordinating one's finger to produce sounds in the right order) is a *capability*.

- Appreciating music is a function of *beliefs and values*.

- Taking on the *identity* of "a musician" is a combination of all of them.

Notice that this type of "hierarchy" involves more than an arbitrary rank ordering of elements. In science and mathematics, for instance, hierarchy is used to denote "a series of ordered groupings of people or things within a system." Usually these groupings have "few things, or one thing, at the top with several things below each other thing," like an inverted tree structure. Examples from computer science include a directory hierarchy, where each directory may contain files or other directories, a hierarchical network, or a class hierarchy in object-oriented programming.

NeuroLogical Levels are "hierarchic" in this way. That is, each level in the hierarchy is related to groupings of phenomena or experiences from the level below it. Thus, the system of levels can be represented as an inverted tree structure.

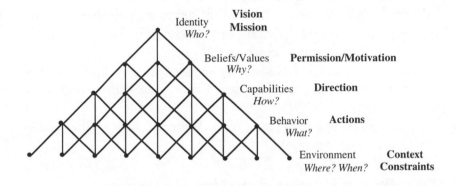

NeuroLogical Levels Can Be Represented as a Series of Ordered Groupings in the Form of an Inverted "Tree Structure."

The implication of this tree structure is that a single identity is shaped by, and reflected in, a particular group of beliefs and values. Each belief and value, in turn, is related to a particular group of capabilities. The capabilities relate to specific groupings of behaviors, and the behaviors ultimately relate to particular clusters of environmental conditions.

At the level of behavior change, physical behavior is the prime focus. Internal representations are only relevant to the extent that they support behavior.

At the capability level of change, internal representations are the primary focus. Behaviors, in the form of accessing cues, are relevant only in so much as they support the establishment or development of internal representations. Once internal representations are formed, behaviors can be generalized.

Change at the level of beliefs and values focuses on the relationships between representations. The content of the representations is much less important than their submodality qualities. This is why changing submodalities produces such significant affective responses. (Changes in submodalities— i.e., making a picture larger, smaller, more colorful, still or moving, etc.—tend to provoke "approach/avoidance" responses such as fear, pleasure, desire, etc.)

Change at the level of identity focuses on the relationships between the beliefs and values which make up a person's belief system.

A change in spirit derives from the collection of identities which make up the "field."

NeuroLogical Levels and the Nervous System

In 1988 I encoded the concept as the model of "NeuroLogical Levels," which relates Bateson's levels of processing to the nervous system. Bateson himself (*Steps to an Ecology of Mind* pp, 249-250) contended that the hierarchy formed by the various levels of learning would correspond to "hierarchies of circuit structure which we may—indeed, must— expect to find in the telencephalized brain," claiming that "we should look forward to a classification or hierarchy of neurophysiological structures which will be isomorphic with [the various levels of learning]." The concept of "NeuroLogical Levels" proposes that different "logical levels" are a function of different types of neurological organization, and mobilize successively deeper commitments of neurological "circuitry."

The level of neurology that is mobilized when a person is challenged at the level of mission and identity, for instance, is much deeper than the level of neurology that is required to move his or her hand. To experience the environment, a person can passively adjust his or her sense organs. To take action in a particular environment, a person needs to mobilize more of his or her nervous system. In order to coordinate those actions in a complex sequence, such as dancing or driving an automobile, a person has to utilize even more of the nervous system. Forming and manifesting beliefs and values about capabilities, behaviors and the environment, requires an even deeper commitment of neurology (including those related to the "heart" and "guts"). A sense of self arises from a total mobilization of the nervous system at all of the other levels. In general, then, higher levels of process mobilize a deeper commitment of the nervous system.

A particular *environment* is made up of factors such as the type of external setting, weather conditions, food, noise level, etc., that surround an individual or group. Neurologically, our perceptions of the environment relate to information coming from our sense organs and peripheral nervous system To perceive a particular environment, for instance, an individual views it with his or her eyes to see any relevant objects, listens with his or her ears to hear significant sounds, smells odors through his or her nose, and feels the temperature of the air on his or her skin. The person also makes many subtle and unconscious adjustments to maintain balance, respond to changes in the intensity of light and sound, acclimate to temperature changes, etc. Thus, the peripheral nervous system essentially relays information related to the environment to and from the brain. It is responsible for producing sensations and purely reflex reactions.

Behavior relates to the specific physical actions and reactions through which we interact with the people and environment around us. Neurologically, our external behavior is a result of activity in our motor systems (the pyramidal system and cerebellum). Non-reflexive behaviors involve the psycho-motor system, a deeper level of neurology than the sense organs. The psychomotor system coordinates our physical actions and conscious movements.

Capabilities have to do with the mental strategies and maps people develop to guide their specific behaviors. While some behaviors are simply reflexive responses to environmental stimuli, most of our actions are not. Many of our behaviors come from "mental maps" and other internal processes whose source is within our minds. This is a level of experience that goes beyond our perceptions of the immediate environment. You can make pictures of things that do not relate to the particular room you are in, for instance. You can remember conversations and events that took place years ago. You can imagine events that may happen years from now. Behaviors without any inner map, plan or strategy to guide them are like knee jerk reactions, habits or rituals. At the level of capability we are able to select, alter and adapt a class of behaviors to a wider set of external situations. Thus, "capability" involves mastery over an entire class of behavior—i.e., knowing *how to* do something within a variety of conditions. Neurologically, developing cognitive capabilities is a function of higher level processing in the cortex of the brain. It is in the cortex (or gray matter) of the brain that sensory information is represented in the form of mental maps, associated with other mental representations, or pieced together in imagination. This type of processing is usually accompanied by semi-conscious micro movements, or "accessing cues" (eye movements, breathing rate changes, slight postural adjustment, voice tone shifts , etc.).

Values and beliefs relate to fundamental judgments and evaluations about ourselves, others and the world around us. They determine how events are given meaning, and are at the core of motivation and culture. Our beliefs and values provide the reinforcement (*motivation* and *permission*) that supports or inhibits particular capabilities and behaviors. Beliefs and values relate to the question, "*Why?*"

Neurologically, beliefs are associated with the limbic system and hypothalamus in the midbrain. The limbic system has been linked to both emotion and long term memory. While the limbic system is a more "primitive" structure than the cortex of the brain in many ways, it serves to integrate information from the cortex and to regulate the *autonomic nervous system* (which controls basic body functions such as heart rate, body temperature, pupil dilation, etc.). Because they are produced by deeper structures of the brain, beliefs produce changes in the fundamental physiological functions in the body that are responsible for many of our unconscious responses. In fact, one of the ways that we know that we really believe something is because it triggers physiological reactions; it makes our "heart pound," our "blood boil," or our "skin tingle" (all effects that we cannot typically produce voluntarily). This is how a polygraph functions to detect whether or not a person is "lying." People show a different physical reaction when they believe what they are saying than when they are being untruthful or incongruent.

It is the intimate connection between beliefs and deeper physiological functions that also creates the possibility for them to have such a powerful influence in the area of health and healing (as in the case of the placebo effect). Because expectations generated by our beliefs affect our deeper neurology, they can also produce dramatic physiological effects. This is illustrated by the example of the woman who adopted a baby, and because she believed that "mothers" were supposed to provide milk for their babies, actually began to lactate and produced enough milk to breast feed her adopted child!

The level of *identity* relates to our sense of *who* we are. It is our perception of our identity that organizes our beliefs, capabilities and behaviors into a single system. Our sense of identity also relates to our perception of ourselves in relation to the larger systems of which we are a part, determining our sense of "role," "purpose" and "mission." In our neurology, our identity can be associated with our nervous system as a whole, and probably involves deep brain structures such as the reticular formation. The reticular formation is a large group of cells deep within the brain stem. Fibers from this area project via thalamic nuclei to large association areas in the cortex. The reticular formation is a regulator of the state of alertness; its destruction at the midbrain level results in a state of coma. (In contrast, large areas of the cortex may be destroyed without a loss of consciousness.)

Identity is also physiologically related to the immune system, endocrine system, and other deep life sustaining functions. Thus, change or transformation of identity can have a tremendous and almost instantaneous effect on one's physiology. Medical research on individual's with multiple personalities (Putnam 1984) shows that remarkable and dramatic changes can occur when an individual switches from one identity to another. For instance, the brain wave patterns for the different personalities are usually completely different. Some people with multiple personalities carry several different pairs of eyeglasses because their vision changes with each identity. Other individuals will have allergies in one personality and not in another. One of the most interesting examples of physiological change with different identities is that of a woman, admitted to a hospital for diabetes, who "baffled her physicians by showing not symptoms of the disorder at times when one personality, who was not diabetic, was dominant . . ." (Goleman, 1985).

Spiritual level experience has to do with our sense of being part of something, on a very deep level, that is beyond ourselves. It is the awareness of, what Gregory Bateson called, "the pattern which connects" all things together into a larger whole. We, as individuals, are a subsystem of this larger system. Our experience of this level is related to our sense of purpose and mission in life. It comes from asking the questions: "For whom?" and "For what?" This is the level that I believe Bateson was indicating when he referred to Learning IV.

Neurologically, spiritual level processes have to do with a type of "relational field" between our own nervous systems and those of other people, forming a type of larger, collective nervous system. The results of this field of interaction are sometimes referred to as a group "mind," a group "spirit," or a "collective consciousness." This field also includes the "nervous systems," or information processing networks, of other creatures and beings, and even our environment.

As Bateson described it:

> *The individual mind is immanent but not only in the body. It is immanent in pathways and messages outside the body; and there is a larger Mind of which the individual mind is only a sub-system. This larger Mind is comparable to God and is perhaps what people mean by "God," but it is still immanent in the total interconnected social system and planetary ecology. (Steps to an Ecology of Mind, 1972)*

It has been speculated that this level of processing and change influences our environment and ourselves through what Rupert Sheldrake termed "morphogenetic fields." It is often used to explain phenomena which involve action at a distance, such as healing through prayer and the effects of "the hundredth monkey"; i.e., situations in which change in a part of a population stimulates change in another member of the population, or the group as a whole, without any direct physical contact.

In summary, NeuroLogical Levels are made of the following "hierarchy" of neurophysological structures:

Spiritual: *Holographic*—Individual nervous systems combining to form a larger system

A. Identity:*Immune system and endocrine system*—Nervous system as a whole, and deep life sustaining functions (e.g., reticular system).

B. Beliefs & Values: *Limbic and autonomic control system* (e.g., heart rate, pupil dilation, etc.)—Unconscious responses.

C. Capabilities: *Cortical systems*—Semi-conscious actions (eye movements, posture, etc.)

D. Behaviors: *Motor system (pyramidal & cerebellum)*—Conscious actions

E. Environment: *Peripheral nervous system*—Sensations and reflex reactions.

The first books formally mentioning this formulation of Logical Levels were *Changing Beliefs with NLP* and *Beliefs: Pathways to Health and Well-Being*, both published in 1990.

The Logical Levels model has continued to be developed and enriched, and has become the basis of many recent NLP processes and techniques. I am planning to publish a more in-depth article soon, describing the history of Logical Levels and its relations to Set Theory, Mathematical Group Theory, hierarchical levels, levels of abstraction, logical types, Arthur Koestler's (also used by Ken Wilbur) notion of "holons" and "holarchy," and simple "chunking."

(To be continued. . .)

Bibliography

Ballard, E., *Three Letters From Teddy*, **A Second Helping of Chicken Soup for the Soul**, Health Communications, Deerfield Beach, FL, 1995.

Bandler, R., **Using Your Brain**, Real People Press, Moab, UT, 1985.

Bandler, R. and Grinder, J., **The Structure of Magic, Volumes I & II**, Science and Behavior Books, Palo Alto, CA, 1975, 1976.

Bandler, R. and Grinder, J., **Patterns of the Hypnotic Techniques of Milton H. Erickson, M.D., Volumes I & II**, Meta Publications, Capitola, CA, 1975, 1977.

Bandler R. and Grinder, J., **Frogs into Princes**, Real People Press, Moab, UT, 1979.

Bandler R. and Grinder, J., **Reframing**, Real People Press, Moab, UT, 1982.

Bateson, G., **Steps to an Ecology of Mind**, Ballantine Books, New York, NY, 1972.

Bateson, G., **Mind and Nature**, E. P. Dutton, New York, NY, 1979.

Campbell, J., **The Power of Myth**, Doubleday & Company, Inc., Garden City, NY, 1988.

DeLozier, J. and Grinder, J., **Turtles All The Way Down**, Grinder, DeLozier & Associates, Santa Cruz, CA 1987.

Dilts, R., Grinder, J., Bandler, R. and DeLozier, J., *Neuro-Linguistic Programming: The Study of the Structure of Subjective Experience, Vol. I*, Meta Publications, Capitola, CA, 1980.

Dilts, R. and DeLozier, J., *Modeling and Coaching*, Dynamic Learning Publications, Ben Lomond, CA, 2002.

Dilts, R. and DeLozier, J., *The Encyclopedia of Systemic Neuro-Linguistic Programming and NLP New Coding*, NLP University Press, Santa Cruz, CA, 2000.

Dilts, R., *Sleight of Mouth: The Magic of Conversational Belief Change*, Meta Publications, Capitola, CA, 1999.

Dilts, R., *Modeling With NLP*, Meta Publications, Capitola, CA, 1998.

Dilts, R. and McDonald, R., *Tools of the Spirit*, Meta Publications, Capitola, CA, 1997.

Dilts, R., *Visionary Leadership Skills: Creating a World to which People Want to Belong*, Meta Publications, Capitola, CA, 1996.

Dilts, R. and Epstein, T., *Dynamic Learning*, Meta Publications, Capitola, CA, 1995.

Dilts, R., *Strategies of Genius, Volumes I, II & III*, Meta Publications, Capitola, CA, 1994–1995.

Dilts, R., *Effective Presentation Skills*, Meta Publications, Capitola, CA, 1994.

Dilts, R. with Bonissone, G., *Skills for the Future: Managing Creativity and Innovation*, Meta Publications, Capitola, CA, 1993.

Dilts, R. B., Epstein, T. and Dilts, R. W., *Tools for Dreamers: Strategies of Creativity and the Structure of Innovation*, Meta Publications, Capitola, CA, 1991.

Dilts, R., *Changing Belief Systems with NLP*, Meta Publications, Capitola, CA, 1990.

Dilts, R., Hallbom, T. and Smith, S., *Beliefs: Pathways to Health and Well-Being*, Metamorphous Press, Portland, OR, 1990.

Dilts, R., *Applications of NLP*, Meta Publications, Capitola, CA, 1983.

Erickson, M. H., *Advanced Techniques of Hypnosis and Therapy, Selected Papers of Milton H. Erickson, M.D.*, Haley, J. [Editor], Grune & Stratton Inc., New York, NY, 1967.

Feldenkrais, M., *The Case of Nora: Body Awareness as Healing Therapy*, Harper and Rowe, New York, 1977.

Freud, S., *A General Introduction to Psychoanalysis*, Pocket Books, New York, NY, 1963.

Gallwey, T., *The Inner Game of Tennis*, Random House, New York, NY, 1974.

Gallwey, T., *The Inner Game of Work: Focus, Learning, Pleasure and Mobility in the Workplace*, Random House Trade Paperbacks, New York, NY, 2000.

Gilligan, S., *The Courage to Love*, W.W. Norton & Company, New York, NY, 1997.

Gordon, D., *Therapeutic Metaphor*, Meta Publications, Capitola, CA, 1978.

Haley, J., *Uncommon Therapy, The Psychiatric Techniques of Milton H. Erickson M.D.*, W. W. Norton & Company, New York, NY, 1973.

James, W., *Principles of Psychology*, Britannica Great Books, Encyclopedia Britannica Inc., Chicago, IL, 1979.

Lakoff, G., and Johnson, M., *Metaphors We Live By*, University of Chicago Press, Chicago, IL, 1980.

McMaster, M. and Grinder, J., *Precision: A New Approach to Communication,* Precision, Los Angeles, CA 1981.

Miller, G., Galanter, E., and Pribram, K., *Plans and the Structure of Behavior*, Henry Holt & Co., Inc., 1960.

O'Connor, J. and Seymour, J., *Introducing Neuro-Linguistic Programming*, Aquarian Press, Cornwall, England, 1990.

Pavlov, I., *Essential Works of Pavlov*, Kaplan, M. [Editor], Bantam Books, New York, NY, 1966.

Rodin, Judith, *Aging and Health: Effects of the Sense of Control*, **Science** Vol. 233, September 19, 1986, pp.1271-1276.

Senge, P., *The Fifth Discipline*, Doubleday, New York, NY, 1990.

Watzlawick, P., Bavelas, J. and Jackson, D., *Pragmatics of Human Communication*, W.W. Norton & Co, New York, NY, 1967.

Index

Note: Numbers in italics refer to main entries.

About the Author

Robert Dilts

Robert Dilts has had a global reputation as a leading behavioral skills trainer, coach and organizational consultant since the late 1970s. He is an internationally known developer and author in the field of Neuro-Linguistic Programming (NLP)—a model of human behavior, learning and communication. In addition to spearheading the applications of NLP to education, creativity, health, and leadership, his personal contributions to the field of NLP include much of the seminal work on the NLP techniques of Strategies and Belief Systems, and the development of what has become known as "Systemic NLP."

Mr. Dilts has done coaching, consulting and training on leadership and organizational development throughout the world to a wide variety of professional groups and organizations. Past clients and sponsors have included Apple Computer, Hewlett-Packard, IBM, The World Bank, Alitalia, Telecom Italia, Lucasfilms Ltd., Ernst & Young, The American Society for Training and Development and the State Railway of Italy. He has lectured extensively on leadership, organizational learning and change management, making presentations and keynote addresses for The European Forum for Quality Management, The World Health Organization, and Harvard University.

Mr. Dilts has been an associate professor at the ISVOR Fiat School of Management for a number of years, helping to develop programs on leadership, innovation, values and systemic thinking. He is also chief scientist and Chairman of the Board for ISVOR DILTS Leadership Systems, a joint venture with ISVOR Fiat. ISVOR DILTS develops and delivers a wide range of innovative leadership development programs to large corporations on a global scale. These programs leverage leading edge e-learning solutions and other new technologies to serve corporate clients around the world.

In 1982 Mr. Dilts co-founded the Dynamic Learning Center with the late Todd Epstein. In 1991 he and Epstein (together with Judith DeLozier and Teresa Epstein) established NLP University, which provides a full range of basic and advanced NLP training. He and Epstein were also the founders of Dynamic Learning Publications and The Academy of Behavioral Technology.

Mr. Dilts is the principle author of *Neuro-Linguistic Programming Vol. I* (1980), and has authored numerous other books on NLP including *Changing Belief Systems with NLP* (1990), *Tools for Dreamers* (1991, co-authored with Todd Epstein), *Skills for the Future* (1993), *Visionary Leadership Skills* (1996), *Modeling with NLP* (1998), *Sleight of Mouth* (1999) and the *Encyclopedia of Systemic Neuro-Linguistic Programming and NLP New Coding* (with Judith DeLozier, 2000), which provides a comprehensive overview of the field of Neuro-Linguistic Programming, including its wide range of applications, techniques and influences.

Mr. Dilts' recent work, *Alpha Leadership: Tools for Business Leaders Who Want More From Life* (with Ann Deering and Julian Russell) describes a new model of leadership that captures and shares the latest know-how on the practice of effective leadership, offering approaches to reduce stress and to promote satisfaction. The Alpha Leadership model supplies tools for managers, consultants and coaches to develop more effective leadership ability.